BIG-
BORE
REVOLVERS

BY MAX PRASAC

Published by

Gun Digest® Books, an imprint of F+W Media, Inc.
Krause Publications • 700 East State Street • Iola, WI 54990-0001
715-445-2214 • 888-457-2873
www.krausebooks.com

To order books or other products call toll-free 1-800-258-0929
or visit us online at www.gundigeststore.com

ISBN-13: 978-1-4402-2856-8
ISBN-10: 1-4402-2856-6

Designed by Dusty Reid
Edited by Jennifer L.S. Pearsall
Cover photography by Kris Kandler

Printed in China

ABOUT THE AUTHOR

Max Prasac was born and raised in sunny, southern California, and spent more time in his local gun shop (the Lock, Stock n' Barrel of San Gabriel, California) than was probably prudent, given the direction his career has taken. But, the blame for his career trajectory lies squarely on the shoulders of his parents for having bought him his first Daisy BB gun (yes, a Red Ryder!) for his eighth Christmas. Max's father gave him his first revolver, when the youth was barely in high school. He joined the NRA as a junior member in the early 1980s, and enlisted in the United States Marine Corps at the age of 17. Max has a Bachelors degree from the George Washington University, and has been writing professionally since the mid-'90s. Formerly, he also spent a number of years as a contractor performing disaster relief work overseas, work that included de-mining, reconstruction, and running food convoys in war zones. Later, he contracted in the security sector.

A member of Handgun Hunters International, life member of the North American Hunt Club, and a Life Member of the National Rifle Associa-

AUTHOR PHOTO

tion, Max writes a column for Boar Hunter and Bear Hunting magazines, and is an occasional contributor to the National Rifle Association (NRA) publications, particularly American Hunter. He hunts whenever possible, making frequent trips south to North Carolina, to test guns and loads on wild hogs. In the winter, he hunts deer and black bear. He hunts almost exclusively with handguns, nowadays, but will occasionally pick up a rifle. He resides in Northern Virginia with his wife, dog, and numerous big-bore revolvers.

ACKNOWLEDGEMENTS

I would like to say a special thanks to the following people who assisted me while clawing my way through this book: Katica, Dick Casull, Ken Jorgensen, John Parker, Jack Huntington, Jason Menefee, Jim Miner, Bill Vaznis, the Lee Martins, Hamilton Bowen, John Linebaugh, Dustin Linebaugh, Jim Stroh, David Clements, Jim Tertin, Mike Rintoul, Tim Sundles, Mike McNett, Bob Baker, Alan Dickey, Vincent Ricardel, Alan Harton, Bill Fowler, Fermin Garza, Gary Reeder, Rod Huelter, Mag-Na-Port, Tom Roach, Ross Seyfried, Scott Olmsted, John Gallagher, Larry Welch, Lynn Thompson, Gary Smith, Milt Turnage, James Swidryk, Darrel Harper, Dr. Larry Rogers, Rob Millette, Ed Folmar, Mike Giboney, Greg Brush, Rene Anderson, Jim Schlender, Jennifer Pearsall, Buddy, Veral Smith, Brian Pearce, Bud Rummel, Otto Candies, Jr., Mike Leeds, Chad Stevenson, Alan Griffith, Mike Winnerstig, #9 Lake Outfitters - Don Burnett, Louise Merrill, and Mike Hogan, Stephen Webb, Todd Corder, Tim Marshall, Glenn Swaggart, Boge Quinn, Wes Daems, and Kraig Pendleton. If anyone was left out, it was unintentional!

DEDICATION

I dedicate this book to the memory of my father who left this world too soon, and who taught us to reach high and accept no limits.

ABOUT THE COLLABORATORS

Louisiana born and bred, John Parker is a master welder by trade and a hunter to the core, not to mention a freelance ballistician and a real live cowboy. John has raised, trained, and shown horses and cattle, and, during high school, had the Louisiana state champion quarter horse. John began handgun hunting in the early 1970s with a Ruger Blackhawk .357 convertible, eventually graduating to a Smith & Wesson Model 29 .44 Magnum. John also shot in IHMSA competitions for a number of years. He says that the writings of Ross Seyfried were truly what fueled his desire to hunt large and dangerous game with a big-bore revolver.

While living and working in Alaska in the mid-'80s, John found the .44 Magnum to be a bit light in the loafers, for Alaska's oversized game, and so he commissioned Hamilton Bowen to build his very first custom revolver chambered for the .475 Linebaugh. John took delivery in 1988, just in time for the fall hunting season. John Parker has the distinction of having stopped an angry grizzly bear with a big-bore

JOHN PARKER AND THE AUTHOR on a hog hunt in Florida. Parker is packing the very first revolver chambered in the .500 JRH, an FA 83.

revolver, and living to tell about it (see account in the last chapter of this book), an encounter that cemented the man's faith in these guns.

Today, John Parker serves as a member of the editing committee for a major bullet manufacturer's annual loading manual. He is a trusted friend, one I know has forgotten more about big-bore revolvers than most will ever know.

Jack Huntington was born and raised in the high desert of Southern California, and he decided early on that his life would revolve around guns. Chasing the dream led Jack through numerous high school courses, including some simple gun work, that culminated in an honor in industrial arts. The next stop took Jack through an undergraduate program in Small Arms Engineering and Ballistic Science. He completed that program with a Bachelor of Science degree, in 1983. Next, working at an entry-level engineering job in a small arms manufacturing firm, where he performed all facets of design, product testing, and planning, Jack was motivated to create.

MASTER GUNSMITH Jack Huntington, owner of JRH Advanced Gunsmithing, hard at work in his shop.

Having an exceptional working knowledge of revolvers, and motivated by the works of earlier master gunsmiths like Dick Casull, Jack made the decision to follow suit and build a five-shot big-bore mega revolver. In 1987, Jack purchased The Rifle Shop from noted African rifle builder Ryan Breeding. As a trained tool and die machinist, Jack performed warranty work for Smith & Wesson, Colt's, Winchester, Browning, Remington, Charter Arms, and Thompson Center Arms, to name but a few. It wasn't an immediate endeavor, thanks to his busy schedule, but, in 1988, the five-shot Jack Huntington revolver was born.

That first revolver was chambered in .500 Linebaugh. Jack followed that one immediately with a .475 Linebaugh built on a Ruger Bisley frame. Simultaneously, Jack was building big-bore bolt-action rifles for hunting in African, heavily influenced by good friend and mentor Gill Van Horn, a permanent fixture in his shop. To complement his rifle work, Jack then started producing all manner of five-shooters.

In 1991, Jack got the bright idea to monkey with the Freedom Arms Model 83 platform. While the Model 83 is a masterful hunk of steel, Jack wanted to shoehorn something bigger than the .454 Casull into the FA's cylinder. After some careful study, it was decided that, by making a smaller rim on a .475 Linebaugh case (at that point, it was still a wildcat using cut down .45-70 brass), the cartridge could and would fit in the limited confines of the Model 83's cylinder. It was time to contact Freedom Arms.

Jack spoke with production manager Randy Smith, who expressed his enthusiasm for the idea of a .475 Freedom Arms Model 83. The fly in the ointment for Randy was the fact that cases had to be modified on a lathe one at a time. In other words, there was no simple commercial solution. Still, Jack continued to convert FA 83s to the new specification .475 Linebaugh, but it wasn't until 1999 that Freedom Arms took real notice, when Tim Sundles of Buffalo Bore acquired the case dimensions needed to make the .475 Linebaugh work in the excellent Model 83. Sundles got Starline to produce properly headstamped brass that featured a smaller rim and a slightly shortened case length, and began commercially producing .475 Linebaugh ammunition. This became the impetus for Freedom Arms to finally offer production Model 83s in .475 Linebaugh, in the year 2000.

JRH Advanced Gunsmithing officially opened its doors in 1997, but Jack had began working on the .500 JRH as a concept all the way back in 1993, when he'd made a dummy in his lathe. His desire was for a full-power .50-caliber round that would fit the limited space of an FA 83. While the .500 JRH didn't initially show any commercial viability, the tides of time brought the .500 Smith & Wesson Magnum case to life. Right on its heels came the .500 JRH case, bearing only a slight change in the rim diameter and case length. With the help of his friend Tim Sundles, and Bobby Hayden of Starline Brass, the .500 JRH was born and displayed for the first time at the Safari Club International show in Reno, Nevada, in 2005. It was at this show that a friendship began between Jack and production manager of Magnum Research, Jim Tertin, and in the months following the show, Jim built a prototype and began offering the .500 JRH in Magnum Research's Precision Center revolvers.

With much time and money invested in the .500 JRH, Jack sought to test his creation on a number of large bovines and found it wanting for nothing. The slow stream of interest in this very useful big-bore cartridge continued to grow, and real life was breathed into the Magnum Research BFR in .500 JRH in 2011, due in large part to the editorial work of this book's author, Max Prasac.

Today, Jack continues to innovate and build exotic pistols, revolvers, and rifles in his northern California shop. When time permits, Jack enjoys hunting large game with a big-bore revolver of his making, preferring the .500 JRH above the others.

CONTENTS

FOREWORD

The first firearm I ever built was a single shot "cap-'n'-ball" pistol made from the broken axle off an old Ford. While the diameter of the bore was approximately ⅜-inch, it was by no means a big-bore handgun, but, rather, a product of the largest drill bit I could get my hands on at the time. I was about 11 years old, then, and my objective was to build a pistol that would serve me reliably during my daily excursions hunting small game in the hills behind my parents' home in Salt Lake City.

The philosopher Plato is credited with the statement, "Necessity is the mother of all invention." During those depressed times that were the years of my childhood, it seemed nearly everything we did was out of necessity. Necessity had me working in my father's garage at a very early age, learning skills and applying principles that would forge the foundation of my life's work. That period of my life also exposed me to some early pioneers of the firearms trade who were instrumental in perpetuating my interests and promoting my passions. All were legends within a proud industry, and each had something to offer that built upon the designs of those who preceded them. Despite my youth, I was a lucky recipient of their friendships and knowledge and, in return, privileged to their challenges.

One of those challenges involved the Colt .45 Single Action revolver. It was a firearm of choice, for me and many of my acquaintances, due to its availability and affordability. Definitely a big-bore, its accuracy was often inconsistent and, from my standpoint, power was anemic. Ever thankful of the skills learned early in life, I often set upon the task of "perfecting" those old Colts. One thing led to another, and pretty soon I was pushing the structural limits in pursuit of "just a little more power." If necessity is the mother of all invention, then passion must be the father of innovation. It is the culmination of necessity and passion that has guided me through the years designing the .454 revolver and cartridge that bears my name.

The unknowing often ask, "Why the need for so much power in a handgun?" Simplistically speaking, it is because it was what I wanted, and I would not be denied! I would bet those same individuals would have asked a similar question when seeing the first wheel. Realistically, the need for big-bores remains unlimited, and the resultant knowledge acquired from their success lends itself to many things, bigger and better yet.—*Dick Casull*

INTRODUCTION

Welcome to Big-Bore Revolvers!

On the surface, it may appear that this book will re-hash material that has been covered ad nauseum, but, in all actuality, I, along with input from my collaborators, firearms and ballistics experts John Parker and Jack Huntington, am bringing you so much more. Of course, I will cover some ground that has already been walked upon something that's unavoidable, but I will focus distinctly and intently on the modern big-bore revolver.

We live in what I consider the "Golden Age" of the big-bore revolver. There are currently no less than four different .50-caliber handgun rounds chambered for production revolvers on the market today! That's big news for the big-bore aficionado. Every single revolver manufacturer today offers a number of big-bore revolvers to the public. There are more commercial big-bore ammunition and bullets available than ever before, and there have been several notable new-comers to the big-bore revolver scene within the last decade, with the introductions of the .480 Ruger, the .500 JRH, the .500 Wyoming Express, and Smith & Wesson's .460 and .500 Magnums. It is a vibrant and constantly progressing hobby. These are truly good times!

But what constitutes a big-bore? It's a relative term, but I draw the line at the .41 Magnum, the third cartridge to bear the "magnum" moniker. I think most will agree that "big" starts around .40-caliber, but it's only fair to include the .357 Magnum in the discussion, as it has played a significant role in where I have landed today—besides, it was the first cartridge to wear the "magnum" title. As to where the evolution of the big-bore ends, I don't know. We have a very dynamic industry that seems to be listening to what the people want—and they want more.

Obviously this book could not be considered complete without looking backwards at the Colt Single Action Army and examining the roots of the guns we have today. The Colt "Peacemaker," as it is also known, is the sire of the single-action revolvers manufactured today. That said, I will offer no more than a cursory glance backwards as we are more concerned with modern design and modern metallurgy.

Our approach will be a bit different still, as I have included a chapter dedicated to the care and feeding of your big-bore revolver and the discussion of terminal ballistics, a topic that has not been explored deeply enough for my taste, and one that is normally a topic addressed only from the perspective of rifle ballistics. Don't let that scare you off, as I have not created a physics text book on the subject, but instead rather hopefully dispensed some of the myths that are frequently perpetuated by the hunting/gun magazine industry as a whole, some of which have been repeated so often as to be considered dogma. I am not being critical of gun/hunting publications, just that when conventional wisdom is repeated so often as to become law, rarely is that piece of wisdom challenged. I intend to challenge some of these "laws" in this book. For instance, one particularly irksome accepted myth I intend to challenge is that of "energy dump" and the declaration that states a bullet that exits an animal has not fully deposited its energy in said animal. Hogwash, I say. Two holes have the potential of bleeding at a much higher rate and volume than one hole, and two holes normally means a higher wound channel volume by virtue of greater length. I hope to get you, the reader, thinking about these issues, if nothing more. But, much more on this later.

The decision to include a terminal ballistics chapter also stems from the constant comparisons that are made between rifle ballistics and those of big-bore revolvers. Rifles, by virtue of their much greater velocities, are subject to a very different dynamic than those of the short-barreled revolver replete with cylinder gap. To repeat and paraphrase a description coined by the gun builder John Linebaugh, a big-bore revolver is nothing more than a long-range punch press—nothing more, nothing less. Any attempt to make a rifle out of your revolver is a recipe for failure. Revolvers were designed for relatively low velocities (save for a couple notable cartridges), and that is where they shine when loaded to take advantage of this limitation, as this book will demonstrate.

I have also thoroughly examined the platforms for these powerful cartridges from the single-action, with its roots firmly entrenched in the Wild West, as well as the more modern iteration of the six-shooter, the double-action revolver. Both are alive and thriving, and so I'll take a look at all of the modern single-action and double-action revolvers available on the new and used market and examine their strengths and weaknesses.

A chapter dedicated to the art of custom gun building will appeal to those who have traveled this route—and those who are drawn to dance outside the lines of stock manufactured guns. This is the realm of anything you want you can have, as long as your bank account carries a sufficient balance. Besides, if it's not offered commercially, why not have it made, for without gun-makers John Linebaugh, to whom we owe much for the big-bore cartridge development of today, we may never have seen cartridges like the .480 Ruger, .500 Smith & Wesson, or .460 come to fruition. John Linebaugh paved the way for manufacturers to climb aboard the big-bore revolver train, and other gunsmiths to build their creations. It must also be said that, without gun scribes like Ross Seyfried, who pursued the blossoming custom big-bore revolver trade in the pages of the popular gun press, the likes of John Linebaugh may have remained in the darkness of anonymity.

I have also taken the time to examine each big-bore revolver cartridge available commercially—and some not. I have included case and cartridge dimensions, but have not included load data, as I don't want this book to be utilized as a loading manual. The information is technical, as well as anecdotal, and is therefore both for your education and, just as importantly, your entertainment.

Holsters and sighting systems are reviewed, and I will spell out to you, the reader, the pros and cons of each system. Sighting systems are particularly important, when it comes to maximizing the effectiveness of your revolver, especially when you take the time to define the use of the gun. Will you be hunting or punching paper? Are you a serious competitor? Defining the use will help you come to a decision with regards to the type of sighting system that will best serve you.

Of course, shooting your big-bore revolver will be covered. I am of the belief that your big-bore revolver should make regular forays out of the protective lair of the safe, and it should be allowed to make some noise—often. So in this book you'll find some tips that better enable you to effectively shoot your revolver, imparting on you even more enjoyment.

I took the time to study those who came before us, blazed a trail, and laid the foundation for all big-bore revolver lovers, in the chapter aptly named "The Pioneers." The great Elmer Keith had a hand in developing one of the greatest big-bore revolver rounds ever, the .44 Magnum, and showed an unsuspecting world that these handguns were more than a "stunt," when it came to hunting. Dick Casull, whose name graces the cartridge he developed, brought us such greats as the .454 Casull and the Freedom Arms Model 83. The late Larry Kelly, who rose from poverty to become an industry innovator, served as a leading ambassador of handgun hunting. I finished up this chapter talking with Ross Seyfried, the gun writer who promoted the ideas of John Linebaugh, and showed us his intestinal fortitude by hunting dangerous African game with a "measly" revolver, all of which found their way into his marvelous stories splashed across the pages of your favorite gun magazines. These men, along with others on the periphery, brought us the modern day big-bore revolver. Without them, you might be reading a book on needlepoint right now (although not penned by yours truly).

Finally, I will take our big-bore revolvers on the hunt. For me, hunting is where these sidearms really shine.

They are effective all out of proportion to what their paper ballistics would suggest. Maybe I can sway some of the doubters and entice them to venture out into the field on the hunt. I have assembled photographs and stories of successful big-game hunts with revolvers, and also discussed using your revolver as a backup in the event that things go wrong and you end up facing an angry fur-bearing critter bent on your destruction. Some hair-raising firsthand accounts of revolvers being used for protection against dangerous animals have also been included in this final chapter.

My love affair with revolvers began at an early age, and my first acquisition was a Smith & Wesson Model 36 .38 Special (a revolver I still have today) that was passed on to me by my late father. Obviously not a big-bore, but a revolver nonetheless, and my imagination made up for its lack of bore size. After a tour in the Marine Corps while attending college, I bought my first true big-bore revolver with the proceeds of my very first professional boxing match (a hobby that admittedly seems incongruous with the pursuit of a higher education). That gun was a nickel-plated Smith & Wesson Model 29 .44 Magnum—just like Dirt Harry Callahan's, save for the finish, of course.

On a student's budget (read "broke"), I also took up reloading at that opportune time. A young former Marine, full of testosterone and low on good sense, I took all of my loads at the top end of those recommended by the manuals—full-throttle all the way! I burned hundreds of pounds of 2400 and beat that poor Model 29 nearly to death, but I still have it, and it still makes appearances at the range, though I rarely hunt with it any more. That was my introduction to big-bore revolvers, and I've been hooked since.

This book is something I have dreamed of writing for some time. I owe my wonderful and lovely wife, Katica, a debt of gratitude for encouraging me to pursue this challenge and colossal undertaking and bearing with me while I pulled my hair out in frequent bouts of frustration. As I mentioned in the beginning, I wrote this book in collaboration with two close friends, John Parker, a big-bore revolver pioneer who boldly went where others feared to go and who challenged my beliefs with the righteousness of hard proof through experimentation, and the brilliant gunsmith Jack Huntington who was forced to change his phone number due to the frequent and annoying calls (at all hours) from yours truly seeking technical information. Sorry Jack! I think there is something here for the beginner, the expert, the weekend warrior, and both the mildly and keenly interested. Sit back, smell the smokeless powder, and enjoy the ride. —*Max Prasac*

CHAPTER ONE

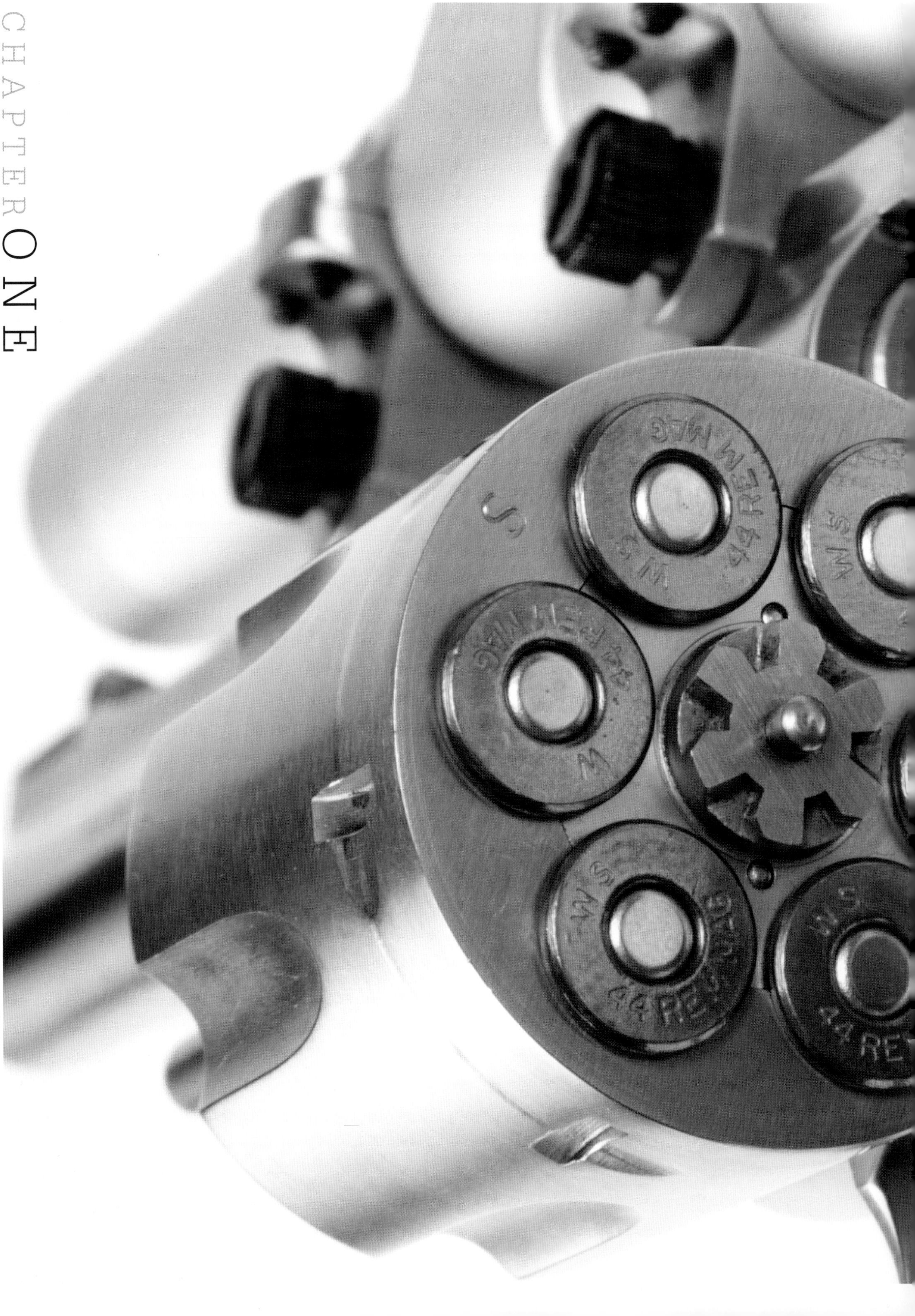

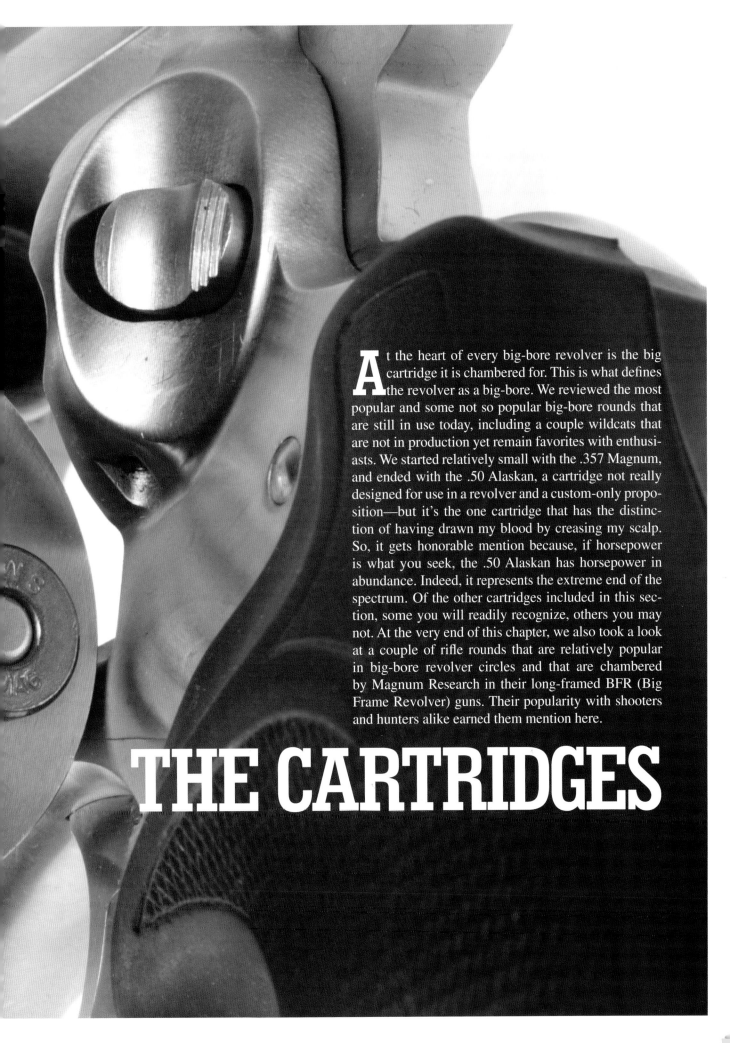

At the heart of every big-bore revolver is the big cartridge it is chambered for. This is what defines the revolver as a big-bore. We reviewed the most popular and some not so popular big-bore rounds that are still in use today, including a couple wildcats that are not in production yet remain favorites with enthusiasts. We started relatively small with the .357 Magnum, and ended with the .50 Alaskan, a cartridge not really designed for use in a revolver and a custom-only proposition—but it's the one cartridge that has the distinction of having drawn my blood by creasing my scalp. So, it gets honorable mention because, if horsepower is what you seek, the .50 Alaskan has horsepower in abundance. Indeed, it represents the extreme end of the spectrum. Of the other cartridges included in this section, some you will readily recognize, others you may not. At the very end of this chapter, we also took a look at a couple of rifle rounds that are relatively popular in big-bore revolver circles and that are chambered by Magnum Research in their long-framed BFR (Big Frame Revolver) guns. Their popularity with shooters and hunters alike earned them mention here.

THE CARTRIDGES

AUTHOR PHOTO

With each cartridge description, we have included our shooting impressions. While this is something completely subjective, we felt you might find it interesting if not helpful in your cartridge selection. A couple we have not shot, and have so stated.

AUTHOR PHOTO

.357 MAGNUM

This is the cartridge with the distinction of being the first to wear the name "Magnum," with its introduction in 1935. While not technically a big-bore, this is one of the first truly high-performance handgun cartridges ever produced, boasting velocities never before seen from a revolver cartridge. Dimensionally, the .357 Magnum is a lengthened .38 Special loaded to much higher pressure levels. The case was lengthened to prevent the uninitiated from loading these more power rounds in the structurally weaker guns chambered only for .38 Special (you can, of course, load .38 Special rounds in any revolver chambered for the .357 Magnum).

While this round has proven as effective as defensive caliber throughout its colorful history, we find it to be on the light side for big-game hunting. Let me rephrase that. Proper placement with a good bullet, matched to the game being

THE VERY FIRST MAGNUM, with the .44 Magnum on the left for comparison.

AUTHOR PHOTO

hunted, will put meat on the table, period. But due to diameter limitations, the .357 Magnum doesn't leave much margin for error. That said, there is still no replacement for placement.

The .357 Magnum is a good starting point for the beginner or novice, as the mild recoil makes mastering a revolver in this caliber a snap. There are many fine makes and models of this caliber available new and used.

Shooting Impressions: Loud. Very loud, if you are not wearing hearing protection (and you should be). Recoil is negligible, even when loaded hot. The .357 makes for a great starter pistol.

Specifications:

Bullet Diameter	.358-inch
Case Length	1.29 inches
Overall Length	1.59 inches
Maximum Pressure	35,000 psi

.357 MAXIMUM

Designed by the late Elgin Gates, the .357 Maximum is merely a lengthened .357 Magnum. It has a maximum case length of 1.6 inches. Unlike the .357 Magnum, which was lengthened to prevent loading in guns of inferior strength, the Maximum was lengthened to increase the payload of the car-

.44 Magnum left, .357 Maximum right.

tridge so that it could throw heavier projectiles at reasonable velocities for metallic silhouette shooting; the .357 Magnum simply didn't provide enough punch to knock over the targets in this style of competition at increased ranges.

Ruger produced a special Blackhawk single-action revolver with a lengthened frame to house the requisite longer cylinder, in 1982. These revolvers were produced for just three years and experienced some purported trouble with flame cutting that was evident only when light bullets at high velocity were used.

Dan Wesson also offered a revolver in the .357 Maximum chambering, a double-action that proved popular, as did one from U.S. Arms, a lengthened Seville model single-action revolver.

The two single-action platforms in this chambering provide the foundations for .475 and .500 Maximum conversions (see the .500 Maximum segment), as well as for the lengthened .475 and .500 Linebaughs (from 1.4 to 1.6 inches), but I have seen only the Ruger Maximum used in this conversion. Factory .357 Maximums are getting harder to find, but they do turn up.

Shooting Impressions: This is a cartridge

PHOTO BY LEE MARTIN III

that, even when loaded with heavy bullets, is comfortable to shoot. This is a good, relatively flat-shooting cartridge for thin-skinned game and another good choice for the neophyte.

Specifications:
Bullet Diameter .... .359-inch
Case Length .... 1.605 inches
Overall Length .... 1.990 inches
Maximum Pressure .... 40,000 psi

.375 SUPERMAG

While not technically a big-bore by the parameters we set, the .375 SuperMag is worth mentioning in this discussion. Another in the series of Elgin Gates' creations, this is a really fine round that, unfortunately, never caught on. It split the difference between the .357 SuperMag/Maximum and the .414 SuperMag. Capable of launching a 220-grain bullet in the 1,700 fps range from a 10-inch barreled revolver, the .375 SuperMag was quite the performer, yet known for its relatively light recoil, flat trajectories, and good knock-down power in metallic silhouette matches. Dan Wesson and U.S. Arms were the only manufacturers of revolvers to offer guns in this specialized caliber. A reload-only proposition, the .375 SuperMag is a unique and rare bird indeed.

Shooting Impressions: This is another one of those cartridges I classify as a pleasure to shoot, even when loaded to full potential. It shot relatively flatly and proved to have good knock-down power in metallic silhouette.

Specifications:
Bullet Diameter .... .376-inch
Case Length .... 1.610 inches
Overall Length .... 2.087 inches
Maximum Pressure .... 40,611 psi

.41 MAGNUM

The "Goldilocks" of the original Magnum triumvirate, the .41 Magnum was meant to fill the gap between the .357 Magnum and the .44 Magnum. If the .357 Magnum was too small and the .44 Magnum too big, the .41 Magnum was just right. Announced in 1964 by Remington at the same time Smith & Wesson announced the Model 57 chambered for this round, the cartridge was originally destined for law enforcement use. It's more than a shame it never caught on like the .44 and the .357 did, as it is a very good and very effective

AUTHOR PHOTO

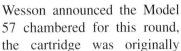

The .44 Magnum left, .41 Magnum right.

round. It does enjoy a loyal following outside the badged world and, in my experience, doesn't give up a whole lot to its bigger brother, the .44 Magnum, but it does perform with less recoil, even when loaded hot.

Some law enforcement agencies actually did press the .41 Magnum into service, but, like many good ideas, lowering standards to the lowest common denominator pushed this large cartridge out of contention. Some of the physically weaker officers evidently had trouble shooting the big revolvers and, thus, were ineffective with them. An officer of the law must absolutely be confident and competent with their sidearm, or it's all for naught. We saw the same pattern of events unfold some years later with the 10mm, when it was adopted by the FBI. That round, too, was emasculated until it disappeared, to be replaced by a weaker sibling, the .40 Smith & Wesson.

Very little is available in factory ammunition for the .41 Magnum today. This lack of on-the-shelf availability makes this round a wonderful handloading proposition, if one is serious about extracting the maximum performance from this cartridge.

Shooting Impressions: I have always found the .41 Magnum to be comfortable, even when loaded with heavy bullets, and it is a considerable recoil step down from the bigger .44 Magnum. I still maintain that it would have been a great law enforcement round (as it was originally envisioned), save for the large-framed gun necessary to house it. This is a good choice for the beginner.

Specifications:
Bullet Diameter .... .41-inch
Case Length .... 1.29 inches
Overall Length...... 1.590 inches
Maximum Pressure.. 36,000 psi

.414 SUPERMAG

Designed by Elgin Gates in the mid-'70s, the .414 SuperMag is merely a .41 Magnum lengthened to 1.61 inches. Dan Wesson was the sole manufacturer of revolvers in

this specialized caliber. As with the other SuperMag calibers, the .414 was originally intended for competition in metallic silhouette. The rarity of this cartridge means you will have to reload, though it will readily digest .41 Magnum fodder.

Shooting Impressions: Loaded to potential, the .414 SuperMag returns recoil like a healthy .44 Magnum.

Specifications:
Bullet Diameter .... .41-inch
Case Length .... 1.610 inches
Overall Length .... 1.975 inches
Maximum Pressure .... 43,511 psi

.44 SPECIAL

This cartridge was a favorite of Elmer Keith's, and his high-performance loading efforts led to the design and introduction of the bigger .44 Magnum. Still a viable performer when loaded correctly, this cartridge is a great big-bore alternative for the recoil-sensitive, as its low pressure delivers relatively mild recoil impulses. Designed primarily as a defensive round, the .44 Special features a .429 diameter like its offspring, the .44

The .44 Magnum left, .44 Special right.

Magnum, and the case length is a nominal 1.16 inches. The .44 Special can be safely fired in any and all .44 Magnum-chambered revolvers. This cartridge does indeed make for a great defensive round, as it is easily handled and delivers a fairly large bullet.

Shooting Impressions: This is the perfect starter big-bore revolver round. Shooting .44 Specials through a .44 Magnum revolver tames the gun and recoil considerably. A common practice is to shoot .44 Special loads through a .44 Magnum, when teaching a newbie how to shoot a big revolver. Recoil is very mild, as is muzzle blast. This round is a pure pleasure to shoot.

The .44 Magnum left,
.445 SuperMag right

Specifications:
Bullet Diameter .... .429-inch
Case Length .... 1.16 inches
Overall Length .... 1.615 inches
Maximum Pressure .... 15,500 psi

.44 REMINGTON MAGNUM

The .44 Remington Magnum made the scene in 1956. Ruger and Smith & Wesson vied for the distinction of being the first one to market with the new high-powered cartridge, the former with the introduction of the Super Blackhawk, the latter with a new N-frame revolver. Both hit the shelves at gun shops nationwide, and the world hasn't been the same since. But the big shot in the arm for the .44 Magnum, from the standpoint of popularity, was the 1971 film, *Dirt Harry*, starring Clint Eastwood as the tough San Francisco detective who carried a Model 29 in a shoulder holster.

Actual diameter for the .44 Magnum is .429-inches, but can you imagine the caché ".429" Magnum would have had? This really is the quintessential big-bore round and, essentially, a threshold cartridge, meaning that it is the upper limit for all but the most hardened handgunner and one that still needs to be approached with caution by true neophytes. The .44 Magnum remained at the top position of power until 1983, then fell victim to the game of one-upmanship, as new and bigger cartridges were introduced.

Still considered the classic big-bore revolver cartridge, the .44 Magnum continues to enjoy a strong following. There is no big-bore round that can claim the variety of available ammunition on the market, with loads ranging from mild to wild. If you don't reload, this is the cartridge for you, as every conceivable variant is available commercially for any and every application imaginable.

Shooting Impressions: The .44 Magnum is the threshold cartridge, in this author's opinion. It can be a true handful, particularly with heavily loaded rounds chambered in a lightweight revolver. This is a great cartridge to come back to after dabbling in the .50-cals, as it then feels .44 Special-esque. Loaded to spec, the .44 Magnum does kick, but I have never found it abusive enough not to over-come, even for novice shooters, as long as you ease them up to full-house levels. Yes, many find the .44 Magnum harsh and difficult to shoot—but I think this is where the fun begins.

Specifications:
Bullet Diameter........ .429-inch
Case Length ...... 1.285 inches
Overall Length ... 1.610 inches
Maximum Pressure ... 36,000 psi

.445 SUPERMAG

The .445 SuperMag, as is the case with all of the SuperMag cartridges, is a lengthened .44 Magnum case, in this case, also to 1.6 inches, which represents a sizeable increase over the parent cartridge in case capacity and velocity potential. The reasoning behind the development of the .445 SuperMag was better knock-down power in metallic silhouette shooting, where it did indeed excel. Only Dan Wesson offered revolvers chambered in this special cartridge, a gun based on the maker's stretched frame.

Shooting Impressions: This is a round that can be loaded to fairly obnoxious levels, particularly with heavy (300-plus-grain) bullets. Not quite in Casull territory, but definitely a sizeable step over the parent .44 Magnum.

Specifications:
Bullet Diameter .... .429-inch
Case Length .... 1.610 inches
Overall Length................................ 1.935 inches
Maximum Pressure ....40,611 psi

.45 COLT

Born in 1873, this old black-powder warhorse never seems to get its just due. Think of the .45 Colt as the Rodney Dangerfield of big-bore handgun rounds. Rarely is it loaded to potential from the factory, because of the number of older revolvers in circulation that are incapable of handling the higher pressure modern smokeless loads that

.44 Magnum left,
.45 Colt right.

would most likely reduce them to shrapnel. Basically, full loads in those old guns are law suits waiting to happen. So, due to liability issues, the .45 Colt is rarely ever viewed in the same vein as the .44 Magnum.

No slouch even in blackpowder form, the .45 Colt in modern times really takes on a different persona. Load it to its full potential and it will give the much-vaunted .454 Casull a run for its money and leave the .44 Magnum sucking wind in its rearview mirror. But before you start rolling out the hate mail, keep in mind that I own at least a half-dozen .44 Mags of all shapes and sizes. It's just that I'm an even bigger fan of the modern .45 Colt. If there ever was a do-it-all cartridge, the .45 Colt would be at the top of the heap.

Gun scribe Ross Seyfried is a also a big fan of the .45 Colt and chose one to use against a Cape buffalo in the 1980s. Ross evidently had a great deal of confidence in the capabilities of this round—when loaded to potential—and his own ability on the trigger. In an article in *Handloader* magazine, while discussing the merits of the .44 Magnum, Ross stated, "In the midst of this I began to work in Africa. It was a handgunner's paradise. Plenty of deer- and elk-like critters could be stalked to within honest handgun range. Many could be taken with the .44 Magnum, but I always felt like I was asking a boy to do a man's job." Almost losing a trophy kudu shot with his trusty .44 Magnum further exposed that round as an overachiever of sorts, one that was somewhat marginal when the game got a bit larger, and Ross' confidence in the .44 Magnum fell.

About this time, a gentleman by the name of John Linebaugh began pestering Seyfried with letters and phone calls touting the .45 Colt as a significant step up and over the legendary .44 Magnum. The two ultimately met, and Linebaugh offered Ross the chance to shoot his .45 Colt over the chronograph. Ross declined, stepping back an adequate distance and taking cover, as he fully expected the revolver to come apart like a grenade in John Linebaugh's hands. But the chronograph told the story—the true story—six times in a row, the 310-grain bullet traveling at 1,500 fps. Remarkable! The biggest shock came when Ross, expecting to pound the surely mangled cartridge cases out of their chambers, was able to lift them out with minimal effort. Linebaugh was definitely on to something, and Seyfried immediately commissioned him to build him one of these super .45 Colts. As for my love affair with this cartridge, what's good enough for Ross Seyfried, is certainly good enough for me (and anyone else for that matter!).

One need not load the .45 Colt to Casull levels to enjoy a leg up in effectiveness. Loaded to much lower pressure levels, the .45 Colt will not leave the big-game handgun hunter needing more. We will examine the .45 Colt and why this is so in more detail later in the book.

Shooting Impressions: In the right revolver, this cartridge can be every bit as obnoxious as the .454 Casull, as it can be loaded to the same pressure levels. That said, when loaded to potential—somewhere in the 30,000 psi range—and even while it reminds you that you have a very potent load in your hands, I find it less bone-jarring than even the benchmark .44 Magnum. Not nearly as "snappy," for lack of a better term, but you will still take notice. Truly a great choice for the big game hunter who is somewhat recoil sensitive.

Specifications:
Bullet Diameter........ .452-inch
Case Length......... 1.285 inches
Overall Length....... 1.60 inches
Maximum Pressure. 14,000 psi

The .44 Magnum left, .454 Casull right.

.454 CASULL

In the early 1950s, while Elmer Keith was hot-rodding the .44 Special, Dick Casull turned his attention to the .45 Colt and building special five-shot cylinders on Colt SAA revolvers. In those days, with limited gunpowder options, one had to get creative in order to achieve high velocities. Dick was able to get a full 2,000 fps out of a 230-grain jacketed bullet (one designed for use in the .45 ACP round), by loading two grains of Unique, 25 grains of H 2400, and three grains of Bullseye. At the time, highly compacted triplex loads were the only path to achieving the pressures necessary to reach the velocities he sought.

Manufacturers of .454 Casull ammunition have remained true to the original design parameters, offering some very high-velocity loads. The Casull also shines with heavy-for-caliber bullets, though care must be taken when loading them at high velocities, for such recipes have a propensity for testing the integrity of the crimp.

In 1983, the Freedom Arms Model 83 was introduced in Dick Casull's souped-up .45-caliber cartridge. Never before had such a high-pressure revolver round been produced, nor a gun that could live under the abuse generated by it. Other manufacturers, like Ruger and Taurus, followed suit years later with their own revolvers chambered in .454 Casull, as this round required a revolver of much stronger construction than any made for the .44 Magnum. This was not only because of the higher pressures, but also because Dick Casull specified a longer case to prevent the accidental (or merely idiotic) use of .454 Casull ammunition in .45 Colt revolvers of inadequate strength. Additionally, Casull specified a small rifle primer pocket, to strengthen the head of the case (by virtue of leaving more material in this spot).

I think of the .454 as the .378 Weatherby of the revolver world, as neither are really pleasant to shoot, when loaded to spec. The .454 Casull generates horrendous recoil and has caused its fair share of disability. Most .454 Casull ammunition manufacturers load the cartridge short of its full velocity and pressure (SAAMI specification) potential, yet paper ballistics sell, and, even loaded down a bit, the .454 can still boast potent numbers. There is no other commercially available cartridge that has a maximum SAAMI pressure specification as high as the .454 Casull, though the .460 and .500 Smith & Wesson Magnums come close.

Shooting Impressions: If the .44 Magnum marks the starting point of heavy recoil, the .454 is where unpleasant begins and lingers a while. The round's 65,000 psi behind a 300-grain bullet will get anyone's attention, even veteran big-bore revolver shooter. Shooting the .454 for extended periods ignites the onslaught of fatigue. While not the most unpleasant, the .454 is definitely in the top 10 percent. The .454 is also very loud, in comparison to other big-bore revolver calibers. Not a caliber for the neophyte, nor for many of the experienced. The recoil impulse is hard and sharp, like a heavy jab. Bring a glove to the range.

AUTHOR PHOTO

The .44 Magnum left, .460 Smith & Wesson right.

Specifications:
Bullet Diameter .... .452-inch
Case length .... 1.398 inches
Overall Length .... 1.765 inches
Maximum Pressure ... 65,000 psi

.460 SMITH & WESSON

Smith & Wesson's long-range wonder cartridge was introduced, in 2005, in the company's X-frame platform. Boasting a case length of a full 1.8 inches, the .460 is basically a stretched .454 Casull with a $^4/_{10}$-inch length advantage. This new cartridge was designed in the same vein as the .454—high pressure, high velocity, long range. The .460 Smith & Wesson has the distinction of being the highest velocity production revolver cartridge in existence, with some factory loads able to exceed 2,300 fps!

With an overall cartridge length of 2.30 inches, the .460 XVR will also safely chamber and shoot .454 Casull and .45 Colt ammo.

Not a terribly efficient round, the .460 excels with both light and with heavy bullets, but will not outshine the .454 Casull by much when midweight bullets are loaded. Similar pressures can be achieved, and, by increasing the payload, the results aren't dramatic. That said, in most factory loads, the .460 pushes a lightweight bullet at high speeds, just as intended. In this iteration, it does well on thin-skinned game, but light, frangible bullets at high-velocity are a recipe for disaster on truly large game. Fortunately, the .460 is very effective loaded with heavy bullets, as well.

The price one pays for choosing the .460 is the size of the revolver necessary to house the oversized cartridge. Then again, every decision in life comes with a price.

The .44 Magnum left, .480 Ruger right.

Shooting Impressions: This caliber is a mixed bag. Many (most) factory loads feature a relatively light bullet pushed to relatively high velocities. In this iteration it is a maiden's caress, particularly when coupled with a long-barreled and consequently heavy X-frame Smith & Wesson revolver. The bulk of the gun, combined with the effective muzzle brake, do tame the big cartridge. Step up to CorBon's 395-grain cast loads at 1,500-plus fps, and you will have awoken a sleeping recoil giant; despite the weight of the revolver, this load will let you know it is serious every time you trip the hammer, and the web of your hand will pay the price. Also worth noting is that this is arguably the loudest revolver I have ever had the pleasure of shooting. You absolutely must where hearing protection with the .460.

Specifications:
Bullet Diameter .... .452-inch
Case Length .... 1.790 inches
Overall Length .... 2.343 inches
Maximum Pressure...............61,931 psi

.480 RUGER

The .480 Ruger is, essentially, a shortened .475 Linebaugh. The first loads offered the public did not show the true potential of this cartridge and were overshadowed by the aggressive marketing of the .500 Smith & Wesson Magnum and .460 Smith & Wesson. To that end, it never really stood a chance, as it could not boast being the biggest

The .44 Magnum left, .475 Linebaugh right.

or fastest. What Sturm, Ruger did create, though, is a relatively mildly recoiling and effective round, that, in the author's opinion, is one of the better all-around choices for the big-game handgun hunter.

Released in conjunction with the Ruger Super Redhawk (SRH), the big revolver was a good platform from which to debut the new round bearing the Ruger name. Recoil, while expectedly stout, still pales next to the .454 Casull, even though the .480 boasts a larger diameter. The .480 can be loaded close to the levels of the .475 Linebaugh, but cannot achieve the higher end velocities. Don't let that fool you into thinking the .480 isn't a serious cartridge. There is no game animal walking this earth the .480 Ruger cannot comfortably take, when loaded appropriately.

Loaded to a SAAMI specification pressure of just under 48,000 psi, only 2,000 psi separates the .480 Ruger from its progenitor, the .475 Linebaugh. Off the market for a number of years, purportedly Sturm, Ruger and Company have plans to bring this outstanding caliber back into production at a later date.

Shooting Impressions: I like this round. Even when loaded with heavy bullets (400-plus-grain), the impulse is mild and creates more of a push than a sharp jab. Start pushing those same-weight bullets up over 1,300 fps and this is where the party really starts (see .475 Linebaugh shooting impressions). Plus, all factory revolver offerings in .480 Ruger are of sufficient bulk to tame even the hottest loaded .480. As a milder version of the .475 Linebaugh, what's not to like? This is another great choice for the person wanting big-bore knock down power without debilitating recoil.

Specifications:
Bullet Diameter .... .476-inch
Case Length............. 1.285 inches
Overall Length .... 1.650 inches
Maximum Pressure .... 47,862 psi

.475 LINEBAUGH

A personal favorite of mine, the .475 Linebaugh was unleashed on an unsuspecting handgun world in 1988 by gun builder, John Linebaugh, whose surname appropriately graces the cartridge. The original parent case of the then-wildcat was the .45-70 cut down to 1.4 inches with a .476-caliber bullet. This cartridge is truly serious and has taken the largest and most dangerous game that Africa and the rest of the world has to offer.

In its first incarnation, it was designed to push a 400- to 420-grain bullet to speeds up to 1,400 fps. The recoil is stout by anyone's standards. This is not a cartridge for the uninitiated, as it kills on both ends.

Ross Seyfried first wrote about the .475 Linebaugh in the pages of the May 1988 issue of *Guns & Ammo*. The article was appropriately dubbed, ".475 Monster Magnum … The 'Outer-Limit' Handgun." If that article hadn't gotten your blood pumping, he followed it up with an essay entitled ".475 Revolver Down Under," in the December 1989 issue of *Guns & Ammo*. In this article, Seyfried succinctly stated, "The .475 revolver cartridge was designed to be the ultimate big-game round for use in handguns. It represents a monumental step up from the .44s and a considerable increase in horsepower over any of the .45-caliber cartridges. This combination of long, heavy bullets and moderately high velocity makes even the highly-touted .454 Casull seem small and ineffective." Ross then proceeded to knock down a modicum of big game in Australia with his John Linebaugh-built Ruger Bisley .475, game that included feral goats, pigs, donkeys, wild cattle, and, last, an Indian water buffalo. Ross' first shot on the water buffalo resulted in two broken front shoulders. The effectiveness of the .475 Linebaugh on big game cannot be argued.

Brass is readily available for the handloader from two sources, Hornady and Starline. Two production revolvers are offered in this fantastic caliber at the time this book goes to print, those

The .44 Magnum left, .475 Maximum right.

being the Freedom Arms Model 83 and the Magnum Research BFR.

Shooting Impressions: We are now into undeniably heavy recoil territory. You need to wear your big-boy (or -girl) pants to shoot this round effectively. The .475 Linebaugh, loaded to potential—that is, a 420-grain bullet pushing over 1,300 fps—will not let you soon forget that you are packing serious heat. The recoil isn't quite the quick jab the .454 Casull exhibits, but more of a heavy push. It can get away from you, so you must concentrate when shooting the .475. You also need to limit the number of rounds you shoot per session with this round. A shooting glove wouldn't be a bad idea.

Specifications:

Bullet Diameter:	.476-inch
Case Length	1.384 inches
Overall Length	1.75 inches
Maximum Pressure	50,038 psi

.475 MAXIMUM

The January 1991 issue of *Guns & Ammo* introduced big-bore handgun nuts to the .475 Maximum (and its bigger brother, the .500 Maximum). Ross Seyfried was once again responsible for the expose, having thoroughly tested the cartridge and the John Linebaugh-built revolver. Also known as the .475 Linebaugh Long, this cartridge was a result of "More's Law"—if some is good, more is better—being applied to the .475 Linebaugh. This round is merely a .475 Linebaugh lengthened $^2/_{10}$-inch to 1.6 inches, and the extra length ensured the new round was able to achieve velocities somewhere around 150-plus feet-per-second more than its smaller counterpart, while maintaining similar pressures.

The .475 Maximum never really caught on, as the discomfort it created when shooting never outweighed the performance gains that could be realized. Ross Seyfried's penetration testing revealed that little more is gained by running higher velocities, and those higher velocities may actually compromise the bullets' integrity. That said, if loaded to .475 Linebaugh (the 1.4-inch case) velocity levels, the resulting lower pressures make for a more reliable cartridge in extreme heat—a definite plus when hunting Africa or other hot climes.

A note for reloaders. Brass at one time was produced by Hornady for the .475 Maximum, but this is a used-market proposition now.

Shooting Impressions: This is a .475 Linebaugh that ate its Wheaties. It's simply the .475, but more. Great care and focus must be taken when shooting the .475 Maximum. The recoil is heavy and pretty sharp, with regards to the recoil impulse. You will need a glove.

Specifications:
Bullet Diameter .... .476-inch
Case Length: .... 1.6 inches
Overall Length .... 1.950 inches
Maximum Pressure .... 50,000 psi

.50 ACTION EXPRESS

This cartridge was actually designed for use in a semi-auto pistol and is not, technically, a revolver round. Having put that up front, I would like to point out that the .50 Action Express (AE) was the first commercially available .50-caliber pistol round, one that inevitably ended up in a couple commercial revolvers. Featuring a heavily rebated rim, and due to the physical limitations of the auto pistol platform, the round has a relatively short loaded length, which necessitates using light bullets. Heavy bullets must be seated deeply, displacing too much valuable case capacity.

.44 Magnum left, .50 AE right.

Freedom Arms offered Model 83 revolvers in .50 AE for a period of time, but no longer. One can still purchase a BFR in .50 AE from Magnum Research but, if a serious caliber for hunting is desired, there are better choices.

Shooting Impressions: The short overall length of this cartridge prevents one from loading the .50 AE to any really heavy levels. As a consequence, it cannot be loaded very hot. While the recoil isn't negligible, it borders on pleasant. This is a very good plinking round, in this author's opinion.

Specifications:
Bullet Diameter .... .500-inch
Case Length .... 1.285 inches
Overall Length .... 1.594 inches
Maximum Pressure .... 35,000 psi

.500 SMITH & WESSON MAGNUM

The biggest of Smith & Wesson's Magnum cartridges, the .500 Magnum was the company's successful attempt at recapturing the crown of most powerful production revolver cartridge. Not only did Smith & Wesson seek to create the biggest cartridge in .50-caliber, it pulled out all stops by also making it amongst the highest of pressure producers; Smith & Wesson didn't want to just take the top position back, they also wanted to put as much distance as possible between the .500 Smith & Wesson Magnum and its nearest competitor. To that end, Smith & Wesson was able

The .44 Magnum left, .500 Smith & Wesson Magnum right.

to boast an excess of 2,500 ft-lbs of muzzle energy from this new cartridge.

Based loosely on the old .500 Maximum, or "Linebaugh Long," as it is also known, the .500 Smith & Wesson Magnum also features a case length of 1.6 inches and a diameter of .500 (unlike the Maximum's .510-bore diameter), necessitating a whole new revolver from Smith & Wesson. Enter the X-frame.

Unlike its parent cartridge, the .500 Maximum, the .500 Smith features a maximum pressure of 62,000 psi, putting it in the company of a small number of revolver cartridges loaded to rifle-like pressures. Loaded to spec, it is capable of impressive velocities, even with heavy bullets. When the .500 Smith and the X-frame debuted, CorBon released two loads, a 275-grain hollowpoint, and a 440-grain flat-nosed hardcast. Now, a wide range of varying loads are available from the likes of

Hornady, CorBon, Grizzly Cartridge, Buffalo Bore, and Double Tap Ammunition, with bullet weights ranging from 275 grains on up to 500.

With the introduction of Smith & Wesson's .500 came a renewed interest in handgun hunting. But, this is definitely not a cartridge for the un-initiated. Even when loaded in a heavy revolver like the X-frame, or even BFR's larger iteration, this cartridge produces significant recoil. You cannot launch bullets this heavy, at these speeds and burning this much powder, without producing sizeable recoil. This round evokes the term "extreme."

Shooting Impressions: Like its smaller brother, the .460 Smith & Wesson Magnum, the .500 is two-faced—think Dr. Jekyll and Mr. Hyde. Many of the factory loads offered really don't recoil very hard, but the muzzle blast perhaps gives one the impression that things are worse than they actually are. The sheer size of all .500 Smith factory revolvers (coupled with a muzzle brake, in most cases) is significant in taming the beast; it has to be, or the .500 Smith & Wesson Magnum would be unshootable, as well as unpopular. The round burns a lot of powder and is loaded to high pressures. Move up to heavyweight bullets loaded to SAAMI spec pressures, and the .500 Smith becomes unpleasant to shoot. I like to think of it as a large .454 Casull. Don't forget your ear muffs, as you are really going to need them and the requisite shooting glove.

.44 Magnum left,
.500 JRH right.

Specifications:

Bullet Diameter	.500-inch
Case Length	1.625 inches
Overall Length	2.300 inches
Maximum Pressure	61,931 psi

.500 JRH

The .500 JRH was the brainchild of Jack Huntington, a gunsmith out of northern California, and a collaborator on this book. Jack wanted a full-power, no-compromise, .50-caliber cartridge that would fit in a standard-framed revolver like the Freedom Arms Model 83, as well as one that had a maximum case length of 1.4 inches. He turned a dummy round in his lathe in 1993, and the .500 JRH became a commercially loaded reality, in 2005, when Starline turned the brass and Buffalo Bore produced the first commercial loads for it. Grizzly Cartridge Company also produces the cartridge, now. Today, it is offered in the standard lineup of revolvers from Magnum Research (the company's BFR line).

The very first revolver to be chambered in .500 JRH was a Freedom Arms Model 83, providing an workable alternative to the .500 Linebaugh, which features too large a case and rim to fit in the rather compact Model 83.

Brass is available from JRH Advanced Gunsmithing (produced by Starline), but .500 Smith & Wesson brass can easily be cut down for use. The specifications call for turning the rim down, but BFR revolvers in .500 JRH will accept the larger rim of the .500 Smith & Wesson brass. One ammo manufacturer (we'll let you guess which one!), in an effort to test the upper load limits of the .500 JRH, saw 1,625 fps with a 440-grain hardcast bullet! The end result was sticky extraction, but the case itself suffered no abnormal wear or damage, and the revolver was unscathed. We don't recommend you attempt to duplicate those levels, but it is interesting to know where the upper end of its limitations are.

Shooting Impressions: Most of the .50-caliber cartridges kick, and the .500 JRH is no exception. The first time I shot my BFR in .500 JRH, I loaded it with the hottest factory load available at the time, Buffalo Bore's 425-grain loads. These loads were chronographed averaging 1,450 fps out of my revolver. That gun wore Micarta grips, and they cut my hands to ribbons. Recoil is sharp and heavy. With the gun wearing rubber grips and handloads pushing a 440-grain bullet to a more manageable 1,350 fps, not only is the revolver usable, but it now kicks a bit harder than the typical .475 Linebaugh loads, meaning that it is heavy, but the push is a little harder and about as sharp.

The .500 JRH is one of my favorite rounds. I settled on a stiff dose of Winchester 296 under a 440-grain cast plain-based bullet (designed by good friend Jim Miner). This load produces 1,350 fps from my 6½-inch-barreled BFR, has produced three-shot groups of a ¼-inch at 50 yards, and has accounted for a number of wild hogs and whitetail deer.

Specifications:

Bullet Diameter	.500-inch
Case Length	1.4 inches
Overall Length	1.80 inches
Maximum Pressure	45,000 psi

.500 WYOMING EXPRESS

This proprietary offering from Freedom Arms is a virtual ballistic twin of the .500 JRH, but instead of the traditional rim of a revolver cartridge, Freedom Arms opted to use a belt for head spacing. The end result is a packable .50-caliber revolver, one with power to spare.

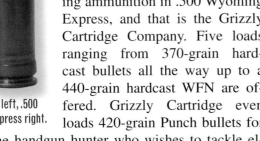

.44 Magnum left, .500 Wyoming Express right.

Currently there is only one commercial manufacturer producing ammunition in .500 Wyoming Express, and that is the Grizzly Cartridge Company. Five loads ranging from 370-grain hardcast bullets all the way up to a 440-grain hardcast WFN are offered. Grizzly Cartridge even loads 420-grain Punch bullets for the handgun hunter who wishes to tackle elephants—or concrete buildings!

Shooting Impressions: This is one I have not shot, but I have shot the equivalent Freedom Arms Model 83 chambered in .500 JRH (this was the very first revolver chambered in .500 JRH) and can report that it is lively to shoot. Recoil is pretty heavy, but manageable if one isn't particularly sensitive and takes the time to work up to this level.

Specifications:

Bullet Diameter	.500-inch
Case Length	1.37 inches
Overall Length	1.765 inches
Maximum Pressure	38,000 psi

.500 LINEBAUGH

Attention was first drawn to the .500 Linebaugh, with the publication of an article by Ross Seyfried in the August 1986 issue of *Gun & Ammo* magazine. The article was appropriately titled, "The .500 Magnum—The "Outer Limits" of Handgun Power." Though not offered in a production revolver, the .500 Linebaugh still boasts a strong following—enough that both Grizzly Cartridge and Buffalo Bore offer a number of production loads for this first .50-plus-caliber handgun cartridge. Brass is available from Starline.

The .44 Magnum left, .500 Linebaugh right.

Loaded to potential, the .500 Linebaugh is a true big-game hammer. Based originally on the .348 Winchester case and cut down to a nominal 1.4 inches, the .500 Linebaugh features a .510-bore diameter. Maximum pressures should be kept in the 33,000 to 36,000 psi range, though it will safely go higher. The beauty of the .500 Linebaugh is that it doesn't need to be pushed hard to work well on large game (with the caveat, of course, that it is loaded correctly and with a good bullet). In fact, through testing we have found that, with cast, wide-meplat bullets in the 500-grain range, even 1,100 fps is more than adequate for even the largest of ungulates. I successfully took a nearly 800-pound moose with a .500 Linebaugh, and the round failed to disappoint in how it did its job.

Shooting Impressions: The .500 Linebaugh, in my experience, offers a heavier push than its smaller brethren, the .475 Linebaugh. I shoot 500- and 525-grain bullets from mine almost exclusively nowadays, as these loads have proven deadly and accurate. That said, my revolver weighs just under three pounds and does a good job of beating up the shooter. While muzzle jump is less than with many of the big-bore revolvers I have shot, the recoil is heavy and jarring. The cumulative affect can be debilitating. This is a caliber you should limit yourself shooting.

Specifications:
Bullet Diameter .... .511-inch
Case Length .... 1.4 inches
Overall Length .... 1.80 inches
Maximum Pressure .... 50,000 psi

.500 MAXIMUM

Also referred to as the .500 Linebaugh Long, this is the cartridge that the .500 Smith & Wesson Magnum is purportedly based upon. This wildcat is typically built on Ruger .357 Maximum frames housing custom five-shot cylinders. Recoil at the upper end of the loading spectrum can best be described as very unpleasant to life altering, particularly when loaded to the 50,000 psi range. The .500 Maximum is capable of throwing 525-grain bullets at a blistering 1,500 fps, and some reports indicate even more velocity. While it is not recommended to feed your Maximum a steady diet of similar loads, it is fully capable of delivering this level of performance. This cartridge is an exercise in excess.

The .500 Maximum (right, with .44 Magnum left) is the cartridge that the .500 Smith & Wesson Magnum was based on and a result of "More's Law," i.e., if the .500 Linebaugh is good, more must be better.

Dedicated and properly headstamped brass is available sometimes on the used brass market (Hornady actually made a run of this brass), but the perfect parent case is the commercially available .50 Alaskan, which can be easily cut down to 1.6 inches.

In the end, the .500 Maximum is the poster child for "More's Law" being applied to the already potent .500 Linebaugh. Is the added velocity potential and resultant abuse on the shooter necessary? No, but we don't always (or even usually) apply the concept of necessity to our hobby. What fun would that be?

I am so enamored—read, "glutton for punishment"—with this oversized cartridge that I have sacrificed a pristine Ruger .357 Maximum to the big-bore gods, and, as this book goes to print, Jack Huntington is putting the final touches on my .500 Maximum.

Shooting Impressions: This one never fails to leave an impression (sometimes on the shooter's forehead). This is a very versatile cartridge for the handloader. You can load it to "mild" .500 Linebaugh levels, or you can concoct proof loads in the 50,000 psi range—and dearly pay a price in very heavy recoil.

The recoil impulse of this round is deceptive. When you think it's finished recoiling, it recoils some more, with an impulse that seemingly never ends. The guns typically chambered in this wildcat round are on the light side, meaning they come in under 3½ pounds. Be careful how hot you load this one, as it is capable of hurting the shooter. Definitely not for the meek! Do not forget your shooting gloves.

.44 Magnum left,
.50 Alaskan right.

Specifications:
Bullet Diameter .... .511-inch
Case Length .... 1.6 inches
Overall Length .... 1.955 inches
Maximum Pressure ... 50,000 psi

.50 ALASKAN

This is a cartridge designed for use in a lever-action rifle, one based on the .348 Winchester case that dates back to the 1950s. It is a big case that stretches out to 2.10 inches and features a .510-bore. The only revolvers large enough to handle this chambering are the BFRs, including the early DMax-framed revolvers (the frames first used to make .45-70 Magnum Research BFR revolvers), but they are custom propositions only, as Magnum Research doesn't chamber for this round.

If horsepower is what you seek,

The mighty .500 Smith & Wesson is dwarfed by the mightier .50 Alaskan on the right.

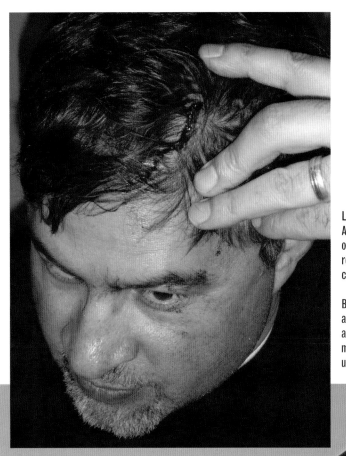

LEFT: The front sight blade of the author's .50 Alaskan revolver created this scalp wound during one shooting session. A revolver with this much recoil requires considerable muscle tension and full mental concentration to avoid becoming injured.

BELOW: A Huntington-built .50 Alaska revolver built on a prototype D-Max frame. The brute has been fitted with a Bisley grip frame and features an 8-inch barrel and muzzle brake. With max loads, this revolver is nearly unshootable.

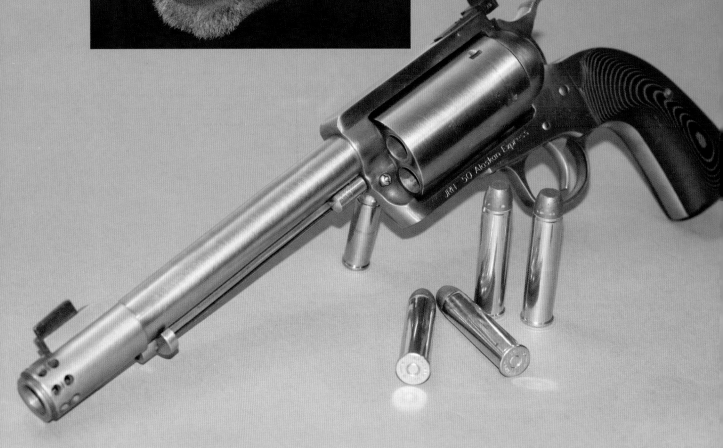

look no further. This cartridge can be loaded to levels no one in their right frame of mind will be able to shoot or want to shoot. The author owns a revolver chambered in .50 Alaskan and can attest to the brutal recoil it produces. Attempts to load this beast down still produce enormous recoil impulses. Many starting loads utilize more than 50 grains of any given powder, and, no matter how you slice it, burning that much powder simply produces a truckload of recoil.

The author has chronographed loads by Buffalo Bore Ammunition, and the results are sobering. The 525-grain bullets exit the muzzle at close to 1,600 fps. This revolver is a lot of gun to control, but it really offers nothing more than bragging rights—and a headache, if it gets away from you. Just let me know if you want to shoot it. You supply the hard hat.

Shooting Impressions: This one is like bringing your own personal severe weather front to the range. Every ounce of your concentration needs to be focused on this cannon. The recoil impulse is huge and violent. If you fail to give it all your attention and all the muscle tension you can summon, it will make contact, and that contact will not be pretty (see photo). My custom revolver in .50 Alaskan opened up a two-inch gash in my scalp, when I let down my guard for one moment. In fact, the DNA of several shooters is on the gun's front sight blade. I recommend a good glove, a helmet, and a saddle to tame this monster. After shooting this one, every other caliber is, quite frankly, mild. Yikes.

The .44 Magnum left, .444 Marlin right.

Specifications:

Bullet Diameter	.511-inch
Case Length	2.1 inches
Overall Length	2.60 inches
Maximum Pressure	46,412 psi

HONORABLE MENTIONS

There are a number of revolver chamberings that are not, technically, handgun cartridges (like the aforementioned .50 Alaskan), but that deserve honorable mention. Magnum Research, under the BFR banner, offers an extended-frame revolver capable of making a home for any number of long rifle cases. BFR made its name with the .45-70 revolver and aptly named it the Biggest Finest Revolver. While this platform is a bit on the cumbersome side, with regards to size and weight, chamberings such as the .45-70 Government, and the .450 Marlin are quite pleasant to shoot, even when loaded hot. Here are three honorable mentions I think are worthy of space here.

.444 MARLIN

Designed in 1964 as a joint venture between Marlin Firearms and Remington Arms, think of the .444 Marlin as a stretched .44 Magnum—an *extensively* stretched .44 Magnum as the photo above clearly shows. It shares the same .429-bore, but features a case length of 2.25 inches. Capable of impressive velocities out of a rifle-length barrel, even in a revolver with its short barrel and cylinder gap, such as the BFR, it still will attain stout velocities.

Shooting Impressions: Recoil is substantial, but by no means overwhelming for this shooter, especially out of a large revolver like the BFR.

The .44 Magnum left, .45-70 right.

Specifications:

Bullet Diameter	.429-inch
Case Length	2.225 inches
Overall Length	2.570 inches
Maximum Pressure	51,488 psi

.45-70 GOVERNMENT

In its nomenclature, ".45" denoted the caliber and "70" the number of grains of blackpowder. This old warrior is still hanging around, more viable and youthful than ever. Introduced, in 1873, at the U.S. Army's Springfield Armory, the .45-70 in modern form is quite the performer, one able to mimic the .454 Casull in a handgun, but at much lower chamber pressures. We are talking about modern smokeless powder loads, here, not the .45-70 in blackpowder form. Granted, it takes a *lot* of revolver to house the big .45-70 round, but the bulk of the BFR serves to tame the cartridge quite a bit over a revolver loaded to similar ballistics in .454 Casull. The nominal bullet diameter is .458 and the case length is 2.10 inches.

Shooting Impressions: My impressions of the .45-70 in the BFR are, well, not what I expected in the least. Loaded to Casull-like levels (300-plus-grain bullets over 1,600 fps), the recoil impulse

couldn't be less Casull-like. This is a good thing. With much lower pressures, the .45-70 delivers potent performance without the noise and drama. This is a great choice for the handgun hunter willing to put up with the added size of the package.

Specifications:
Bullet Diameter: ....458 inch
Case Length .... 2.10 inches
Overall Length .... 2.55 inches
Maximum Pressure .... 28,000 psi

The three-way brawl, two Rugers far left and center, chambered in .44 Remington Magnum and .45 Colt, respectivley, up against a Freedom Arms in .454 Casull.

.450 MARLIN

Essentially a hot-rodded, higher pressured, modern .45-70, the .450 Marlin was a joint effort by the engineers at Marlin Firearms and Hornady Ammunition. Actually based on the .458 Winchester Magnum case, it features the same case length as the .45-70 Government at 2.10 inches. It also features a belted rim.

Shooting Impressions: This one recoils much like the .45-70, though potentially heavier, as the SAAMI spec calls for higher pressures. The long-framed BFR platform really tames the recoil of the .450 Marlin to acceptable levels, but recoil is largely dependent on your loading practices.

Specifications:
Bullet Diameter .... .458-inch
Case Length .... 2.10 inches
Overall Length .... 2.55 inches
Maximum Pressure .... 47,862 psi

AUTHOR PHOTO

The .44 Magnum left, .450 Marlin right.

Cartridge Bullet (grains)	Velocity (avg fps)	Velocity (Act fps)	Pressure (psi)
.44 Magnum 300 WFN	1,325	1,362.6	36,000
.44 Magnum 320 WLN	1,300	1,364.4	36,000
.45 Colt 300 LFN	1,250	1,326	30,000
.45 Colt 335 WLN	1,150	1,365	30,000
.454 Casull 300 LFN	1,750	1,539	59,000
.454 Casull 335 WLN	1,550	1,538	59,000
.454 Casull 360 WLN	1,450	1,467	59,000

PENETRATION TEST - .44 MAGNUM VS. .45 COLT VS. .454 CASULL

Bullet/Cartridge	Velocity (fps)	Penetration (inches)	Notes
300/.44 Mag	1,362.6	20.5	straight line
300/.44 Mag	1,345.6	24	straight line
320/.44 Mag	1,361	26	straight line
320/.44 Mag	1,364.4	25	straight line
300/.45 Colt	1,326	26	straight line
300/.45 Colt	1,309	28	straight line
335/.45 Colt	1,365	27.5	straight line
335/.45 Colt	1,341.6	26	straight line
300/.454 Casull	1,525.8	25.5	straight line
300/.454 Casull	1,539	30.5	straight line
335/.454 Casull	1,538	29	straight line
335/.454 Casull	1,534.3	25	straight line
360/.454 Casull	1,456.6	32	straight line
360/.454 Casull	1,467	24	straight line

THE MAGNIFICENT .45 COLT

This segment is dedicated to what I think is one of the finest revolver rounds to ever take a head of game, the magnificent .45 Colt. The .45 Colt was born in the 1870s as a blackpowder round. In its original form, it was no slouch, able to sling 250 grains of lead at nearly 1,000 fps—it accounted for many a human life lost in many a shootout. Times have changed, and so has the .45 Colt. No longer a blackpowder-only proposition, the .45 Colt has matured into a powerful revolver cartridge able to take even the largest game without breaking a sweat.

We will show you that the .45 Colt is the Goldilocks of all the revolver cartridges—not too hot, not too small, but just right. It will handily outperform the .44 Magnum with similarly weighted bullets, though at considerably lower pressures. It will also leave the .44 stepping on its tongue when loaded with heavy bullets, as the .44 is incapable of launching such mass with any meaningful velocity. We will also compare the modern .45 Colt to its younger progeny, the .454. We are not advocating turning the .45 Colt into a .454 Casull, which is actually easy enough to do with a five-shot revolver (with modern brass, the same pressures can be attained by the .45 Colt as in the .454 Casull). But, the .45 Colt doesn't need to mimic the Casull, as it is a round lacking nothing loaded to the 30,000 psi range.

We ran a penetration test between the heavily loaded .44 Magnum (300-grain bullets are the accepted heavy bullet weight), the .45 Colt, and the .454 Casull. Does the extra speed of the .454 buy you more penetration? Let's see.

For the penetration test, we utilized wet newsprint soaked for 24 hours prior to the first shots fired in testing. We positioned the penetration "box" approximately 10 feet in front of the benchrest, firing all shots over a chronograph and recording all velocities and penetration (see chart).

We tested nothing but hardcast, flat-nosed bullets, as we were interested in maximum penetration. We chose factory loaded ammunition from the Grizzly Cartridge Company for all testing, as the loads were all know commodities, with tested and confirmed pressure levels. No guesswork here, and no pitting one ammo manufacturer against another. One note. We do not possess the capacity or capability to test pressures, and, in this test, pressure is an important facet. That said, the Grizzly Cartridge Company stepped up with two .44 Magnum loads, a 300-grain WFN at a claimed 1,325 fps, and a 320-grain WLN at a claimed velocity of 1,300 fps. The second load represents the upper reasonable limit in effective bullet weight for the .429-diameter and the twist rates of production .44 Magnum revolvers. (See Chapter 5, where we tested extreme bullet weights in the popular .44 Magnum.)

The .45 Colt loads from Grizzly Cartridge consisted of a 300-grain LFN at a rated 1,250 fps, and a 335-grain WLN at 1,150 fps. None of these loads exceed 30,000 psi in pressure.

The .454 Casull was well represented by Grizzly's 300-grain LFN at an advertised 1,750 fps, a 335-grain WLN at an advertised 1,600 fps, and the 360-grain WLN at an advertised 1,500 fps.

As a side note, the .454 is a brutal cartridge, as you will see me mention a number of times in this book. The high pressure, relatively high velocity, and violent recoil impulse all lead to unpleasant recoil. This aspect of the .454 in and of itself will keep many away from this cartridge.

Three revolvers were used in this test. The .44 Magnum was represented by a Ruger Bisley Hunter, and we had a Ruger Vaquero in .45 Colt and a Freedom Arms Model 83 in .454 Casull. All revolvers had 7½-inch barrels.

As you can see from the chart, all three cartridges performed well. The biggest disparity was clearly between the 300-grain .44 Magnum load and the 300-grain .45 Colt load. The .45 Colt demonstrated a significant step up in penetration, surely not a deal-breaking gain, but keep it in mind. The .45 Colt 300-grain load penetrated deeper, with less pressure and less velocity, even though the velocity was close.

Despite the popular belief that sectional density plays a significant role in determining what bullet will penetrate deeper, we have seen in independent testing that this is not the case in many instances. The lower sectional density number of the 300-grain .45 Colt compared to the 300-grain .44 Magnum bullet seems to play no role in the deeper penetration.

Recoil was about the same, but the .45 Colt makes a discernibly larger hole. Yes, some will say we are splitting fine frog hairs here, yet those same folks will point out the greater diameter of the .475 over the .45, even though the size is roughly the same. The 335-grain load also outperformed the heavier 320-grain .44 load, though not by much. The .454 showed some gains, but keep in mind the fact that we were using bullets that are better suited to lower velocities in order to maintain their nose shape—when the nose degrades, penetration suffers. In cartridges with faster velocity potential, a hardcast bullet may not be the best choice, particularly when engaging a lot of bone. That said, if you keep the velocities in a particular range, they are very hard to beat. If hardcast bullets are the bullets you choose to use, the higher velocities of the .454 really aren't necessary, and all you really gain is recoil, muzzle blast, and the possibility of a reduced level of penetration due to the limitations of the bullet material.

In conclusion, there is little about the .45 Colt not to like, and I can say the only real criticism one can objectively level at the old warhorse is commercial availability. The .44 and, to a lesser extent, the .454, have the .45 Colt covered in spades, but there are a few manufacturers of really fine, high-performance .45 Colt ammunition, and this will not leave you at a disadvantage.

This chapter will be broken into two major parts: big-bore single-action revolvers and big-bore double-action revolvers. Some are currently in production and available new, while others are no longer produced but somewhat readily available on the used gun market. I believe there is something here for everyone's taste. First up is the oldest design, one that has actually changed very little through the years, the ubiquitous single-action.

THE PLATFORMS

A TRIO OF BIG-BORE REVOLVERS in .50-caliber, from top to bottom: Smith & Wesson .500 Magnum, Freedom Arms Model 83 .500 Wyoming Express, and the BFR in .500 JRH.

SINGLE-ACTION REVOLVERS

Single-actions derive their name from the fact that they can be fired only by cocking the hammer and squeezing the trigger, each and every time. The double-action, conversely, can be fired either in the same manner as the single-action or by simply squeezing the trigger to fire without first cocking the hammer, hence, there are two actions, or "double-action."

All modern-day single-action revolvers are based, however loosely, on the Colt's Single Action Army (SAA). So prolific was this design that it is still in wide use today. There are a number of manufacturers of single-action revolvers, including Ruger, Freedom Arms, Magnum Research, Uberti, USFA, and Colt's. There are also a number of models that are no longer in production but still very viable, like the Virginian Dragoon, and the Sevilles and El Dorados produced by the now defunct United Sporting Arms. In all, single-action big-bore revolvers are more popular than ever, and the single-action lover has many options to choose from, new and used.

RUGER'S FIXED-SIGHT Vaquero in .45 Colt.

Sturm, Ruger and Company

Probably the most produced modern single-action revolver in circulation is Sturm, Ruger and Company's Blackhawk and its .44 Magnum derivative, the Super Blackhawk. Strongly built and affordable, this is the single-action revolver for the masses. They have a number of innovative design features that set them apart from other revolver makes in modern form, particularly the transfer bar safety system, which was introduced with the "New Model" designation, in 1974. The transfer bar allows the revolver

to be safely carried with a live round under the hammer.

When discussing Ruger single-action revolvers, we must draw the distinction between the old and new models. The old model revolvers were produced from 1955 to 1974. There were three distinct frame sizes then, but we will concern ourselves only with the medium- and large-framed revolvers. The medium-frame was used by Ruger for the .357 Magnum cartridge and was of the same stature as the Colt's Single Action Army. The large-framed revolver was chambered in larger calibers, most notably the .44 Magnum.

The New Model revolvers were introduced in 1974. At that time, the medium-framed revolver was dropped from Ruger's lineup; instead of producing the .357 Magnum in a medium-framed revolver, it was now made on the Blackhawk's large frame.

The year 1983 marked the introduction of the .357 Maximum, a cartridge developed by the late Elgin Gates, for use in the popular metallic silhouette competitions. The .357 Magnum was deemed a bit too light to knock down the steel silhouettes, but the lengthened case of the Maximum—from 1.29 to 1.6 inches—allowed for heavier bullets at adequate velocities. To accommodate this longer case, Ruger built a special run of Blackhawk revolvers with a stretched frame. The effect is subtle and easy to

A LONGER CYLINDER and stretched frame were necessary to accommodate the new .357 Maximum cartridge, which featured a 1.6-inch case length compared to the .357 Magnum's 1.29-inch case. The difference in cylinder length is seen here.

AUTHOR PHOTO

overlook, if a buyer is not paying much attention. Problems with flame cutting, which reared its head only when lightweight bullets at high velocities were incorporated, led to the eventual termination of production a mere three years after introduction.

The Super Blackhawk Hunter series of revolvers was introduced in 2002. These are dedicated hunting pieces, as the name clearly suggests. Chambered at one time in .41 and .44 Magnum, a limited run was also chambered in .45 Colt. Built with integral scope mounting points (scallops) along the dedicated rib on top of the barrel, the only barrel length offered is 7½ inches. The revolver can be had in two different grip con-

THE RUGER BISLEY HUNTER offers the handgun hunter a dedicated revolver for the task at hand, one featuring a 7½-inch barrel and this wonderful grip frame that allows for better control of heavy recoil. Most custom revolver builders retrofit single-action Rugers with this grip frame.

AUTHOR PHOTO

RUGER GRIP FRAMES—THE PLOW AND THE BISLEY (OR THE FARMER AND THE ENGLISHMAN)

Ruger revolver arguments nearly always center on the grip frames collectively grouped into two types, the so-called "plow handle" and the "Bisley." Big-bore revolver enthusiasts are seemingly equally divided as to their preferences, except when moving up to the really heavy recoil producers, where the Bisley seems to be the preferred grip type.

But, let's talk plow handle first. This is a generic term encompassing three different and yet similar grip frames, the XR3, XR3-RED (RED for redesign), and the "Dragoon-style." Many pages can be dedicated to the Ruger single-action grip frame discussion, but I don't want to burden you with the minutiae. (For an absolutely detailed rundown of the grip frames used by Ruger over the years, I would recommend the excellent piece by Bill Hamm, with photography by Bill Hamm and Boge Quinn, on www.Gunblast.com. It is the most definitive work I have seen to date.)

Anyhow, for this discussion, the XR3 was first introduced in 1953 on the Single Six and the .357 and .44 Flat Top Blackhawks. The Dragoon-style grip frame, with its squared-back trigger guard, made its debut on the Super Blackhawk in 1959. This grip frame is longer than the XR3's towards the bottom of the grip. The XR3-RED made its first appearance in 1962, on the Single-Six, Super Single-Six, Hawkeye, Old Army, and, most importantly for this discussion, the Blackhawk. All three of these plow handle grip frames share a similar contour, the main differences being in the length of the grip. I am admittedly and horribly oversimplifying here, so please save your hate mail, but there have been so

Ruger's excellent Bisley grip frame (top) compared to the Dragoon-style plow handle grip frame (bottom).

AUTHOR PHOTO

many variations that we simply don't have the luxury or space to explore them all here. (And for those of you wondering, I have purposely left the "birds head" grip frame out of this discussion, as I personally feel it doesn't belong anywhere on or near a revolver that generates debilitating recoil.)

The Bisley grip frame is patterned loosely on Colt's Bisley model, but, on the Ruger, it bears a more vertically profiled grip. Ruger's Bisley debuted in 1986. Master gunsmith Hamilton Bowen states in his excellent book, The Custom Revolver, "With its longer, more vertical grip, the ultra big-bore revolver boom would never have materialized. The .475 and .500 Magnum guns would be unshootable fitted with any other grip frame." I agree completely with this sentiment, though one of the most common complaints leveled at the Bisley is the close proximity of the shooters fingers to the trigger guard, which often leads to uncomfortable contact.

Which one is better? This question is subjective, at best. The plow handle tends to pivot upward in the hand, while the Bisley acts somewhat like a double-action revolver, pushing back into the web of the hand. I find it much easier to control a Bisley grip frame-equipped heavy recoiling revolver than one fitted with a plow handle grip. Just a preference, mind you, and each individual will require something different. I would recommend trying both before drawing a conclusion. I have found that a custom set of grips made for your hands goes a long way towards making any revolver more controllable and, thus, enables the shooter to shoot more accurately.

PHOTO BY BRIAN BAKER

THIS BEAUTIFUL example of a Colt Single Action Army belongs to Brian Baker of Plano, Texas, and was manufactured in 1923. The original caliber is unknown, but the Colt was, at some point, converted to chamber the .44 Special using Colt parts. Hamilton Bowen cleaned up the action and added period-correct markings.

figurations, the standard Ruger Super Blackhawk (plow handle), or the Bisley grip frame. Which is better? It boils down to preference. I personally prefer the Bisley, particularly when the gun has a chambering with heavy recoil, as this grip design moves around less in the hand.

Colt's

The company that really started it all still produces a version of the famous Single Action Army (SAA) today. Sometimes called the "Peacemaker," virtually all modern single-action revolvers are loosely based on Colt's classic design. One of the most iconic pieces of Americana, the Colt's Single Action Army is probably the most recognizable gun in American film history. Three "generations" of Colt's SAAs have been produced, since its inception in 1873.

The first generation was produced from 1873 through the start of World War II. During this time frame, the classic army-style revolver was available and later joined by the Sheriff and Storekeeper models that featured shorter barrels without ejector housings. In the late 1880s, a flat-top SAA target model was added to the lineup. The Bisley model, a competition-style revolver, was introduced in the early 1890s. It featured a distinctly vertical grip frame and low-spur hammer, fixed or adjustable rear sight, and a removable front sight blade.

Production of Colt's SAAs ceased during World War II and didn't begin again until 1956. When general production ensued, it did so with the army-style model, with its only variation being the New Frontier model, a target-style revolver with modern, adjustable iron sights introduced in 1961. Production ended for the single-actions again in 1974 or '75, then resumed just two years later, in 1976. It was at this point that significant changes in design were made, marking the departures from the originals as what's now known as the third generation guns. These changes included a different barrel shank thread pitch and a solid cylinder bushing. By 1982, regular production faltered, even though the factory custom shop continued producing revolvers on a special order basis. By 1993, the Colt's Single-Action Army was back in Colt's catalog and continues to be available today.

PHOTO BY VINCENT RICARDEL

THE BFR by Magnum Research chambered in .500 JRH.

Magnum Research's BFR

Magnum Research entered the revolver building business in 1999, with the introduction of the BFR—the "Biggest Finest Revolver"—chambered in the ubiquitous .45-70 Government. Magnum Research has since re-designated BFR to stand for "Big Frame Revolver." As you are well aware, it takes a large cylinder and equally large frame to house a cartridge as big as the .45-70 and, so, the BFR has comic book proportions. Today, Magnum Research produces both long- and short-framed revolvers in a range of calibers to suit just about everyone's needs.

Let me start out by saying that today's consumer would be very hard pressed to find a higher quality and more accurate firearm without spending twice what the BFR sells for. In appearance, they look like a Ruger Super Blackhawk on steroids, having been beefed up in key areas such as the bottom of the frame and the top strap. Consequently they weigh a bit more than similarly sized revolvers, but are second to none with regards to strength.

Made entirely of 17-4PH stainless steel, the BFR features the plow handle grip frame like standard Ruger Blackhawks and Super Blackhawks. The counter-bored, smooth-sided (non-fluted), five-shot cylinder features a free-wheeling pawl, making loading and unloading a snap. The transfer bar safety system is borrowed directly from Ruger, allowing for safe loaded carry in the field. The barrels are sourced from Badger and feature a fast 1:15 or 1:16 twist rate, depending on caliber. All BFR frames come pre-drilled and tapped for a scope base and come with an aluminum Weaver-style scope base, an extra taller front sight, and a padded soft case. You can also specify rubber or ivory or black Micarta grips.

Magnum Research offers BFRs in a variety of "standard calibers." The short-framed models house the .44 Magnum, .454 Casull, .50 AE, .475 Linebaugh, and .500 JRH. Long-framed revolvers can be had in .45-70, .450 Marlin, .460 and .500 Smith & Wesson Magnums, and even in .30-30 Winchester. Custom revolvers from the Precision Center (Magnum Research's custom shop) can be ordered in a number of less mainstream calibers including .45-90 Winchester, .38-55 Winchester, .375 Winchester, and .50 Beowulf. Customers can also specify barrel length, the action gets some extra atten-

MAGNUM RESEARCH'S long-framed revolver in .500 Smith & Wesson Magnum is capable of delivering outstanding accuracy.

THE FREEDOM ARMS Model 83 in .454 Casull.

tion, and Precision Center guns also receive an 11-degree crown.

My only criticism of the BFR is rather subjective. The grip frame, as mentioned above, is the standard Ruger plow handle. I am a self-professed Bisley man. That said, the Bisley grip frame is not for everyone, and, if you ask 10 handgunners their preferences, they will likely come down on one of the two sides evenly. Changing the grip frame on the BFR is a custom proposition only, as it requires extensive massaging to fit the Bisley grip frame.

Overall, BFRs are outstanding revolvers delivering reliable performance at a reasonable cost. In my opinion, BFR should stand for "Bang For the Revenue."

Freedom Arms

These guns are the Cadillacs of the single-action revolver world. Freedom Arms was started by entrepreneur Wayne Baker, with a revolver design brought to the table by the veteran designer and originator of the modern, high-pressure, five-shot revolver, Dick Casull, in 1978. The first guns manufactured by Freedom Arms were actually mini revolvers of Casull's design. The biggest and most noticeable result of that union was the Freedom Arms Model 83 released in, you guessed it, 1983, and chambered for Dick Casull's wonder cartridge, the .454 Casull. The introduction of the Model 83 also debuted the .454 as an honest-to-goodness production cartridge. Freedom Arms takes its name from the location of its plant in Freedom, Wyoming.

Though a traditionally styled single-action re-

volver, the FA 83 is all modern on the inside and produced of modern materials (17-4PH stainless steel), though in a five-shot configuration (a lesson learned by Dick Casull, after decades of experimentation and development). When handling a Freedom Arms revolver, the lack of cylinder play becomes readily apparent. The company prides itself on hand assembling each and every unit to tight and exacting tolerances. It is a true "custom built" production revolver, and the tolerances are tight enough to necessitate regular cleaning to avoid problems like moving parts, well, not moving (a condition that could prove detrimental when facing an angry fur bearer higher up on the food chain than the user).

Unlike other commercial revolver producers, Freedom Arms has the distinction of performing machine work that is normally a custom shop-only proposition, a procedure known as line boring. Once the cylinder has been externally machined and fitted to the frame, the cylinder is heat-treated. Once heat-treating is complete, the cylinder is then placed in the frame of the revolver, a face-boring fixture is fitted where the barrel will attach, and each chamber is drilled through this fixture (which is mimicking the barrel). Thus, each hole is bored in precise alignment with the barrel, and it is one of the reasons Freedom Arms revolvers shoot as well as they do. All this extra attention will cost the buyer more, but perfection never comes cheaply.

The grip frame bears mention here. It is not at all like the plow handle of single-action revolvers of old (and some new), instead being much

FREEDOM ARMS' excellent Model 97 on top, and the Model 83 on bottom.

more like the Bisley interpretation by Ruger in that it angles down much sooner than the traditional plow handle grip frame that sweeps back before plunging down. And, much like the Ruger Bisley, the FA 83 grip frame handles recoil much better, in my opinion, than the standard single-action grip frame, as it is not designed to roll up in the hand. This is very beneficial when shooting a revolver that generates considerable recoil.

With the debut of the .454 Casull came the obvious need for ammunition, as a significant number of big-bore revolver fans do not reload and the .454 was a brand new cartridge. Freedom Arms addressed this need with a number of its own premium loads, one featuring a 240-grain bullet rated at 1,875 fps (from a 7½-inch barreled revolver), a medium velocity 250-grain load at 1,300 fps, a 260-grain jacketed flat-point (truncated cone) load at 1,800 fps, and, lastly, a load featuring a 300-grain jacketed flat-point at 1,600 fps. The semi-jacketed design of these last two featured a core and nose of an alloy heavy in linotype, which is very hard. These bullets were designed to expand very little, if at all, and were very effective on game. Unfortunately, these loads are no longer available, and though Freedom Arms still sells the 260-grain bullets, supplies are limited.

Fast forward to 2011, and Freedom Arms not only continues to produce the FA 83, but it does so in a number of different calibers and in two different grades, Field and Premier. The 83 is available in .22 LR (Field Grade only), .357 Magnum, .41 Magnum, .44 Magnum, .454 Casull, .475 Linebaugh, and .500 Wyoming Express. The Model 83 Premier Grade features a brighter brushed finish, fully adjustable rear sight, laminated hardwood grips, and a limited lifetime warranty. Field Grade revolvers have a matte finish, a rear sight that can only be adjusted for elevation, a one-year warranty, and rosewood grips.

Freedom Arms also produces a smaller framed revolver, the Model 97, for those who wish for a trimmer package on their hip. The 97 is available in .17 HMR, .22 LR, .224-32 FA (a wildcat of Freedom Arms' design), .327 Fed-

WHILE FREEDOM ARMS was getting ready to unleash the Model 83 in .454 Casull, United Sporting Arms produced less than 100 of these Seville .454 "Magnums."

UNITED SPORTING ARMS produced stretch-framed revolvers in a number of calibers. This one is chambered in the popular metallic silhouette cartridge, the .375 SuperMag.

eral, .357 Magnum, .41 Magnum, .44 Special, and .45 Colt. Introduced in 1997, this revolver departed from the Model 83 mechanically, in that it featured a transfer bar safety system similar to Ruger's design and which allows for safe carry with a round under the hammer. Also of note is the size difference between the 97 and the 83. When newly introduced, the 97 was of the same stature as Colt's famous SAA. Originally only offered as a six-shot .357 Magnum, the line was later expanded to include the .41 Magnum and the .45 Colt in a five-shot configuration. Tim Sundles, of Buffalo Bore Ammunition fame, even loaded special .45 Colt ammo for the smaller 97, with a 300-grain bullet at moderate velocities and pressures and loaded to a shorter overall length to accommodate the shorter cylinder. The 97 makes for a really fine packing revolver!

These revolvers have no equals, with regards to fit and finish. Tolerances are very tight and the grip frame is superb. Just like single-action Colt's of old, the FA 83 should not be carried with a cartridge under the hammer, or an accidental discharge can result. Loading and unloading is performed with the hammer in the half-cock position, allowing the cylinder to spin—another nod to the Colt's Single Action Army. Freedom Arms recommends carrying the 97 with an empty chamber under the hammer as well, to eliminate any possibility of an accidental discharge. In all, Freedom Arms produces true modern-day classics.

United Sporting Arms

While no longer produced, the Seville and El Dorado lines of revolvers from U.S. Arms are still available on the used gun market. These revolvers are single-actions of modern design and metallurgy, but theirs is a story of financial difficulty, broken friendships, and unfulfilled potential wrought by the dogged and tenacious pursuit of firearms perfection.

The history and chronology is a bit convoluted, but it all began in 1972, when Sig Himmelman, gun designer and builder, and Forrest Smith, a retired aircraft engineer, founded United States Arms in Riverhead, New York, and designed the Abilene revolver in .44 Magnum. Keep in mind that these were the days long before CNC machinery and computer design software, necessitating countless hours on a Bridgeport to produce moulds. The goal was to blend the classic lines of the Colt's New Frontier with the modern strength of the Ruger Blackhawk. In 1974, Sig and Forrest broke away from United States Arms and formed United Sporting Arms, Inc., also based in New York, and created the Seville, a blued revolver in .44 Magnum that was close in design to the original Abilene. By 1976, Sig and Forrest had brought forth the El Dorado, the first completely 17-4PH stainless steel revolver. It was also chambered in .44 Magnum.

The year 1979 brought about another move, but this time it was only Sig Himmelman packing his bags. Moving west to Tombstone, Arizona, he

THIS REVOLVER is an early stainless steel .44 Magnum. United Sporting Arms was the first manufacturer to produce and sell an all-stainless steel .44 Magnum revolver.

MOSSBERG ASSEMBLED approximately 200 U.S. Arms Abilene single-action revolvers in .45 Colt.

set up a second assembly site in the drier climes of the American southwest. No parts were manufactured there, with Sig instead relying solely on parts manufactured by United Sporting Arms, Inc., in New York. In fact, Sig's "facility" consisted of a small tin shed behind a warehouse. By late that year, Sig again picked up his operation and moved to Bisbee, Arizona, with the promise of more assembly space and funding from local businessmen. Those promises fell through, yet production continued, though less than 200 Sevilles (including the approximately 40 Qwik-Kit guns with interchangeable barrels and cylinders). Concurrently, Mossberg, the shotgun manufacturer, purchased United States Arms of Riverhead, New York, and continued producing the Abilene line of revolvers from leftover stock until 1983, when the parts supply ran dry.

In 1980, Sig Himmelman made a final split from United Sporting Arms, Inc., in New York, and moved his operation over to Tucson, Arizona. His new company was dubbed Sporting Arms, Inc. Meanwhile, in New York, United Sporting Arms, Inc., decided to simplify its life by renaming itself El Dorado Arms, and went about the business of primarily building stainless steel .44 Magnums.

Under the Sporting Arms banner, Sig Himmelman began offering Seville revolvers in many different calibers, and in both blue and stainless finishes. Calibers included the ubiquitous .44 Magnum, .45 Colt, .357 Magnum, .45 Win. Mag., 9mm Win. Mag., .454 Magnum (Casull), and .41 Magnum. In 1982, the maker stretched the frame to house the new 1.6-inch cased .357 Maximum. Sig was a close friend of Elgin Gates, and the pair worked together to bring about this new long-framed revolver, actually beating Ruger to market (though not by much). The stretch-framed theme continued and, by late '83, Sporting Arms had prototyped two .375 SuperMags revolvers. But the debut of these prototypes coincided with big financial problems, and the company was sold to investors out of Pittsburgh, who

ONE OF THE MOST innovative products to come out of United Sporting Arms was its "Qwik Kit" Sevilles with interchangeable barrels and cylinders. The kits got the buyer a .357 Magnum, .44 Magnum, and a .45 Colt in one revolver, all housed inside a brief case!

THE UBERTI 1873 Callahan New Model Target in .44 Magnum. Uberti has a well-earned reputation for strong, reliable handguns, selling its creations under its own name, as well as under others, such as Beretta.

returned the company to its old name, United Sporting Arms. El Dorado Arms closed its doors for good, in 1983.

United Sporting Arms, under the new investment group, continued producing stretch-frame revolvers and the standard blued and stainless steel Sevilles to include the .454. But this venture didn't last long and, by late 1985, this company, too, closed its doors. An investment group out of Post Falls, Idaho, subsequently bought all of United Sporting Arms' asscts and produced Sevilles through 1986. Sadly only about 200 guns were produced and shipped.

In 1988, one of original owners, Forrest Smith, along with Russell Wood, a former partner of the original United States Arms and El Dorado Arms, moved to Chimney Rock, North Carolina, to reform El Dorado Arms. It is important to note that the revolvers from the North Carolina iteration of El Dorado Arms were the makers' highest quality revolvers produced to date. All of them were hand fit and assembled. Meticulous manufacturing techniques accounted for the low production numbers (only 700 to 800 revolvers were built to ship from El Dorado of Chimney Rock, North Carolina). The company produced stainless steel (17-4PH) and blue El Dorados, with both fixed and adjustable sights, in all the standard big-bore chamberings. It also produced stretch-framed re-

volvers in .357 Maximum and .375 SuperMag. In 1997, Forrest Smith's health began to fail, and El Dorado arms closed its doors for the last time.

SAA CLONES

A number of quality Colt's Single Action Army copies or clones are available on the new and used gun market. I don't want to spend too much time on these, as their use is limited to lighter loads (with an exception or two), but they are worth mention because they are sometimes an economical way for the enthusiast to get into a real live big-bore revolver.

Uberti

Oddly enough, some of the finest reproduction American Old West guns are produced in Italy. Uberti, a subsidiary of Benelli, offers a whole line of reproduction Colt's 1873 Single-Action Army revolvers made of modern materials. These fine reproductions are economical, pleasing to look at, and of good quality. Like their progenitor, you have to place the hammer on half-cock in order to rotate the cylinder for loading and unloading.

We ordered an 1873 Callahan New Model Target in .44 Magnum directly from Uberti and were more than pleased with the overall fit and finish. This revolver is more of a modern interpretation

AUTHOR PHOTO

WE REALLY LIKE the attention to detail by Uberti, like these counter-bored chambers that allow the cartridge case head to sit flush in the cylinder.

of the Single Action Army, not only by virtue of its modern caliber (.44 Magnum), but also for the quality adjustable sights perched on top, a six-shot, counter-bored cylinder, and a spring-loaded cylinder pin retainer that makes cylinder removal a snap. Cylinders are non-fluted, and the guns come with a nice one-piece walnut grip. Due to its light weight, our sample was a bit lively with heavy loads, but it proved accurate out of the box using factory ammunition. It particularly likes Double Tap Ammo's 320-grain WFN loads (and I can't wait to see what it will do with handloads). What a bargain! Time will tell how it stands up to the abuse meted out by yours truly, but to say I am pleased is an understatement of epic proportions. I really like this gun!

U.S. Fire Arms

You will be hard pressed to find a nicer reproduction Colt's SAA than those produced by U.S. Fire Arms. These revolvers are faithful reproductions using modern materials and production techniques that result in first-rate workmanship, fit, and finish. Every possible variation from Flat Top Targets, Bisleys, and bird's heads models to Cowboy Action-specific competition models are available, as are revolvers from U.S. Fire Arms' Custom Shop. The possibilities and options are seemingly limitless. Each single-action revolver series revolver is built to your specifications, the option list including seven calibers from .32 WCF to .45 Colt, and three barrel lengths (4¾, 5½, and 7½-inches) with ejectors. A special ejector-less Sheriffs model is also available. Hard-rubber grips come standard, but U.S. Fire Arms offers a large selection of grip options to include stag, walnut, and genuine elephant ivory, to name but a few, so the customer can truly have the revolver they wish for. You can have your single-action in a color case-hardened finish or nickel plated, engraved, with dual chamberings (e.g. .45 Colt/.45 ACP), and many other options than we have room to list. At U.S. Fire Arms, you can truly have it your way.

DOUBLE-ACTION REVOLVERS

There are a number of quality big-bore double-action (DA) revolvers from Smith & Wesson, Sturm, Ruger and Company, Colt's, Dan Wesson,

TURNBULL MANUFACTURING, best known for correct, faithful, and top-shelf restorations of vintage firearms, tuned this USFA SAA (in .45 Colt) with the full Turnbull treatment to include color case hardening the frame and hammer, rust bluing of the cylinder, grip frame and barrel, tasteful and subtle engraving, and a special Turnbull serial number. This beautiful revolver is owned by Boge Quinn of Gunblast.com and was purchased through CDNN Sports, Inc.

and Taurus available on the new and used market. While Colt's no longer produces a big-bore double-action, their Anaconda revolver is a fine specimen worth owning. There are many out there on the used gun market, though they fetch a premium.

Double-action revolvers offer a couple distinct advantages over their single-action counterparts, to include the ability to fire by simply pulling the trigger without having to pull the hammer back first, as well as the ability to swing open the entire cylinder for loading/unloading that's much easier compared to a single-action revolver and its gate-accessed one-round-at-a-time design. Oddly enough, many who have double-action big-bore revolvers don't shoot them double-action. This sort of negates that advantage a bit, but, that said, I would rather have a double-action revolver if underneath an animal trying to take my life, as that advantage would then surely become more than pronounced.

Smith & Wesson

Smith & Wesson builds its revolvers only as double-actions, but these guns are some of the finest of their type in the world. The two we are most interested in discussing in this book are the N-frame, which was the largest frame offered by Smith & Wesson until 2003, when the company then introduced the X-frame. Smith & Wesson revolvers are known for their quality fit and finish, as well as their distinctive actions. Distinctive how? The word "superb" comes to mind. They are characteristically smooth and only become smoother with use.

N-Frame

The N-frame was first introduced in 1908 as the Hand Ejector model in .44 Special. That gun has experienced a number of iterations in its production history, but it wasn't until 1956, with the introduction of the .44 Remington Magnum, that these revolvers became famous, and these are the models we are most interested in discussing.

Of special note is the Model 29. With the release of the film *Dirty Harry,* which starred the Model 29 in .44 Magnum—oh, and Clint Eastwood, playing a "supporting role"—the gun gained rapid fame. The big Smith features some of the nicest lines to ever make their way down a revolver production line. It feels good in the hand and well balanced, even with a longish 6-inch barrel. The Model 25s in .45 Colt are also of interest to the big-bore revolver enthusiast and, aside from caliber, are identical to the Model 29. The model designation changed to "629," when production changed to stainless steel.

Smith & Wesson has the distinction of of-

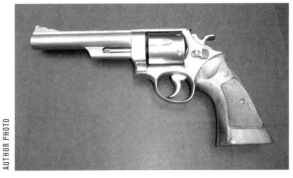

SMITH & WESSON'S instant classic, the Model 629, with a 6-inch barrel, wood grips, and stainless steel metal.

SMITH & WESSON'S Model 29 Classic DX is one of the finest N-frames ever produced, in the opinion of the author. The Classic features a full underlug and a rounded grip frame.

fering the only forged steel frames in the industry, with the N-frame as no exception. They are strong, relatively light in weight, and will deliver the user years of reliable service, if not abused. Many iterations of the Model 29 have been created in the five and half decades of production.

X-Frame

The X-frame is the largest-framed revolver Smith & Wesson has ever built, its sheer mass necessitated by the decision to build revolvers around the new, oversized Smith & Wesson cartridges, the .460 and .500. Large and heavy, the X-frame isn't for everybody.

It was 2003 that marked the year Smith & Wesson snatched the "Most Powerful Handgun" crown back from the .454 Casull. In 1983, when the Casull made its first appearance as a production cartridge in the debut of the Freedom Arms Model 83, the crown was unceremoniously stripped away from the ubiquitous .44 Remington Magnum. And that's where it stayed for 20 years, until S&W rolled out a whole new super-sized platform, the X-frame, chambered in a really big cartridge, the .500 Smith & Wesson Magnum. Not only was the crown back on Smith & Wesson's head, it was cemented in place.

Based loosely on the .500 Maximum, or .500 Linebaugh Long, a wildcat created by Wyoming gun builder John Linebaugh, the .500 S&W Magnum took its case length from the Maximum, a full 1.6 inches, but with a slightly smaller diameter of .500-inch, compared to its parent's .510-inch diameter. Here's the rub: the SAAMI pressure spec for Smith & Wesson's wonder cartridge is a full 62,000 psi!

In 2005, the .500's smaller sibling, the .460, was unleashed on the public, this round featuring a full case length of 1.8 inches and a ceiling operating pressure of 62,000 psi, just like the .500 Smith & Wesson Magnum. The addition of this round to its lineup completed Smith & Wesson's one-two punch on the big-bore revolver world.

If you have never seen or handled an X-frame Smith & Wesson, you may be surprised by the sheer size of the piece. The X-frame, is the largest and strongest frame Smith & Wesson has offered to date, handily unseating the N-frame in sheer bulk. We tested Smith & Wesson's .460 XVR a number of years ago, and the first impression was that it is a no-nonsense, long-range hunting tool. Weighing in at 72.5 oz. empty with an 8⅜-inch barrel, this five-shot revolver appears in a satin stainless steel finish and comes with interchangeable compensators (one for jacketed bullets, one for cast). With an overall length of 15 inches, this is not a revolver you can stick in your jacket pocket or wear comfortably on your hip (I know, I tried). Then again, it was never meant to. With its extra-long barrel featuring gain-twist rifling (meaning the rifling twist rate progresses down the length of the barrel, a design that purportedly aids in the stability of bullets), Smith & Wesson sought to produce the highest velocity production revolver in the world. It succeeded

AND YOU THOUGHT the N-frame was a big revolver! The .460 XVR dwarfs the Model 29 not only in size, but in power.

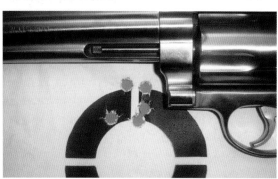

THE SMITH & WESSON .460 XVR returned outstanding accuracy, like this 1⅛-inch five-shot group at 50 yards. This revolver is capable of great long-range accuracy.

in spades, with some factory loads achieving an incredible 2,300 fps!

Of course, this gun has long-range applications written all over it, but what constitutes long range? If your eyes are as bad as mine, I would say anything over 100 yards, with open sites, but within this discussion, I would actually say 200 yards. Game starts looking really small at that range, and open sites become a real challenge, despite the excellent HIVIZ

front sight blade and adjustable rear sight. Then again, this is a gun that truly deserves a scope.

I didn't have as much ammo on hand to wring out this revolver the way I had wanted to, thanks to an editorial deadline, but even with an abbreviated test, I was able to see the tremendous potential the .460 XVR has to offer. I had on hand a box of Magtech 225-grain solid copper hollowpoints that leave the barrel at a scorching 2,132 fps—and that's hauling the mail for *any* revolver. The .454 Casull used to be the velocity king, but those days are gone, since the .460 has made the scene. Wearing a green HIVIZ front sight blade, I was able to get a 1⅛-inch group at 50 yards off of sandbags (I never test any firearm at distances under 50 yards, as 25 yards is just too close to experience the limitations of a gun). With carefully tailored handloads, I can almost guarantee that one could better these groups, but this is outstanding performance no matter how you cut it.

Recoil is negligible, as the muzzle brake does

AUTHOR PHOTO

SMITH & WESSON'S .460 XVR (Xtreme Velocity Revolver) chambered in the high-velocity .460 Smith & Wesson.

an effective job at keeping the kick down to more than acceptable levels, as does the excellent wrap-around rubber grips the XVR wears. The trigger is typical Smith & Wesson, meaning that it is very good and will only get better once the revolver is broken in. It exhibited no creep and broke cleanly. Another issue worth mentioning is the noise generated by this gun. In a word—loud. *Really* loud. Do not under any circumstances shoot this piece without substantial hearing protection.

A rather versatile chambering, the .460 X-frames boast the ability to safely shoot three types of ammunition, the .45 Colt, .454 Casull, and the .460 Smith & Wesson. You may not see optimal accuracy using the shorter cased siblings of the .460, but they can be used in a pinch. Best accuracy will be seen with the full-length case of the .460.

Picking up Smith & Wesson's .500 X-frame, one cannot help noticing the mass of the revolver and its cumbersome weight. Upon firing, the "why" behind the bulk becomes clear. When you are burning that much powder to push a heavy bullet at high speed, it *has* to kick, there's no other choice. It's physics, pure and simple.

AUTHOR PHOTO

WE REALLY LIKE the looks of the .500 Smith & Wesson with the 6½-inch barrel. With its partial underlug, it is reminiscent of the Model 29s of yesterday, just a lot bigger.

With high nominal pressures on the menu, Smith & Wesson addressed the issue of strength in its new X-frame by super-sizing the entire package and attaching what amounts to a K-frame grip frame to the new large frame. As I've mentioned, Smith & Wesson has the distinction of being the only revolver manufacturer to make its frames from forgings. While stronger than castings in the direction of the grain, they really don't offer a

LIGHT HEAVYWEIGHT

Smith & Wesson has been building .44 Magnum revolvers since 1956, when it unleashed the venerable Model 29 N-frame on the shooting world. This first truly high-performance, big-bore double-action revolver evolved over the years, culminating in the high-tech space metal 329PD.

Smith & Wesson produces other scandium-framed, lightweight revolvers, but we were interested in testing the biggest in the series in one of our favorite calibers, the .44 Remington Magnum.

If you have never handled a 329PD, let me warn you, there is shock value in picking it up for the first time, as it comes in at 25 ounces unloaded! Featuring a scandium alloy frame and a cylinder made of titanium alloy—a material stronger than most steels, it is corrosion resistant and used extensively in the aerospace industry—Smith & Wesson created a revolver that is both strong and very light in weight.

The 329PD holds a traditional six rounds and sports a four-inch barrel topped with a light-gathering red HIVIZ front sight. An adjustable V-notch rear sight is standard. The 329 comes with two grips, a nice finger-grooved wooden grip, and a recoil-absorbing rubber set. We tested all loads with the rubber grips. Though a bit on the heavy side, the trigger was typical Smith & Wesson in that it broke cleanly, but it clearly needs some breaking in, as all revolvers do. The revolver is finished in a matte black finish—all business.

Surely, that much punch in such a lightweight package must produce severe recoil, shouldn't it? Well, yes and no. While it kicks considerably more than my all-steel Model 29s, I never found it debilitating—then again, I may not be the best judge, so let's just say that it kicks less than it should!

We ordered a whole bunch of different loads from Double Tap Ammunition of Cedar City, Utah, a producer of fine ammunition in a large variety of calibers. We tested a number of loads all the way up to my favorite, Double Tap's 320-grain WFN load (which, incidentally, recoiled the most of all we tested). We have used this load successfully in the past on a number of wild hogs. Stepping down a bit, the .44 Special loads were downright pleasant.

I was unable to produce good groups at my usual 50 yards, as the HIVIZ sights are an up-close combat sight and thereby a close-range proposition. At 25 yards, this revolver is at home, and so I envision the 329PD as a back-up piece. It is really quick to press into action, due to its light weight and superior Smith & Wesson double-action ergonomics. It comes up on target easily, and the sights are a snap to acquire.

The most accurate load tested was the 225-grain XPB load that printed a half-inch five-shot group at the aforementioned 25 yards. This gun was a pleasure to use for quick-fire drills. In fact, I can say the Smith & Wesson 329PD is the most pleasurable big-bore revolver I have ever carried afield. You don't even know it's there, when strapped to your side. I have had a long love affair with Smith & Wesson's Model 29s in every flavor and owned them for decades, and this one is no exception. Big power, great handling, light package. It may just be the ultimate backup revolver.

SMITH & WESSON'S space-age, lightweight, scandium frame 329 PD.

strength advantage over a quality investment casting. Still, testimony to the strength of the X-frame is the fact that these guns can operate all day long at the pressures created by the .460 and .500 cartridges. The X-frame is a large, uncompromising gun that makes no apologies.

Sturm, Ruger & Company

If there is one thing Ruger is known for, it's over-engineering. Strenuous, if not excessive, testing is *de rigueur* for Sturm, Ruger and Company.

Ruger currently produces two big-bore double-action revolvers, the Redhawk and the Super Redhawk, which complement the company's full line of single-action revolvers. Introduced in 1980 and often considered a bit on the bulky side, the Redhawk, and later the Super Redhawk, double-action revolvers are built like tanks, for lack of a more imaginative term. They are known for their strength, and some specialty ammunition companies actually offer Ruger-only loads. That reputation for strength is well founded. By simply handling a Redhawk, its substantiality is readily apparent, particularly alongside similarly sized revolvers from the competition. This is also a point of criticism by some, but I personally like the security of knowing there is no commercially loaded ammunition that can upset a Redhawk! Hamilton Bowen noted that the Redhawk was the "first double-action properly scaled to the .44 Magnum cartridge."

While I do not condone the activity, back in the 1980s, it was a fairly common practice by some to re-chamber production Redhawks from .44 Magnum up to the high-pressure .454 Casull. Typically, the stock barrel was rebored, as was the stock .44 Magnum cylinder. I know of no instances of catastrophic failure with such a conversion, a testimony to the brute strength offered by the Redhawk.

The Super Redhawk was introduced in 1988, in .44 Remington Magnum. The Super Redhawk (SRH) features an extended frame from which integral scope mounts are promi-

RUGER'S REDHAWK in .44 Magnum is on the left, and a Smith & Wesson Model 29 is on the right. The picture clearly shows the additional material in the cylinder of the Ruger, contributing to that gun's strength and weight.

nent. Ruger designed the SRH after determining scopes are best not mounted on the barrel. Ruger also added the superior GP 100 grip frame to the SRH, allowing for better and easier action tuning.

The introduction of the .454 cartridge to the SRH lineup called for something a bit different. Ruger wanted to maintain a six-shot cylinder configuration, instead of the typical five-shot norm for production revolvers chambered in the high-pressure .454 Casull round (roughly a 30,000 psi increase in pressure moving from the .44 Magnum to the .454). The challenge was presented by the company president, at the time, Bill Ruger, Jr., to use the best materials available to make this design come to fruition. Type 410

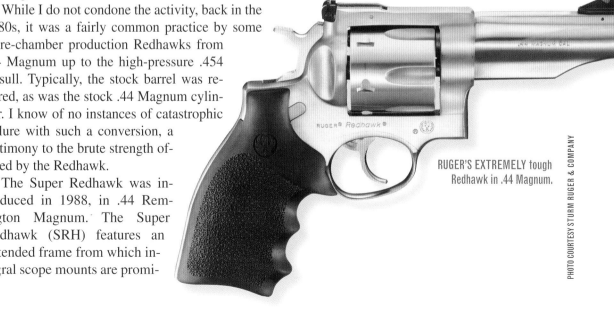

RUGER'S EXTREMELY tough Redhawk in .44 Magnum.

RUGER'S .357 MAXIMUM was only produced for a short period of time. The Blackhawk frame was stretched to accommodate the 1.6-inch long .357 Maximum case. This particular revolver was sacrificed to the big bore gods and is now a .500 Maximum.

stainless steel was tested, but found to be lacking under the repeated abuse the .454 proof loads can inflict. Ruger engineers next consulted Carpenter Technology Corporation metallurgist Humberto Raposo for his assistance in selecting appropriate materials for the project, and he suggested Carpenter's then-new Custom 465 stainless steel.

Ruger made a cylinder from Custom 465 stainless steel and purportedly had a devil of a time drilling the chambers. As I said, Ruger takes testing very seriously, and the new .454 SRH was no exception. Proof loads were created that generated a whopping 92,000 psi of pressure—nearly a full 30,000 psi over the SAAMI specification pressure for the .454 Casull. And the SRH wasn't subjected to just a few of such rubble-reducing loads—a full *300* loads were tested, 50 rounds per chamber! In the end, no measurable damage was

inflicted, giving the Ruger SRH a large margin for error.

In 2001, Ruger unleashed the .480 Ruger SRH on the handgun public, also in a six-shot configuration, it's cylinder likewise constructed of Carpenter's 465 stainless steel. Both the .454 and .480 iterations of the Ruger Super Redhawk were constructed with an interesting finish called "Target Gray." The gray hue actually was the result of the tumbling process used by Ruger and was accidental. Fortunately, it proved tough and resistant to corrosion. Folks seem to either love it or hate it. I like it for its durability and uniqueness.

They say beauty is in the eye of the beholder, and the Super Redhawk seems to fall under this rule. Personally, I like the functionality of the design and appreciate the business-like appearance and durability built into Ruger's flagship revolver.

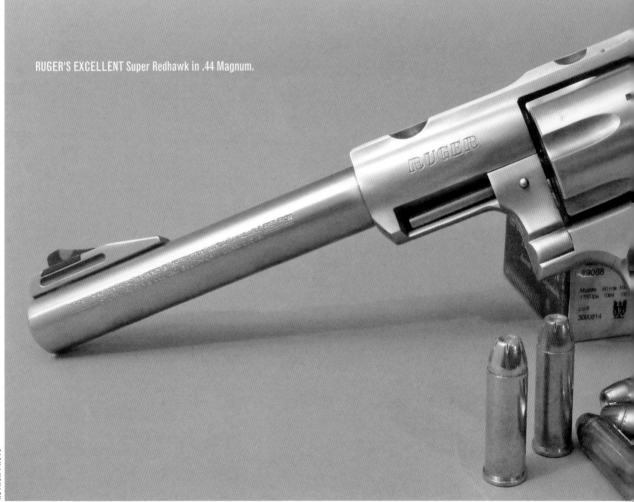

RUGER'S EXCELLENT Super Redhawk in .44 Magnum.

TAURUS

With manufacturing facilities in Brazil, Taurus offers a full line of big-bore revolvers for many uses. There are three models with three different frame sizes we need to discuss, the Raging Bull, the Tracker, and the Judge series.

Taurus' Raging Bull line of revolvers is the company's largest-framed revolver. It is of particular interest to this discussion, as it has been chambered in the past in some of the most powerful revolver cartridges in production, including the .480 Ruger, .454 Casull, and the mighty .500 Smith & Wesson Magnum. While the most powerful Raging Bull currently in Taurus' production lineup is the .454 version, there are plenty of these revolvers in other calibers available used. The Raging Bull can be purchased new in a six-shot configuration in .41 and .44

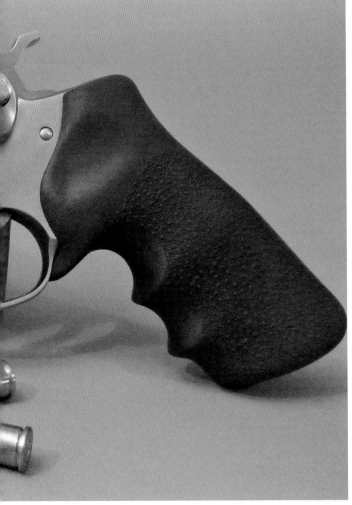

Magnum, and in a five-shot platform in .454 Casull. New or used, Taurus' Raging Bull offers good value for the price of admission.

Introduced in 1998, the Raging Bull is all business. Available in high-polish stainless, matte stainless, or blue finish, Taurus made sure there was something for every enthusiast, even those with the most discerning taste. The Raging Bull is fitted with a bull barrel available in five-, 6½-, and 8⅜-inch lengths, with a full underlug and a vented rib, adjustable sights, and effective rubber grips (effective in that they provide a good cushion to the shooter's hand). Barrels all feature porting, to cut down on felt recoil with the stoutest loads. The porting also serves to up the noise quotient, so one should always wear hearing protection (and, unfortunately these guns cannot be had without the porting). The package is rounded out with a large, five-shot cylinder. The Raging Bull certainly looks the part and lives up to its name.

The Tracker series is my favorite of the Taurus offerings. It is considerably smaller in stature than the Raging Bull, but also of a five-shot configuration. The Tracker is available in .41 and .44 Magnum calibers and offers an easy packing for field use. Available in matte stainless steel or blued steel, with a 2½- or 4-inch barrel, the Tracker is quite an attractive package. The four-inch .44 Magnum version weighs in at a light 34 ounces empty. Trackers also come equipped with Taurus' excellent "Ribber" rubber grips.

Another Taurus revolver of recent introduction, the third frame type, and one that has exceeded all expectations as far as popularity is concerned, is the Judge. This long-framed revolver is chambered in .410-bore and .45 Colt. A variety of different configurations are available to the public, culminating in the Public Defender Polymer Judge, an ultra-high-tech revolver, with a steel frame and a polymer exterior over-molded onto the steel frame. The popularity of the Judge series of revolvers has spurred the design and production of "Judge-only" .410 shotgun loads that accommodate a focus on home-defense.

Performance with either .45 Colt cartridges or .410 shotshells in the Judge has proven to be a bit

THE SUPER REDHAWK lends itself well to customizing and converting to larger calibers than offered by the factory, due to its inherent strength. These two five-shot custom Ruger Super Redhawks were built by Jack Huntington (JRH Advanced Gunsmithing), one chambered in .475 Linebaugh, the other in .500 Linebaugh.

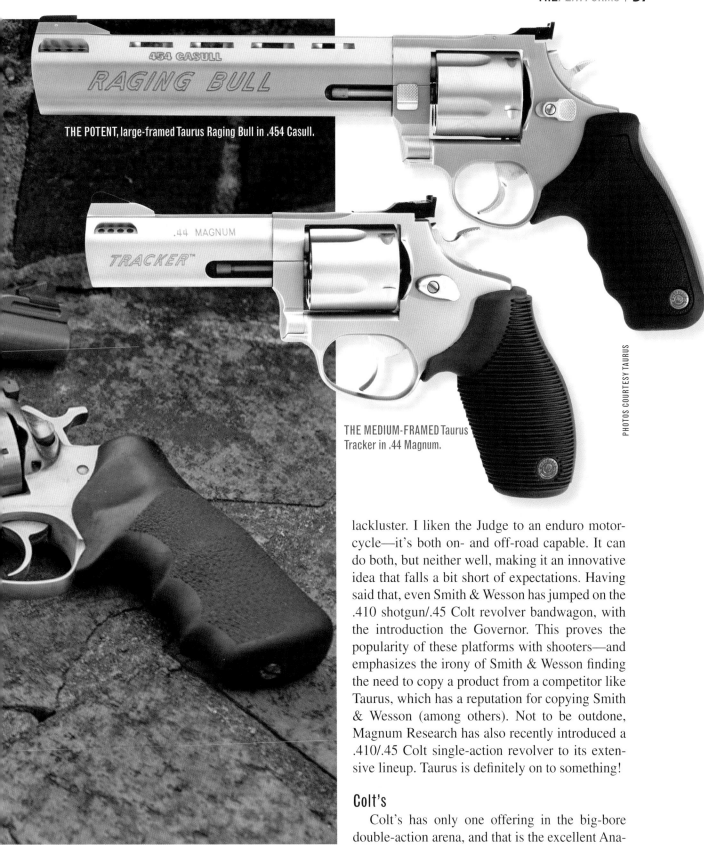

THE POTENT, large-framed Taurus Raging Bull in .454 Casull.

THE MEDIUM-FRAMED Taurus Tracker in .44 Magnum.

PHOTOS COURTESY TAURUS

lackluster. I liken the Judge to an enduro motor-cycle—it's both on- and off-road capable. It can do both, but neither well, making it an innovative idea that falls a bit short of expectations. Having said that, even Smith & Wesson has jumped on the .410 shotgun/.45 Colt revolver bandwagon, with the introduction the Governor. This proves the popularity of these platforms with shooters—and emphasizes the irony of Smith & Wesson finding the need to copy a product from a competitor like Taurus, which has a reputation for copying Smith & Wesson (among others). Not to be outdone, Magnum Research has also recently introduced a .410/.45 Colt single-action revolver to its extensive lineup. Taurus is definitely on to something!

Colt's

Colt's has only one offering in the big-bore double-action arena, and that is the excellent Ana-

THE EVER POPULAR TAURUS JUDGE,
chambered in .45 Colt and .410-bore shotgun.

THE EVER POPULAR TAURUS JUDGE (below)
chambered in .45 Colt/.410-bore shotgun.

conda. Produced from 1990 to 1999, the Anaconda represented Colt's foray into the double-action .44 Magnum revolver production as competition to Smith & Wesson's Model 29 and Ruger's Redhawk. Looking like a scaled-up Python (which in and of itself is a good thing), the Anaconda features a full underlug, a six-shot cylinder, ribbed barrel, adjustable sights, and an all-stainless steel construction. Unlike the competition from Smith & Wesson and Ruger, the Anaconda was never produced in blue, though Colt's did offer it in a Realtree camo version for a time.

Dan Wesson Arms

Founded by the great-grandson of D.B. Wesson, cofounder of Smith & Wesson, Daniel B. Wesson established Dan Wesson Arms, in 1968. Born in 1916, Daniel worked in the family business (Smith & Wesson) from 1938 until 1963, when Smith & Wesson was acquired by Bangor Punta.

Featuring a number of innovations, Dan Wesson's revolvers were known for quality, durability, and, most importantly, accuracy, an asset that made them a favorite in metallic silhouette shooting. Dan Wesson big-bore revolvers were inherently accurate, strong, and on the heavy side, making them among the most pleasant to shoot, even with hot loads.

Certain innovations set Dan Wesson revolvers apart from others, most particularly their switch-barrel capability. Imagine purchasing a revolver that comes with a number of replaceable barrels, enabling you to turn your revolver from a short-barreled carry piece into a long-barreled unit for a silhouette match in just minutes! Ingenuity was a trademark of Dan Wesson Arms.

Dan Wesson also offered stretch-framed revolvers specifically designed for the popular long-range metallic silhouette competitors of the late '70s and early '80s, those guns chambered in Elgin Gates' .357, .375, and .445 SuperMags. Ruger also jumped into the metallic silhouette game, with a production revolver in its version of the .357 SuperMag, the .357 Max-

PHOTO BY JODY BALDWIN

A STAINLESS STEEL Dan Wesson Model 745 in .45 Colt.

imum (same cartridge). Only a small number of .414 SuperMags made it out the door before Dan Wesson closed shop.

By 1983, Dan Wesson Arms was no longer family owned and was in financial trouble. Quality suffered as a result, and there was also a decline in the popularity of silhouette shooting to contend with. Looking more and more like Dan Wesson Arms would close its doors for good, Seth Wesson, the son of Dan and Carol Wesson, took control of the company and renamed it Wesson Firearms Company.

Even with new energy, the company soon faltered and, after a few years, the name was purchased by the company New York International, which had the intent of producing Dan Wesson-designed revolvers once again. Included in the acquisition were the necessary tooling, patents, trademarks, intellectual properties, and all remaining inventories. It was only the old manufacturing machinery that wasn't purchased, as it was both dated and worn out, so it was amply evident that producing the same high-quality firearms would require new tooling.

The new Wesson Firearms tooled up anew, and by December of 1997, the first revolvers were shipped. The fit and finish of that first run were of excellent quality. The production pro-

cess continued to improve, and 1999 marked a year of growth for the company, with two new large-frame revolvers added to the lineup, as well as the reintroduction of the .414 Super-Mag. The Pistol Packs and Hunter Packs returned to production at this time, as well, but with new refinements.

The Pistol Packs bear mention, as they really set Dan Wesson apart from other manufacturers. These revolvers come with three different barrels of different lengths and with their accompanying barrel shrouds, two sets of grips, and the necessary feeler gauge and barrel wrench for swapping barrels. This was truly a great innovation.

When the year 2005 rolled around, CZ-USA purchased Wesson Firearms, adding more depth to CZ's quality lineup. CZ-USA offered a .445 Alaskan model, but generally dialed back on revolver production to focus on semi-automatic pistols, including the ones designed by Wesson Firearms prior to CZ-USA purchasing that company. A number of years later, now, CZ-USA has shelved all revolver production. Will they again offer the excellent Wesson designs? Only time will tell.

A BOWEN CLASSIC ARMS-built Colt's Single Action Army.

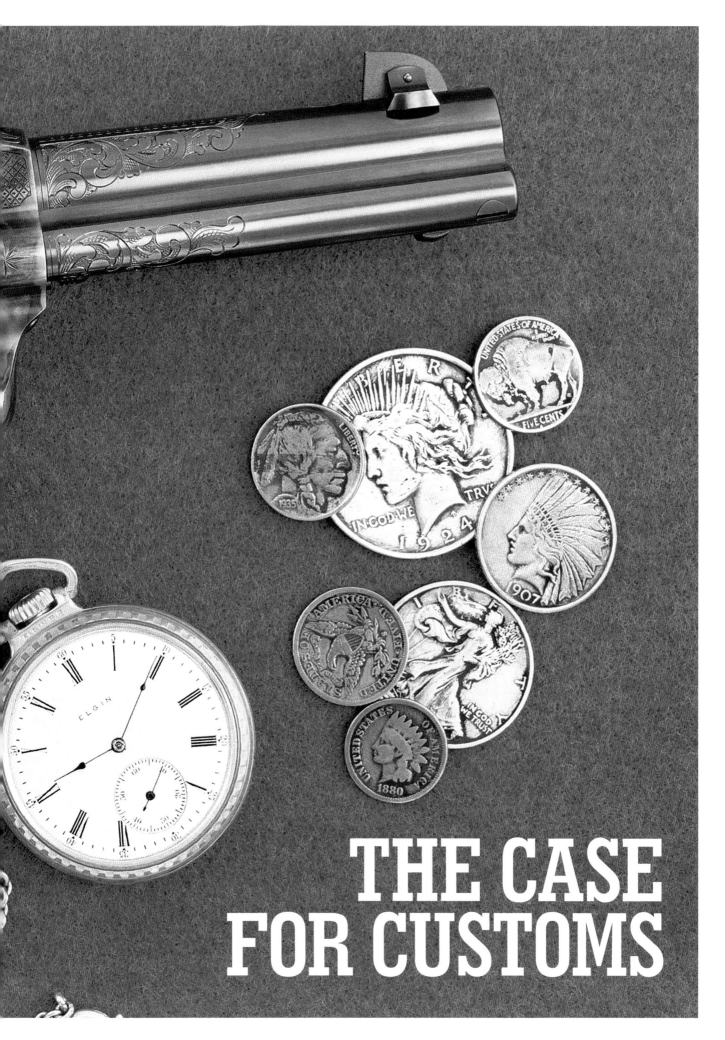

THE CASE
FOR CUSTOMS

There was a time when owning a true big-bore revolver—excluding the .44 Magnum and the .45 Colt— was a custom proposition only. Many custom revolvers were built on Ruger platforms in cartridges that, 20 years ago were wildcats, but which now are production calibers. Those days are gone, but you can still take any factory big-bore revolver and improve upon it significantly. Or simply personalize it. It may not necessarily be about making it better or more reliable, but rather making it more to your liking. Examples might be custom grips that fit your hand perfectly, sights that are easier on your eyes, or a trigger pull that is lighter and smoother than the one the revolver left the factory with (and nothing improves shooting confidence like a smooth trigger that's easy for the shooter to control).

No discussion of custom revolvers would be complete without looking at Elmer Keith's famous No. 5 Colt's revolver, probably the first custom to grace the pages of the popular gun media of the late 1920s. Keith's No. 5 was a collaborative effort between a number of talented individuals, but the brainchild of Harold Croft of Philadelphia, Pennsylvania.

Before the No. 5 was born, though, four other revolvers from Croft were unveiled in the September 1928 issue of the *American Rifleman*. These numbered variations, based on Colt's Single Action Army revolvers, featured modifications to the receivers, sights, hammers, and grip frames, turning them into high-performance, lightweight, self-defense guns. Keith had the good fortune to shoot extensively a number of Croft's Colt's SAA creations and came away impressed not only with Croft's innovation, but also the workmanship of gunsmiths Neal Houchins and R.F. Sedgley. Clearly, these guns ignited a fire in Elmer Keith that got him thinking out loud on the pages of the *American Rifleman* about what would make the perfect revolver for the dedicated outdoorsman.

The result of all of Keith's vocal speculation became what is known as the Keith No. 5 Colt's. This gun made its debut in the April 1929 issue of *American Rifleman*, in Keith's column "The Last Word." The No. 5 Colt's, in .44 Special, embodied many of Croft's innovations, along with a number of Keith's, resulting in what has been described by Hamilton Bowen, in his book *The Custom Revolver*, as "what was probably the first practical, dedicated revolver for the serious outdoorsman." The Keith No. 5 was undoubtedly the most influential and most photographed custom revolver ever built, and the virtual progenitor of all custom single-action revolvers to come.

One of the first true customs I remember reading about was the .45 Colt Seville that Ross Seyfried commissioned John Linebaugh to build in the mid-1980s. The Seville started life as a .44 Magnum and was fitted with a custom, oversized six-shot cylinder and a Douglas barrel. It was able to handle loads that were unthinkable in any other platform of the day, to the tune of those in the 60,000 psi range. Ross Seyfried truly pushed the limits, when loading his .45 Colt Seville, but it held up well. That Linebaugh Seville was made famous in the pages of *Guns & Ammo*, the pinnacle of that fame occurring with the successful take of a Cape buffalo by Seyfried, in Africa.

There are a number of great gun builders and gunsmiths who can turn the ordinary into the exotic, creations limited only by your imagination, the capabilities of your chosen gunsmith, and the depth of your pockets. Yes, custom work is costly, but a revolver is not an object whose function should be taken lightly. It is a serious piece of equipment that requires a skilled hand to modify.

Without a doubt, the most popular platforms on which custom big-bore revolvers are based are the Ruger Blackhawk and Super Blackhawk single-action revolvers. The "new models" are built strongly and provide a tough foundation. While rough in factory trim, they can be massaged to perfection, and their transfer bar safety is a reliable one, making for safe loaded carry in the field and reliable ignition.

We have profiled a number of talented gunsmiths in this segment. Some you will immediately recognize, some you may not, but I hope they'll become familiar to you after you read about them and that you'll consider them for your next custom big-bore revolver project. We have appropriately started with John Linebaugh, whose name

OWNED BY TIM MARSHALL of Sandy, Utah, this stainless steel Bisley was built by John Linebaugh and features a 5½-inch banded barrel. It is chambered in .475 Linebaugh.

graces a couple of the greatest big-bore revolver cartridges to ever be developed—the .475 and .500 Linebaughs.

JOHN LINEBAUGH

This segment would be incomplete without acknowledging the extreme contributions and influences John Linebaugh has wielded on our hobby.

The one word that comes to mind when the name John Linebaugh comes up is "humble." Well, humble and persistent. Missouri born and bred, John Linebaugh was a full-time cowboy in the early '80s, and he also drove a concrete truck during the winter. When the sun went down, he built revolvers.

It was the ubiquitous .45 Colt that provided John with the inspiration he needed to eventually develop such iconic cartridges as the .475

and .500 Linebaughs. Armed with an old Uberti revolver in .45 Colt, John soon realized that gun was capable of doing things the .44 Magnum wouldn't, and at significantly lower pressures. In his words, the .45 Colt would "do more work with less pressure." Soon enough, John and his posse were riding the .45 Colt for all it was worth, with modern brass and oversized six-shot cylinders.

In the early '80s, John used nothing but Sevilles and El Dorados as foundations for custom six-guns, as Rugers during that period were of shoddy quality, according to John. All of this changed in the mid-'80s, when El Dorados and Sevilles were out of production and inventories were drying up. John then realized that the Ruger Bisley was everything he could hope for as a platform, one that offered strength and a grip frame well suited to heavy recoil—and even better suited to the recoil that was on the horizon. The writing was on the wall.

John's big break came when he talked Ross Seyfried into shooting one of his hot-rod .45 Colt creations (at least after he demonstrated that it was

This .475 Linebaugh Bisley was built by John Linebaugh during the brief period when the maker had moved his business back to Missouri. The gun and features a gold bar front sight and beautiful walnut grips by John's son Dustin Linebaugh.

PHOTO BY JOE VANDEMARK AND TODD CORDER

This bevy of John Linebaugh-built Ruger Bisley revolvers is owned by Todd Corder, Joe Vandemark, and Clay Hinderliter of western Illinois. Top is a Ruger Bisley Vaquero with a 5-inch barrel in .500 Linebaugh, bottom right a Ruger Bisley .500 Linebaugh with a 6½-inch barrel, and lastly bottom left is a Ruger Bisley in .38-40 with a 6½-inch barrel.

safe to push his custom Seville to never before seen levels). Ross was so taken aback by the .45 Colt's newfound performance that he commissioned John into building him a Seville with an oversized six-shot cylinder in .45 Colt. Ross eventually took this Linebaugh creation to Africa, where he killed a Cape buffalo without the safety net of a PH backing him up—well, he had a PH with him, but his backup weapon was a camera! All was recorded and immortalized on the pages of *Guns & Ammo* magazine. John Linebaugh had arrived.

Perhaps John Linebaugh's greatest contributions to the hobby are the two cartridges that bear his name. He is credited with the creation of two big-bore cartridges that have set the performance bar, the .475 and .500 Linebaughs. The .500 predates the .475 by a couple years and is based on a .348 Winchester case cut down to 1.4 inches and possessing a .510-inch bore diameter. The .475 Linebaugh, now a commercial offering, was based on a .45-70 case cut to 1.4 inches and having a .476-inch bore diameter. (These two cartridges are discussed in detail in Chapter 2).

John is also known for hopelessly infecting his son and fellow gunsmith, Dustin, with the big-bore revolver affliction. And he has some notoriety for his "Linebaugh Seminars" (discussed in detail elsewhere in this book), that he has been hosting for more than a decade to demonstrate the effectiveness of these big revolver cartridges. Coming from humble roots never put a damper on the dreams and ideas of John Linebaugh, and his creations are sure to live on in history.

Linebaugh Custom Sixguns: P.O. Box 455, Cody, WY 82414; (307) 645-3332; www.customsixguns.com.

JIM STROH AND ALPHA PRECISION, INC.

Located in Comer, Georgia, Alpha Precision is owned and operated by Jim Stroh. With a BS

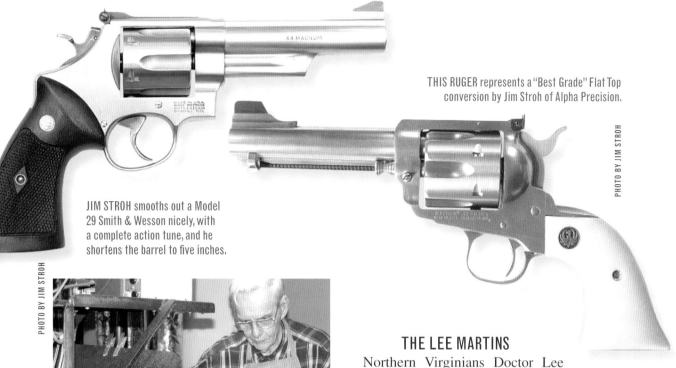

THIS RUGER represents a "Best Grade" Flat Top conversion by Jim Stroh of Alpha Precision.

PHOTO BY JIM STROH

JIM STROH smooths out a Model 29 Smith & Wesson nicely, with a complete action tune, and he shortens the barrel to five inches.

PHOTO BY JIM STROH

in chemistry from the University of Detroit, and graduate studies in both chemistry and metallurgy, Jim began dabbling in gunsmithing in the late 1950s and has been a full-time professional gunsmith since 1981. Jim is an officer in the American Pistolsmiths Guild and was voted Pistolsmith of the Year in 1996.

Alpha Precision specializes in custom Ruger single-actions in both five- and six-shot configurations up to .475 Linebaugh (this last cartridge in a five-shot). Jim also customizes Browning and Walther semi-auto pistols, as well as the ubiquitous 1911. Smith & Wesson and Ruger double-action revolvers also receive custom treatment at Alpha Precision. All of Jim's work is guaranteed, and he offers more than 200 services.

Alpha Precision, Inc.: 3238 Della Slaton Road, Comer, GA 30629; (706) 783-2131; www. alphaprecisioninc.com.

THE LEE MARTINS

Northern Virginians Doctor Lee Martin, Jr., and his son, Lee Martin III, started building Ruger cylinders from scratch right around 1990, when they weren't tearing up the competition at their local drag strip. Their first father-son effort was a .22-250 Winchester on an Old Model Ruger Blackhawk, followed up with a .44-40 on a Super Blackhawk. But, this wasn't the Martins' first go-around at gunsmithing, as Doctor Lee built his basement machine shop in the late '60s and began building custom Mauser 98s. Over the years, Dr. Martin built everything from varmint rifles to big-game rifles on P-17 Enfields. By the late 1970s, the good doctor was building Contender barrels.

By the 1980s, the senior Martin became heavily involved in benchrest shooting, which influenced the direction of his gunsmithing. At the same time, he began making his own reamers and reloading dies. This activity eventually led to him designing his own benchrest actions. The first was a shellholder bolt model, the second a port action with a Remington-style extractor. Both were machined from round bar stock and fully heat-treated in-house. The Martins usually fitted the home-built actions with Shilen or Hart barrels, Jewell triggers, and McMillan stocks. A variety of chamberings were

THIS BRACE OF WILDCAT CARTRIDGES was designed by Dr. Lee Martin and his son Lee. They are from left to right the .32 Martin Meteor, .375 Atomic, .401 Bobcat 1.29-inch, .458 Devastator, and the .450 Bonecrusher.

THE MARTINS built this custom Super Blackhawk back in 1993 in their .45-caliber wildcat dubbed the .458 Devastator. The cartridge is based on .458 Win. Mag. brass cut down to 1.4 inches.

DR. LEE MARTIN, JR., and son, Lee Martin III, in their basement machine shop.

THIS RUGER SUPER BLACKHAWK was built by the Martins and fitted with a five-shot cylinder chambered for the pair's .450 Bonecrusher, a .500 Linebaugh necked down to .458-caliber and wearing a 30-degree shoulder. This round will routinely throw 350-grain bullet at 1,700 fps.

built, including 6mm BR, .219 Wasp, .308 Winchester, .30-350 Remington, and 7mm BR, to name but a few. Eventually, one thing lead to another, and the Martins eventually built a rather large iteration of their rifle action to accommodate one of the most serious of long-range cartridges, the .50 BMG. They even designed their own muzzle brake to tame the recoil of that behemoth cartridge.

By the end of the tumultuous 1980s, the Martins decided to tackle single-action cylinders, prototyping a Ruger single-action cylinder out of aluminum on their Bridgeport mill. Once they figured it out, it was game on, and the Martins began churning out Ruger cylinders made with 4140 barstock. As with their rifle actions, the Martins perform all heat-treating in house. Around 1996, the Martins expanded into stainless steel, using 416 and 17-4PH. Since 1990, the pair have produced dozens of revolver cylinders in five- and six-shot configurations for a whole slew of known calibers, from .218 Bee all the way up the .500 Maximum, as well as some creations of their own design, like the .240 Incinerator, .375 Atomic, and .450 Bonecrusher.

The junior Martin has one of the most informative websites to grace the Internet, called, appropriately, www.singleactions.com). Featuring a number of great forums on which readers can discuss and trade ideas (and the occasional

PHOTO BY JOHN SPARKMAN

THIS BEAUTIFUL stainless Clements-built Ruger Bisley in .500 JRH is owned by John Sparkman and features an octagon barrel. The grips are caramel ebony, by Scott Kolar.

THIS STUNNING pair of Ruger .500 Maximums was built by Dave Clements for a couple of brothers from Missouri. Doug Turnbull color case hardened the frames, hammers, and triggers, and Scott Kolar (SK Grips) made the Bisley grips. The five-shot cylinders are countersunk for recessed cases, and both revolvers have Belt Mountain locking base pins. The revolver on top has a six-inch barrel with a band, the other a five-inch barrel. Both have Bowen Rough Country rear sights and Dave's trademark patridge front sight.

blow), the site also offers a number of technical articles written by Lee Martin III, including a complete tutorial on building a custom five-shot revolver cylinder. Being a Seville aficionado, the junior Lee has also compiled the most complete (and probably only) chronological history of the production of the Seville and El Dorado lines of revolvers. It's a site worth visiting, perusing, and joining.

CLEMENTS CUSTOM GUNS

Hailing from Amory, Mississippi, David Clements established Clements Custom Guns some 18 years ago. Nine years ago, he relocated it east to Woodlawn, Virginia. Though a one-man show, Clements possesses one of the best-equipped gunsmithing outfits in the United States, one featuring a bevy of CNC machines that the gunmaker uses to full capacity. With a background in tool and die making, Clements possesses the skills to produce some of the nicest custom revolvers available to mortal man.

It all began with David reading about the .475 and .500 Linebaughs in the popular gun media. He decided that he would build one himself, knowing he had the skills to make it come to fruition. David has come a long way since then, and his philosophy is that, if there is a part he cannot find and that he needs, he simply makes it. This mantra led to the produc-

THIS DIXIE FIREARMS-built Ruger Vaquero, belonging to Ed Folmar, has been fitted with Bisley parts and converted to a .475 Linebaugh in a five-shot cylinder. The frame and grip frame have been color case hardened, and the barrel was dovetailed for a rifle-type ivory bead front sight.

PHOTO BY ROD HUELTER

THIS DIXIE VAQUERO provides big punch in a small package. The 3½-inch barreled Ruger is chambered in .500 Linebaugh!

tion of hammers for single-action Rugers, and numerous other parts unavailable aftermarket. Whether you want to tune up your Single Action Army or convert your Blackhawk to .475 Linebaugh, you can rest assured that Dave will handle it personally, and the job will be done correctly and artfully.

Clements Custom Guns: 2766 Mt. Zion Road, Woodlawn, VA 24381; (276) 238-8761; www.clementscustomguns.com.

DIXIE FIREARMS

Hailing from California, Rod Huelter, proprietor of Dixie Firearms, got bitten by the gun and hunting bug around the age of 12. Even though no one in his immediate family hunted or participated in any shooting activities, nothing would deter the young Rod's budding interests.

He began his endeavors into the shooting sports by acquiring a compound bow, teaching himself to shoot. At age 14, the family moved to Oregon, where Rod had uncles and other family members who furthered his education and stoked the fires burning inside. In time, he became quite the accomplished bow hunter, with both compound and recurve bows.

In 1985, Rod joined the Navy and served as a Machinist Mate on a fast-attack submarine. Once out of the service, he began working on cars and developed a love for drag racing. For the next two decades or so, he stayed focused on the automotive business, along with a little time spent learning to wrench on fixed- and rotary-winged aircraft and industrial electric motors. All of these activities provided Rod the solid mechanical foundation that would govern the next chapter of his life.

A divorce followed by a remarriage in the late '90s brought Rod into direct contact with in-laws who were avid hunters. Life and fam-

ily soon got in the way of his drag racing habit, but, in its place, Rod discovered the joys and challenges of handgun hunting. With this new-found interest came the desire to explore different types of handguns and ever larger calibers.

The year 2007 was a turning point for Rod. A back injury from 1989 had caused him minor problems over the years and, in 2004, he had his first back surgery. In 2007, Rod's doctors classified him as disabled, and since then, he has had six more procedures on his back and neck. Rod had to make some big changes in his life or risk everything.

"Disabled, but not dead," stated Rod. He learned to deal with the pain and its limitations. Many friends and family members knew how much Rod loved firearms and the mechanical skills he possessed. Gunsmithing, they suggested, was the rational thing to do, especially since production guns had always failed to please him fully. Rod weighed the pros and cons of starting a new career at that stage in his life, but one

DIXIE FIREARMS built this Bisley Ruger and it is the personal firearm of owner Rod Huelter. It is chambered in .500 Linebaugh and wears a Leupold 2X scope on a Weigand base. The durable finish is Cerakote in a modified tiger stripe pattern. The grips are ebony.

SINGLE-ACTION PERFECTION, a lightweight Bowen-built Ruger Vaquero in .50 AE.

PHOTO BY HAMILTON BOWEN

man's encouragement pushed him over the top. That man was Dale Adams, an avid handgun hunter, confidant, and sounding board. Dale also had terminal cancer. So inspired was Rod by the example Dale had set with his positive attitude and approach to life, that Rod decided to move forward with his new vocation.

Enter Dixie Firearms. Rod performs all types of gunsmithing work to all manner of firearms, including custom work and five-shot caliber conversions to revolvers. Dixie Firearms is a one-man show, which guarantees the boss handles every single aspect of the work.

Dixie Firearms: 1615 Makinster Road, Tillamook, OR 97141; (503) 354-2274; www.dixiefirearms.net.

BOWEN CLASSIC ARMS

Tennessee born and bred, Hamilton Bowen is one of the most respected gunsmiths, if not the most respected gun maker in the industry. Despite his own attempts to steer his life in other directions, Hamilton got into gunsmithing for all of the right reasons—he couldn't stay away from it.

Hamilton didn't start out gunsmithing. Instead, he went to college after high school, earning a degree in History and English before heading to law school (the one "skeleton in my closet," as Hamilton likes to joke.) A self-professed "gun nut" growing up, Hamilton simply couldn't leave firearms alone. Wanting to scope a Ruger revolver he'd had as a teen, he found

PHOTO BY HAMILTON BOWEN

FROM THE BEGINNING, Hamilton Bowen liked Ruger's Redhawk platform for its barrel shank diameter. The gunsmith still offers big-bore Redhawk conversions, like this one in .500 Linebaugh.

there were no aftermarket tools or parts to pursue such endeavors. So, Hamilton bought a drill press and did the work himself. And that is how it all started. After his higher education, Hamilton enrolled in gunsmithing courses at Trinity State Junior College of Trinity, Colorado, and, after more than a year of formal gunsmithing education (which, to Hamilton's chagrin, focused more on rifles than handguns), he struck out on his own and opened his shop in 1980.

His shop and work weren't very refined at this stage, but the focus was on basic revolver work. Repairs put food on the table and helped Hamilton pay for more equipment in order to outfit his shop. Hamilton credits "indulgent parents who didn't mind a 28-year-old kid monkeying with guns in the basement," with the direction his life has taken. By the mid- to late '80s, Hamilton Bowen's core technology was in place, and he started refining his technique.

Even though Hamilton Bowen builds "package" guns, he still considers his business a custom shop. The reason for offering packages was simple, as they allowed Hamilton to spend more time building guns than haggling over specs on the phone. Hamilton determined that he was losing time and money, splitting fine frog hairs with customers who were having trouble making decisions over minute details. Bowen stated, "I have two kids in college, therefore I have no time for going back and forth!" Still, with the extensive list of options he offers, there is virtually something for everybody. Also, a large portion of the business is dedicated to parts production, such as pins and rear sights. In fact, the Bowen rear sights are an industry standard for the custom revolver.

While Hamilton's favorite platform for a custom revolver is the Ruger New Model single-action, he reports that he has recently begun working on Freedom Arms products. Hamilton told me, "They are so precisely made, that I don't have to build the platform, so to speak. I can do the stylistic work—the work I really like to do." Hamilton now also teaches summer gunsmithing courses that are supported by the National Rifle Association (the same courses that Hamil-

BOWEN CLASSIC ARMS has recently started working its magic on Freedom Arms' wonderful Model 97, turning a great revolver into an even better one.

PHOTO BY HAMILTON BOWEN

ton credits with giving him his affliction). Hamilton Bowen has come full circle.

The consummate gentleman, Bowen credits John Linebaugh with providing the impetus for the big-bore revolver movement.

"Back then, we had to build everything largely from scratch," said Bowen about the early years of the business.

While nearly everyone in the business has contributed something, according to Bowen, John Linebaugh did all of the ballistic work in the early days. Indeed, Hamilton and John Linebaugh really had the trade to themselves for nearly a decade, but Hamilton says he enjoys the competition he faces with the many quality gunsmiths building custom revolvers today, and says, "I like competition, it makes me work that much harder." Having seen the results personally, we cannot imagine building on perfection.

Bowen Classic Arms Corp.: P.O. Box 67, Louisville, TN 37777; (865) 984-3583; www. bowenclassicarms.com.

GARY REEDER CUSTOM GUNS

Just talking to Gary Reeder will give you a clue into his previous vocation, his voice betray-

GARY REEDER BUILDS guns to the customer's specs or packaged customs like the Grim Reaper. The Grim Reaper is built on Reeder's stretched stainless steel frame and can be chambered in a number of 1.6-inch cased cartridges up to the .500 Smith & Wesson.

GARY REEDER with good friend John Linebaugh (left).

ing him instantly. Clearly, his pipes are those of a radio personality and disc jockey, a 22-year career of a former life.

Born and raised outside of Nashville, Tennessee, Gary grew up on firearms and hunting with his dad and took to handgun hunting at a very early age. Gary began his transition into the firearms industry building custom XP100s and T/C Contenders in his garage at night while still spin-ning records in Florida. In 1985, he quit riding the radio waves and got into building custom guns on a full-time basis.

Gary got his first big break in 1987, with feature articles on his new custom revolver, the Black Widow, in the pages of *Guns* and *American Handgunner* magazines. The Black Widow was the first of many series to come and was an instant success, once the gun public saw it in the popular firearms media. In 1989, another article featuring the guns of Gary Reeder hit the newsstands, and with it came even more popularity. In 1994, Gary made the move to the Southwest, winding up in Flagstaff, Arizona, where he set up permanent shop.

Ruger single-action revolvers are this artist's canvas, and Gary now offers more than 70 different series guns. But package guns make up only 50 percent of Gary's workload, the other half consisting of straight custom work. The multifaceted Reeder is also a manufacturer, offering revolvers built on three unique and distinct frames that are licensed to him, the first based on the dimensions of the original Colt's Keith No. 5 and with all Ruger internals, the second a somewhat beefier Blackhawk-sized frame, and the last a stretch-frame able to accommodate the 1.6-inch or "Maximum" cartridges to include Smith & Wesson's raucous .500. Reeder has also developed his own grip frame, one that is based loosely on the Bisley and which he calls the "Magnum" grip frame. This grip frame design moves the trigger guard forward to give the shooter more clearance between his delicate fingers and the trigger guard, this area being a place of common woe among Bisley shooters.

Unlike many others, Gary is intimately involved with his client base. Reeder has his own forum on his website (www.reedercustomguns.com), where he interacts with his customers on a daily basis. You get the distinct impression that the participants aren't merely customers, but members of an extended family. Gary also hosts group hunts, allowing him to not only get to know his customers, but to befriend them, as well. As a customer, you have instant access to Reeder, a business model that has proven quite successful. You'll be hard pressed to find a business owner in any industry with such a hands-on approach, and it is an approach that breeds loyalty.

Gary Reeder Custom Guns: 2601 E. 7th Avenue, Flagstaff, AZ 86004; (928) 527-4100; www. reedercustomguns.com.

MAG-NA-PORT INTERNATIONAL, INC.

To learn more about the roots of Mag-Na-Port International, I have profiled the man behind the company in the Pioneers chapter of this book. Still, a little background is necessitated here.

The story of Larry Kelly is the classic tale of the American dream. A primary school dropout,

THE ULTIMATE BLACK WIDOW is an updated version of the original Black Widow, which made its debut in the late 1980s. Reviews in *Guns* and *American Handgunner* magazines in 1987 put Gary Reeder's name on the map and made him a star in the industry.

THIS CONVERSION PACKAGE from Mag-Na-Port is called the Deluxe Predator and is the most popular package. Performed on your Ruger Super Blackhawk, the package includes an inverted muzzle crown, porting, C-More front sight, Omega white outline rear sight, action job and a Velvet Hone finish.

Kelly was a man whose hunting and guiding skills provided him and his family with life-giving sustenance while he was unemployed. His journey to Mag-Na-Port began when he happened upon an idea while working for a company that made fuel guidance control valves for the Apollo space program, and that idea translated to Larry figuring out a way to cleanly cut ports in the barrels of firearms through use of Electrical Discharge Machining (EDM). This porting reduced recoil considerably, without any negative side effects on performance. Larry was a man of action, and his activities didn't go unnoticed. In fact, his exploits with a handgun in the game fields graced the pages of the most popular gun magazines. Thus, Mag-Na-Port International was born of humble roots, big ideas, hard work, and a major dose of intestinal fortitude.

Today, Mag-Na-Port International offers a host of services to include Mag-Na-Porting on handguns, shotguns, and rifles, construction of muzzle brakes (called the Mag-Na-Brake), and handgun conversions in package form or piecemeal. Though Larry is no longer with us, he left the company in the capable hands of his son Ken, who continues the tradition of excellence.

Mag-Na-Port International, Inc.: 41302 Executive Drive, Harrison

PHOTO BY MAG-NA-PORT

THE FREEDOM ARMS STALKER PACKAGE from Mag-Na-Port includes cutting and crowning the barrel to 3 3/8 inches (from 10 inches), porting, action job, SSK Three-Ring mount and base, Velvet Hone finish, a sling, swivels and studs.

Township, MI 48045-1306; (586) 469-6727; www.magnaport.com.

DUSTIN LINEBAUGH

As luck would have it, custom gun builder Dustin Linebaugh was born into custom revolver royalty. Dustin reports that growing up in his dad's shop was always interesting, with never a shortage of unique people around. The August 1986 issue of *Guns & Ammo* magazine, featuring an exposé on the then-new .500 Linebaugh, really drew attention to the work of John Linebaugh and put him on the map. Dustin was exposed to all of this in his most formative years, so it was only natural for Dustin to follow in his dad's footsteps.

On-the-job training consisted of working for dad after school. He came on board full-time after graduating high school and was tasked with building numerous Maximum revolvers—the .458, .475, and .500—on Ruger .357 Maximum frames, when he realized that controlling the recoil of these monsters was all in the grip.

All the Maximums that came out of John Linebaugh's shop were fitted with Bisley grip frames, but it wasn't enough to merely replace the plow handle grip frame. This is where Dustin derived his inspiration and the drive to make grips that really work on revolvers that deliver a lot of horsepower and debilitating recoil. He felt that there was no one building grips correctly for

PHOTO BY DUSTIN LINEBAUGH

THIS DUSTIN LINEBAUGH-built stainless steel Bisley in .500 Linebaugh features a 5½-inch octagon barrel, a Bowen rear sight, and Dustin's own exhibition-grade walnut grips.

the big Maximums, yet he figured out early on what worked and what didn't. Of course, he was a kid fresh out of high school, invincible, high on testosterone, and wanting more and more horsepower, so it was a logical progression. Dustin has been making first-rate custom grips, now, for more than 15 years, and to this day he builds grips for his father, as well as Hamilton Bowen.

Dustin struck out on his own seven years ago and has built quite a following. A full-time rancher by day (his "agricultural habit," as he calls it), he treats the building of custom revolvers as pleasure he partakes in on the side. He churns out less than a dozen custom revolvers a year, as he is in the trade purely for the love of the guns. He still

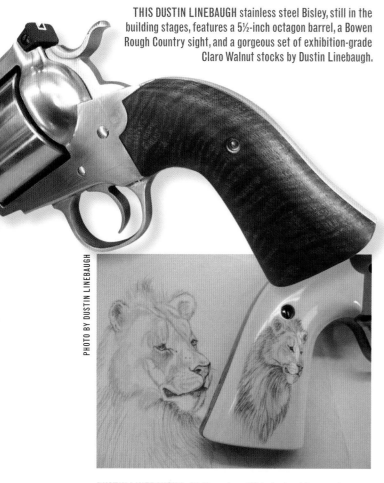

THIS DUSTIN LINEBAUGH stainless steel Bisley, still in the building stages, features a 5½-inch octagon barrel, a Bowen Rough Country sight, and a gorgeous set of exhibition-grade Claro Walnut stocks by Dustin Linebaugh.

PHOTO BY DUSTIN LINEBAUGH

DUSTIN LINEBAUGH built these beautiful elephant ivory grips, while the scrimshaw work was performed by Linda Burwick of Cody, Wyoming. You can always expect this level of workmanship, when you commission Dustin Linebaugh to build a revolver.

THIS JOHN GALLAGHER-built Ruger Super Blackhawk features an octagon barrel, Bisley grip, and color case hardening. This is a beautiful example of the gunsmith's workmanship.

has one of the first revolvers he ever built, a Ruger Vaquero in .475 Linebaugh, a personal favorite and what he considers the most well-rounded and versatile cartridge for the serious handgun hunter.

Quite the accomplished big-game handgun hunter, Dustin took his first big trophy, a mule deer, at the tender age of 14. (You can read about one of his exploits in the final chapter of this book.) Dustin plans to continue at the unhurried pace he has set for himself, emphasizing quality and perfection over quantity. He treats every revolver individually and gives each one his personal touch. A custom big-bore revolver by Dustin Linebaugh is money well spent.

Dustin Linebaugh Custom Conversions: P.O. Box 263, Cody, WY 82414; (307) 899-5368; www.dustinlinebaugh.com.

JOHN GALLAGHER FIREARMS

Hailing from Midland, Texas, and in typical Texas fashion, John Gallagher dreamed big and turned his desire into reality. You see, John worked in the oil industry of West Texas for 10 years before he decided it just wasn't the life he wanted, so he moved on to ranching in Montana, an endeavor he undertook for the next nine years. Then he figured out what he really wanted to toil over, and that was single-action revolvers. John

PHOTO BY JOHN GALLAGHER

PHOTO BY JOHN GALLAGHER

PHOTO BY JOHN GALLAGHER

THIS GALLAGHER-BUILT Bisley is chambered in a proprietary cartridge of John Gallagher's design that he named the .458-400 Express. It is based on a .45-70 case cut down to 1.4 inches, but maintaining the .45-70's .458-inch diameter bullet. It was loaded with a 400-grain bullet flying at a velocity of 1,300 fps.

comprised a niche market, John also does a sizable amount of work on rifles. A dedicated big-game hunter, when work and time permits, John reports that he favors handgun hunting to all else, likening it to bow hunting, but with results that are "more predictable."

John Gallagher Firearms: 3923 Bird Farm Road, Jasper, AL 35503; (205) 384-5229; www. gallagherfirearms.com.

had the good fortune of getting the opportunity to handle a fine custom Ruger in .475 Linebaugh, one made by John Linebaugh himself, and he knew he had found his calling. John then pursued his dream through three years of gunsmithing school at Trinity College, before opening the doors of John Gallagher Firearms, in 1994.

Realizing that custom big-bore revolvers

SINGLE-ACTION SERVICE

Single-Action Service honcho and native Texan Alan Harton spent 34 years as a master machinist during his first career. He took only two years off to participate in an inconvenience in Southeast Asia, better known as the Vietnam War, where he fought with the U.S. Army. In the 1990s, while

ANOTHER ALAN HARTON creation this time for consummate handgun hunter, Dick Thompson, in .480 Ruger, exhibiting the usual excellent workmanship of Single Action Service. This revolver has accounted for countless head of big game in the capable hands of Dick Thompson.

THIS ABSOLUTELY STUNNING .44 Special Blackhawk, built by Alan Harton of Single-Action Service, is owned by Ed Musetti.

JOHN GALLAGHER BUILT this gorgeous color case hardened Ruger Vaquero in .44 Magnum.

working in a machine shop on a full-time basis, a good friend, who liked building 1911s, planted a bug in Alan's ear. You see, Alan has been a single-action revolver nut since he was child, hooked on a variety of TV westerns. When Alan's buddy began customizing his own 1911s, the gears began turning in Harton's head. He had an extensive ma-

chinist background, so why couldn't Alan make a living working on the guns he loves?

Alan sought to answer that question. He set up half his garage as a machine shop and went about restoring a second generation Colt's SAA. The finished product was shown to friends, local gun shows, and anyone willing to look and, before he knew it, folks were asking Alan to do work on their revolvers. Eventually, Alan had enough gunsmithing work lined up to quit his day job as a machinist and open his own full-time business. He registered his business name, acquired a tax ID number and, in the year 2000, Single-Action Service was born. Alan reports it's been foot to the floor since the "Open for Business" sign was hung.

TOM CASSELMAN, of Jamestown, South Carolina, is the proud owner of this Harton-built .445 SuperMag on a Ruger Maximum frame. The revolver was fitted with a Bisley grip, hammer, and trigger and features an octagon barrel.

PHOTO BY TOM CASSELMAN

PHOTO BY JOHN GALLAGHER

Single-Action Service is a full-service shop, specializing in single-action revolvers. One niche Alan has filled is with the cowboy action shooters, who largely shoot period-correct replica Colt's SAAs. Most SAA replicas are correctly fitted with fixed sights, creating an issue for a revolver that doesn't actually shoot where aimed, definitely a problem in competition. Alan's fix is a barrel bending hydraulic press that rides in the back of his pickup truck. He will then take his client's gun, load of choice, and predetermined distance the client requires his zero to be to his local range. Typically, within 30 minutes, the revolver is dead on, ready for competition, and no worse for wear.

Another service provided by Harton is to bolster the strength of the internal parts on Colt's SAA replica revolvers, particularly the Italian-sourced guns that have rather soft internal parts that tend to wear out rather quickly, when subjected to the rigorous grind of cowboy action shooting competitions. Many internal parts of these popular revolvers are not heat treated, and, where Alan is able, he performs this treatment. Many parts on these guns also benefit from grinding out the soft metal and welding in H13 tool steel. The parts (like the sear, hammer cam, etc.), are then reshaped with a diamond cutter. The finished product is a revolver that is as tough internally as it is externally, giving a lifetime of service after the modifications are performed.

Alan quickly credits his success with customers turned good friends, such as Fermin Garza and Dick Thompson, who have spread the word of his prowess to whoever is willing to listen.

THIS OLD MODEL RUGER SUPER Blackhawk, Belonging to Fermin Garza, was completely revamped by Alan Harton to include a Bisley grip frame. Only the frame and cylinder remain from the original gun. The beautiful grips are Amboyna Burl.

ANOTHER JRH creation is this Freedom Arms Model 83 in .500 JRH with an octagon barrel.

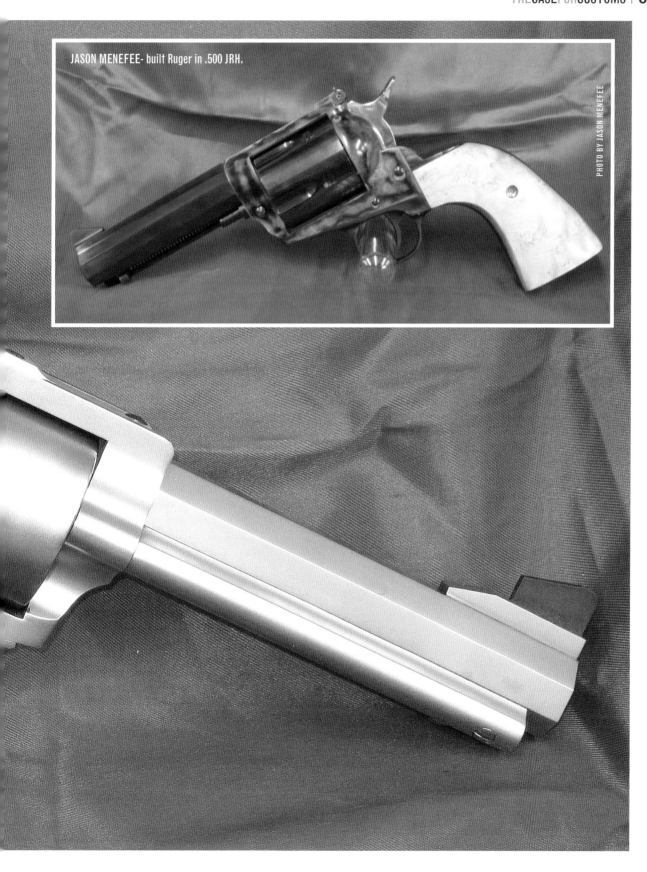

JASON MENEFEE- built Ruger in .500 JRH.

PHOTO BY JASON MENEFEE

Samples of Alan's and Single-Action Service's work can be viewed on www.gallery.mac.com/aharton, an online photo gallery.

Single-Action Service: 8822 Jackwood Street, Houston, TX 77036; (713) 907-6031; aharton@hotmail.com.

JRH ADVANCED GUNSMITHING

JRH Advanced Gunsmithing, of Grass Valley, California, officially opened its doors in 1997, but proprietor Jack Huntington (the JRH in the company name), has been churning out custom five-shot big-bore revolvers since 1988. Having decided at an early age to pursue a career in the firearms industry, the Southern California native earned a bachelor's degree in Small Arms Engineering and Ballistic Science that formed the theoretical foundation for his chosen vocation. Various machining jobs provided Jack the

THIS .475 LINEBAUGH was built by Jack Huntington and features a five-shot cylinder, Bisley grip frame and a 5 1/2" barrel with barrel band.

practical abilities necessary to transform his ideas to reality.

Jack's first five-shot big-bore was a Ruger Bisley in .500 Linebaugh, immediately followed by a Bisley in .475 Linebaugh. Jack is also one of the few gunsmiths who builds custom five-shot double-action revolvers, which are more complex

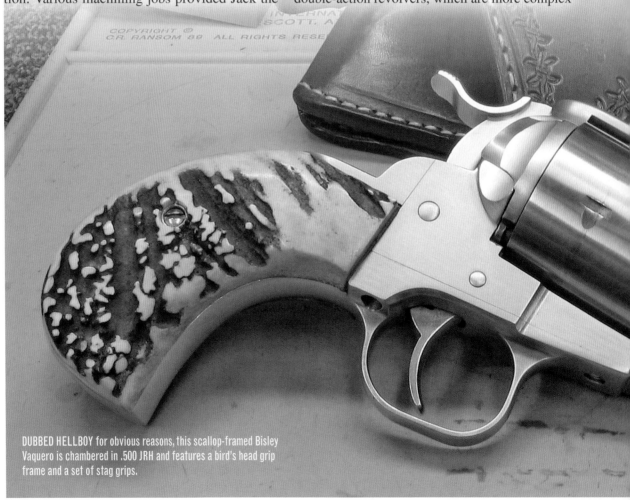

DUBBED HELLBOY for obvious reasons, this scallop-framed Bisley Vaquero is chambered in .500 JRH and features a bird's head grip frame and a set of stag grips.

PHOTO BY THOMAS KELLY

THIS JRH-BUILT Vaquero in .480 Ruger was commissioned by John Sparkman. It is now owned by Thomas Kelly.

PHOTO BY JASON MENEFEE

NAMED THE FANNER, this revolver was actually set up to fan. The stainless Bisley is a best-grade revolver from JRH Advanced Gunsmithing, featuring a tritium insert-equipped adjustable front sight and chambered in .500 JRH.

PHOTO BY JOHN MENEFEE

in nature than their single-action counterparts. But Jack's repertoire isn't exclusively revolvers, having had Gil Van Horn as a mentor. Jack also builds, repairs, and modifies rifles (to include doubles), shotguns, and semi-automatic pistols. Basically, if it goes *bang!* Jack works on it.

Jack was the first to chamber Freedom Arms Model 83s in .475 Linebaugh (the commercial specifications for the cartridge designed by him to fit the tight quarters of the FA 83), even before Freedom Arms made the decision to offer production line .475s. Jack also produced the first .50-caliber Freedom Arms Model 83s, before they became a factory reality.

With four talented employees under Jack's watchful eye, JRH Advanced Gunsmithing can churn out quality products in relatively short time.

JRH Advanced Gunsmithing: 21854 Meyer Ravine Road, Grass Valley, CA 95949; (530) 268-6877; www.jrhgunmaker.com.

CARE AND FEEDING OF YOUR BIG-BORE REVOLVER

TERMINAL PERFORMANCE

When this book was a mere discussion and an under-developed idea, the subject of terminal bullet performance came up and culminated into a heated debate. Should we open this can of worms? Will we draw fire from those on the other side of the terminal performance divide? You bet! We don't claim that this will be the last word in terminal performance, just that we believe we can clarify some common misconceptions and, hopefully, get the reader to question some of what has become conventional (and sometimes unwarranted) wisdom.

Terminal ballistics is a sub field of ballistics, and the study of the behavior of a projectile when it hits a target. In this case, a live target is mainly what we are concerned with. Let's get started.

CHAPTER FOUR

GETTING STARTED

Now that you've taken delivery of your big-bore revolver, you need to decide how you will feed it. Obviously, proficiency with your revolver (like any firearm, but more so with a big-bore revolver), will require extensive shooting to familiarize yourself with it, grow accustomed to the sizeable recoil, and get accurate with it. The revolver's use will also dictate how you load. If the handgun is for punching paper, then the nod to accuracy is first and foremost over terminal potential. Or you may be pressing your big-bore revolver into service as a defensive piece, in which case accuracy will also be at the forefront of your ammunition needs. For them, factory ammo is an option, but, to really extract the full potential from your chosen sidearm, you need to take up reloading.

Until you do reload, there are a number of specialty ammunition manufacturers that can supply you with quality ammunition for your big-bore, including Grizzly Cartridge, CorBon, Hornady, Double Tap Ammunition, and Buffalo Bore Ammunition. These companies offer dedicated loads for large-caliber handguns. Not only will this save you a bundle of money (excluding the initial cash outlay for the gun itself, of course), you will get the opportunity to tailor your load to your particular revolver, something that is not possible with one-size-fits-all factory ammunition. I am not denigrating factory ammunition, as it is a difficult task manufacturing ammunition for the masses that works as well as it does. I often start with factory loads, when I acquire a new firearm, in no small part so that I can build a sufficient inventory of once-fired brass, and then I purchase loading dies, powder, primers, etc., and begin the load development process. It is well worth the initial expense and the effort to make your own ammunition from this point on, particularly if you plan on shooting a lot.

Another important issue is loading for accuracy. No matter how you plan on using your big-bore revolver, it will generate a lot more fun for you if the gun is accurate. All else is moot if you cannot hit what you are aiming at. I tend to load for accuracy, and, then, as an afterthought and bow to curiosity, I break out the chronograph. What does it tell me? The chronograph can give a good indication of acceptable pressures, when compared to published load data using the same components, when velocity is in the same ballpark.

BULLET SELECTION

Let me put this up front. Attempts to turn revolvers into rifles by loading light bullets on top of max powder charges usually fall short on big game—not a situation you want to find yourself in when hunting bear or any other animal capable of bringing a fight to you. Handguns do not have the necessary physical attributes of a rifle to achieve rifle-like velocities, therefore they cannot be loaded the way a rifle is loaded—and I am talking specifically about revolvers and revolvers only and not the single-shot specialty pistols chambered in rifle calibers.

We are now talking about hunting with your revolver, as bullet selection for this endeavor is most critical. There are basically two types of bullets that are in use by handgun hunters, those that expand significantly and those that expand minimally. To further break this down, when we talk about expanding bullets, we are usually referring to jacketed soft-nose or hollowpoint bullets.

Minimal expanders consist of the family of hardcast lead bullets, as well as a number of high-quality jacketed bullets designed for deep, uncompromising penetration. These are more resistant to deformation than even a hardened lead bullet and are better able to withstand both high velocities and impacts with hard surfaces. Hardcast bullets derive their name from the composition of their alloy, as well as the hardening process—water-quenching or heat-treating—they are subjected to after casting that enable them to maintain their shape even when striking hard objects, such as bones.

There are many high-quality expanding jacketed bullets available to the handloader that are also offered in factory loaded ammunition. The preference is a stoutly constructed jacketed bullet that will not over-expand upon striking a game animal. While violent expansion works well on thin-skinned game, such as deer, you don't want a bullet that expands at the expense of penetration.

There is a very fine line between enough expansion and adequate penetration. Fortunately, there are very good offerings from the likes of Hornady that provide a limited yet significant amount of expansion, while still ensuring penetration. Lynn Thompson, of Cold Steel fame, took a number of large wild hogs and Asian water buffalo with a Ruger .44 Magnum stoked with Hornady's 300-grain XTP hollowpoint load. The minimal expansion enabled the bullets to penetrate deeply and perform impressively against the large bovines in particular. (Of course it doesn't hurt that Lynn Thompson is one helluva shot!)

The most reliable performers in this category are flat-nosed hardcast bullets and their jacketed counterparts, like Belt Mountain's Punch bullet, Barnes' Buster, and CorBon's Penetrator line of bullets. (We will discuss all three of these in more detail later.) The LBT-style of hardcast bullets feature a wide "meplat" (the flat nose of the bullet). The blunt nose crushes and tears tissue, creating a wound channel much bigger than the original diameter of the bullet. Flat-nosed hardcast bullets are popular with savvy handgun hunters and offer an economical alternative in a bullet that has unparalleled penetrative ability, due to a resistance to big expansion. Also keep in mind that a bullet from a true big-bore revolver—.45-caliber-plus—doesn't require much expansion, as they start off "pre-expanded," as Ross Seyfried so succinctly stated.

All flat-nosed bullets aren't created equal. Many feature a rather narrow meplat. A wide meplat not only creates a larger wound channel, it also helps the bullet stabilize in flesh and thereby penetrate in a straight line. What is a large meplat? In independent testing, we have found that a surface area between 75 and 80 percent of the overall bullet diameter seems to be optimal. Below 70 percent, the wound channel size is compromised, as is stability. (We will talk more about this later.) A small or narrow meplat will also sometimes tumble in flesh or veer off course, as round-nose bullets are also wont to do, not only inhibiting penetration, but also decreasing the likelihood of the projectile going straight through to the vitals. Thus, for straight-line, deep penetration, a large meplat is recommended.

When choosing a bullet or factory load, bullet weight must be taken into consideration. Light-for-caliber bullets, while able to achieve impressive velocities, do not possess the momentum or penetrative ability of a heavy-for-caliber bullet, all else being equal. A well-known handgun hunter, Larry Kelly, once had a grizzly bear break into his cabin, in Alaska. Larry emptied his .44 Magnum sixgun into the offending bear, but the 240-grain bullets failed to even slow Mr. Bear down, before his hunting partner and guide took a rifle to the beast and ended the burglary. The lack of penetration offered by the 240-grain bullets made Larry a convert to heavier slugs. (You can read more about this incident in the final chapter of this book.)

What is heavy-for-caliber? Heavy-for-caliber is heavier than the normally accepted standard loads, the standard range demonstrated by the following:

- .41 Magnum: 230- to 265-grain
- .44 Magnum: 265- to 320-grain
- .45 Colt/.454 Casull/.460 S&W: 300- to 400-grain
- .475 Linebaugh/.480 Ruger: 400-grains +
- .500 S&W/.500 Linebaugh/.500 JRH: 440-grain +

In all fairness, these were the weights utilized during the original cartridge and load development, but we have seen a trend develop over the years, where handgun hunters seeking to increase the terminal performance of their big-bore revolvers have moved up considerably in bullet weight. Randy Garrett, of Garrett Cartridges, stated, "The importance of selecting a heavy bullet is twofold. First, heavier bullets penetrate deeper than lighter bullets. Second, since heavier bullets cannot be driven as fast as lighter bullets, they experience less impact stress and are therefore less likely to fracture on impact." Of course, Garrett is referring to cast bullets and considers them the only option for defensive purposes in dangerous animal encounters. This is important to keep in mind, particularly when loading your

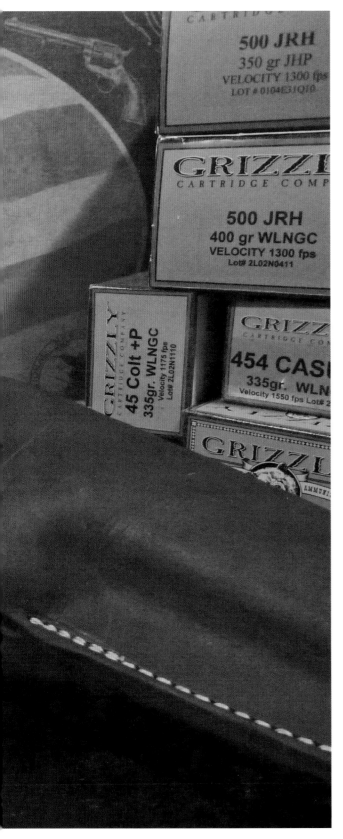

big-bore revolver to protect against large, dangerous animals. The Belt Mountain Punch bullets, CorBon Penetrators, and the Barnes Buster series bullets are even less likely to lose their nose shape on impact with heavy bone.

In a hunting situation, if using a bullet designed to expand significantly, you may have to pass on shots—and that's a problem if the trophy bear, elk, or deer of a lifetime makes an appearance. I personally choose bullets that can kill a large animal from any and every angle presented, and hardcast, flat-nosed bullets allow me to do just that. Expansion is alright, but not at the expense of adequate penetration. You need to reach and destroy the vitals in order to kill an animal cleanly and quickly. Granted, smaller animals typically offer less resistance and don't necessarily require maximum penetration, but if big game is on the menu, you shouldn't skimp on penetration.

No matter what type of bullet or load you ultimately choose, accuracy is paramount. No amount of horsepower or terminal bullet performance in the world will make a lick of difference if you can't hit your intended target. When you find that perfect load, you owe it to yourself and the animal you are hunting to be as proficient as possible with your revolver of choice. No one I know wants to follow a wounded bear into the briar. Your first shot must be well placed, and that requires an accurate load and a practiced shooter. There is still no replacement for placement.

THE PLAYERS

We've mentioned several bullet manufacturers, as well as many of the major players in completely factory loaded rounds. Let's take a look at some that are making their mark in truly high-performance ammunition for big-bore revolvers.

Grizzly Cartridge Company

Grizzly Cartridge front man Mike Rintoul is a mechanical engineer by trade. His approach to ammunition manufacture is scientific, precise, and methodical—exactly what you'd expect from an engineer! Having retired from the oil fields of Alaska, he needed something to do with his free time, and, on a whim, he created the Grizzly Car-

PHOTO COURTESY DOUBLET TAP AMMUNITION

tridge Company, in 2003. Mike and his wife have expanded the company broadly since then, their desire to offer a better product with first-rate customer service. We think they have succeeded in spades, and here's an example why.

In the early days of the Grizzly Cartridge Company, Mike used Cast Performance bullets exclusively, as he felt they were the best product of their kind on the market. When Cast Performance came up for sale in 2005, Mike jumped on it and brought it under the wing of Rintoul Enterprises.

Mike, a handgun hunter himself, began his new endeavor by offering ammunition for revolver and lever-action hunters, but has expanded his line exponentially to include calibers ranging from .32 all the way to .500 Nitro Express and just about everything in between, with more than 350 different loads in all. His big-bore revolver offerings are significant and nearly all inclusive. Grizzly Cartridge offers everything the discriminating big-bore revolver owner could ever want, particularly with top-

shelf ammunition for the more obscure calibers like the .475 Linebaugh, .500 Wyoming Express, and even the .357 Maximum.

Prior to retirement, Mike was hunting feral hogs with a .44 Magnum stoked with his own handloads bearing Cast Performance bullets. He shot a 650-pound slab of bacon at a measured 12 yards, killing the animal. A necropsy revealed the bullet lodged between vertebrae in the neck. Mike was a bit underwhelmed by the .44's penetration, and that provided him with the motivation to step up to something bigger and more decisive, from a killing standpoint. After thorough and exhaustive research, Mike settled on the .500 Linebaugh and commissioned Hamilton Bowen to build him one on a Ruger Redkhawk frame. Mike reports that his .500 Linebaugh has no trouble in the penetration department.

In 2011, Mike acquired Punch Bullets from Belt Mountain. Mike feels the Punch Bullet is the best for maximum penetration and performance on dangerous game. (Do you see a pattern here?)

He is dedicated to the sport of handgun hunting, giving him a unique insight into the needs of such hunters, and so he takes the development of loads and the manufacture of ammunition very seriously. One day, Mike shot a full 300 rounds of full-house .500 Smith & Wesson Magnum loads during a development session. He couldn't even pick up a pencil for two weeks, following the testing. We call that dedication to his craft.

Note: Mike's expertise and high-quality products were used extensively in the research and testing for this book.

Grizzly Cartridge: (503) 556-3006; www. grizzlycartridge.com.(503) 556-3006.

Double Tap Ammunition

Owner and CEO of Double Tap Ammunition, Mike McNett, of Washington State, grew up handloading with his dad. After high school, Mike went on to earn a degree from Gonzaga University, in Spokane, and then a career in advertising followed. So, it wasn't until the year 2000 that Mike realized he wanted to start his own business and do something he truly enjoyed.

Prior to this, Mike had discovered and developed an immediate crush on a then-new offering called the 10mm. Mike's dad had brought home a Colt's Delta Elite in 1987, started handloading for it, and from there, Mike's crush blossomed into a full-time love affair with this high performance cartridge. (In 1991, he bought his first Glock 20 in 10mm—after 150,000-plus rounds through it, Mike humanely retired the old workhorse.) When the FBI adopted the 10mm as its caliber in 1988, it was quickly found to be too hot for agents of smaller stature and so was steadily emasculated to the point that it morphed into the .40 Smith & Wesson. Mike had observed this cartridge's demise, but the straw that broke the camel's back for him and solidified his resolve to get into ammunition manufacture was when CorBon reduced its 10mm ammunition velocities. That company had been the last full-power 10mm ammunition producer standing.

Mike was schooled well, saw the need, and set out to fill it—classical Marketing 101. He promptly developed four 10mm loads—four *full-power* 10mm loads—working in his garage for a year, before he officially opened his doors in 2002 and called his business Double Tap. After six months, Mike had sold enough ammo to quit his marketing job and produce ammunition full time. In 2005, after twice outgrowing his manufacturing facilities, Mike moved Double Tap to Cedar City, Utah, at the base of the Rocky Mountains. Then, in 2007, Mike purchased the company providing his hardcast bullets, bringing hardcast manufacturing capabilities in-house.

Mike's company has grown in leaps and bounds and, as of this writing, is celebrating its ninth anniversary. Double Tap Ammunition offers a very wide range of calibers (59, to be exact) and nearly 300 loads for all occasions. The standard big-bore revolver cartridges are well represented in Double Tap's lineup, some of our favorites being the 320-grain .44 Magnum load and the 360-grain .45 Colt load. Mike was kind enough throughout the production of this book to supply us with his vast knowledge and a variety of loads and bullets for testing purposes.

Double Tap Ammunition: (866) 357-10MM; www.doubletapammo.com.

Buffalo Bore Ammunition

Tim Sundles, of Boise, Idaho, is the proprietor of Buffalo Bore Ammunition. An enthusiastic handgun hunter, Tim has the distinction of bringing the fabulous .475 and .500 Linebaughs to legitimacy, with the very first factory ammunition ever offered, effectively turning his hobby into his life.

It didn't start out that way, as he was a contractor in California, before making the move to the ammunition manufacturing industry. Tim credits Ross Seyfried with the patience and willingness to impart on him the finer points in load development, theory, and practical application.

AUTHOR PHOTO

WHEN BULLETS PULL CRIMP, as this photo demonstrates, the revolver will tie up, leaving it inoperable. Not a good place to be when being mauled by an angry animal.

Tim started out in 1983, with the release of the FA 83 in .454 Casull, buying six of them and experimenting with a variety of loads. Prior to the release of the FA 83, Tim had been playing with heavy .44 Magnum and .45 Colt loads. Then he got to know John Linebaugh, and was subsequently introduced to the .500 Linebaugh. In those days, brass and bullets were hard to come by, but Tim commissioned John to build him a number of .475 and .500 Linebaugh revolvers. Tim performed a lot of load development for these cartridges, and John kept sending his customers to Tim to load ammunition for them. The writing was on the wall, and, one day, John Linebaugh asked Tim to go into the business of manufacturing specialty ammunition, particularly for John's signature cartridges, the .475 and .500 Linebaughs. Tim contacted Starline to make brass, and, in 1997, he opened the doors of Buffalo Bore Ammunition.

Tim started out by making .475 and .500 Linebaugh ammunition, but soon added the popular .44 Magnum, .45 Colt, and .454 Casull. Eventually, Tim contacted Bob Baker of Freedom Arms and pestered him to build a revolver in .475 Linebaugh. By the time Freedom Arms offered the Model 83 in .475, Buffalo Bore had ammo on its shelves ready to supply the masses. Today, Buffalo Bore offers quality ammunition in 50 or so calibers and more than 160 different loads.

Buffalo Bore Ammunition: www.buffalobore. com.

STOPPING AN ANGRY FOUR-LEGGED ADVERSARY

As you can see, there are several makers out there producing high-quality offerings for your big-bore wheel-gun. So, now, back to the original question posed at the beginning of this chapter, to wit, how should you load your back-up revolver?

As I've said, there are two ways, with either

AUTHOR PHOTO

IF YOU DON'T ROLL YOUR OWN, there are a number of commercial hardcast and jacketed minimally expanding options available for use on bear or other potentially dangerous animals. From left to right: .44 Magnum, .454 Casull, .480 Ruger, .475 Linebaugh, .500 JRH, and the .500 Linebaugh.

expanding bullets or minimally expanding bullets. Many folks think that expansion is a plus, when trying to stop an angry adversary, but penetration is actually far more important. Expanding bullets may slow too much, hindering the bullet's ability to reach the vitals. Keep in mind that the calibers we are discussing are already starting out at a large diameter, negating the need for exponential expansion.

We spoke with Mike McNett, proprietor of Double Tap Ammunition, who supplies four of Alaska's state parks with ammunition for their rangers to carry in its 10mm and .40 Smith & Wesson service pistols. While Double Tap supplies controlled-expansion bullets for dealing with bad humans, the Park Service specifies minimally expanding, flat-nosed, 200-grain jacketed

bullets with a wide meplat, for use in dispatching bear, moose, or other large animals, for this is where penetration is crucial.

Don't look at paper ballistics when choosing your load; even the mildest rifle loads make revolver cartridges look meek. Muzzle energy is a poor measure of a cartridge's ability to kill effectively (this will be discussed more in detail later in this chapter). As we've already covered, a heavy-for-caliber bullet with a large meplat, and traveling at moderate velocity, will penetrate adequately from any angle, ensuring that the vitals can be reached when placed properly.

One note is needed here. We have referred to hardcast bullets as "minimally expanding" bullets which may be raising a red flag in your mind. The reason we use this term is that, technically, all handgun bullets sold in the United States are "expanding bullets" by law. Hence, expanding and minimally expanding. I think you get our drift.

Remember again, that there still is no replacement for placement—and I will continue to repeat this mantra in hopes that everyone reading this realizes this fact. This leads to the issue of reliability.

UTTER AND ULTRA RELIABILITY

You have decided a revolver is what you will carry with you in the field as protection against dangerous animals. You have also decided the platform and the caliber, and you have started experimenting with loads. Now you must test your chosen combination thoroughly to expose potential problems that could lead to you getting maimed or killed. We will touch upon this later in the book, when we talk about Alaskan fishing guide Greg Brush's brush (I couldn't resist) with a hungry grizzly bear. Greg actually experienced ammunition failure in his revolver—obviously he was successful in ending a very precarious situation, as he lived to tell me about it—but had the last shot needed to put the animal down failed to fire, you would be reading his obituary here and not a story of survival.

What kind of failure did Greg experience? You will see that, after his last shot, his revolver tied up, meaning he could not advance the cylinder to the next and final shot. This would have presented a big problem, had he needed the next round.

The failure he experienced was that a bullet "pulled crimp"—that is, became slightly unseated from the case—and it did this enough that it put a halt to using the revolver until the offending bullet was pushed back down into the case enough that the user can open the cylinder and remove the round. We sometimes experience this phenomenon with heavy recoiling revolver rounds. The recoil is so severe that the bullets are pulled out of the case under inertia. The .454 Casull has been guilty of this more than most, as it is a round often utilizing heavily compressed loads of powder. This puts additional strain on the crimp around the bullet even before recoil comes into play, not to mention that the recoil is, of course, rather violent. In all fairness, any high-powered revolver cartridge can experience this phenomenon, but we do tend to see it more frequently in the .454 with heavily compressed loads and heavy bullets.

I had two batches of commercially loaded .454

THIS BARNES 375-GRAIN XPB performed as advertised, taking one very large brown bear.

Casull ammunition from two different manufacturers pull crimp in testing. We were on the range shooting for accuracy and measuring velocity. The test revolver (a single-action) only allowed for one or two shots before becoming tied up and inoperable (and it generally *doesn't* take much to tie up a revolver when a bullet pulls crimp).

One of my contributors to this book, John Parker, used to carry a small wooden dowel or screw driver in his back pocket, whenever he went out in the field with his .475 Linebaugh, because pulled crimps weren't uncommon with the heavy kickers and older brass. Keep in mind the early .475 Linebaughs used cut down .45-70 brass and not the dedicated cases we have today. Exacerbating the problem, it was also conventional wisdom, at that time, that the .475 Linebaugh should be loaded to maximum velocities with heavy bullets for maximum effectiveness on game. Anyway, John would simply push the bullet back down enough to open the cylinder and remove the round.

Carrying a tool of some sort to address this issue is still a good idea. You need to be prepared for the worst at all times. I used these same two batches of ammo in another test, this time in a Ruger Redhawk (one that had been fitted with the cylinder out of a Super Redhawk in .454 Casull), and, in the case of both types of ammo, it took four or five shots before the bullets pulled enough to tie the gun up. Undoubtedly the bullets began pulling immediately, but due to greater clearances between the front of the cylinder and the frame, we were able to fire it a number of times more before the inevitable tie up. The pulled crimps would have been obvious a little faster, had we been shooting over a chronograph, as the rounds that had experienced crimp pull would have lost velocity. I believe this is what happened with Greg Brush as well. There is obviously an advantage to having a longer cylinder and/or a little more clearance in the unfortunate instance where ammunition pulls crimp. Even better, of course, is ammunition that doesn't pull crimp.

Keep in mind that this is an ammunition problem and not a problem with the firearms tested. *High-quality ammunition should not pull crimp.* Sure enough, further investigation revealed that it was likely a bad batch of soft brass that was the culprit in our testing failures. In subsequent testing with new batches of the same ammunition, we were not able to duplicate the problematic incident.

Due to the .454's propensity for pulling crimp (again, with heavily compressed, heavy bullet loads), Tim Sundles, owner of Buffalo Bore Ammunition, loads his 360-grain .454 Casull loads to lower velocity and pressure levels, as a nod to reliability for the folks he knows carry the .454 for protection against dangerous animals (and why else would someone put up with the .454's recoil? Lord knows they aren't plinking with this caliber!). He also uses a proprietary crimp, as a double insurance policy. In reference to this crimp, Buffalo Bore's .454 bullets have been redesigned in the crimp groove area. Typically, hardcast bullets have a gently sloping crimp groove angle/edge. Sundles had the crimp grooves cut with a squared bottom edge so that, when the crimp is applied, it has an edge to grab.

When asked about the reduced or rather subdued velocities of Buffalo Bore's 360-grain .454 loads, Tim stated, "We could have run these bullets faster, but have found that at 1400 to 1500 fps, they'll penetrate lengthwise through any bear." Another reason for the his reduced velocities is that Tim also feels you will shoot your .454 better and more accurately if you're not afraid of its punishing recoil, and he couldn't be more

right in that thinking. Tim told me, "When you drive up the .454's speeds, it becomes unruly and unreliable."

Sundles lives in bear country and finds the topic of bear protection no laughing matter. Great care goes into manufacturing the .454 ammunition by Buffalo Bore, as any mistake or carelessness in the assembly process could lead to crimp pull—which could result in a fatality. All the firepower in the world will do you no good if you can only get off the one shot before another round pulls crimp. This is why it is so important to test the equipment you choose to use in the field. When a bear or mountain lion is closing the distance between itself and its next meal at a high rate of speed, it is a poor time to find out that your chosen combination isn't reliable. Reliability rules the roost.

BULLET TYPES

We touched upon this earlier in general terms, but now it's time to explore the two major types of bullets for big-bore revolvers in greater detail. The two categories of bullets as we see them are jacketed expanding bullets, and cast (lead alloy) bullets, and we will focus on premium bullets.

Jacketed Expanding Bullets

There are a number of very good, toughly constructed, jacketed expanding bullets available to the big-bore revolver shooter and hunter. In fact, the offerings have never been better, in this author's opinion. In the past, bullets of this type tended to be entirely too frangible for reliable use on big game (though they were perfectly adequate for anti-personnel use). They also tended to be of a lighter weight than is preferential in a big-game killing scenario. The newest iterations of these bullets are now trending towards heavier weights and much tougher construction than in the past. This is a double-edged sword, actually—the tougher jacket, that is. The tougher jacket ensures that the bullet will stay together, even with high-impact velocities, but they may also hinder expansion. That being said, limited expansion is good for penetration; it is *violent* expansion that absolutely hurts penetration at revolver velocities. But, an expanding bullet that fails to expand at all, even though it still penetrates well, will not deliver the wound channel that a good cast bullet with a wide meplat is capable of producing. In other words, they do a poor impersonation of a flat-nosed cast bullet. Ultimately, a controlled minimal-expansion is the perfect scenario for the jacketed expanding bullet.

Hornady's XTP line of jacketed expanding bullets (flat-nosed and hollowpoint) has come a long way over the years. Criticized for over-expansion in its original form, the XTP has evolved into an outstanding bullet. We have rather extensively tested the 300-grain .44 Magnum XTP load from Hornady and found that the secret to its significant penetration is the rather limited expansion it provides. Hornady has definitely engineered this particular load very well, as they have kept the velocity to a very moderate level, ensuring minimal expansion and thereby almost guaranteeing deep penetration. One only has to watch Lynn Thompson's (owner of Cold Steel) video, *Handgun Hunting Down Under*, to see just how lethal Hornady's 300-grain XTP .44 Magnum load actually is on large game. Lynn puts a number of water buffalo down, with a combination of great bullet performance and expert shot placement.

Sierra produces what I consider to be one of the finest jacketed expanding bullets for handguns in existence. Its bullets feature a tough, thick jacket and a higher antimony lead alloy in the back end, non-expanding portion of the bullet. This ensures adequate expansion up front, while the hardened rear remains intact for deep penetration. Sierra's hollowpoints are also constructed with a thick jacket and a high antimony lead core content for hardness.

Barnes' monometal XPB line of hollowpoint bullets are perfect for those who hunt in some of the lead-free zones of the golden state of California. These bullets are exceedingly tough and will stay together even when pushed to relatively high velocities. Two perfect candidates for their use are the .454 Casull and Smith & Wesson's velocity champ, the .460 Smith & Wesson Magnum.

All of the bullets mentioned here are ideal for deer and other thin-skinned game animals. They will work on larger and tougher game, as well, but more care must be taken to choose shots that avoid heavy bone. But more on this later.

Cast Bullets

As the name suggests, cast bullets are cast from lead, or, more accurately, lead alloys. The term that is most associated with big-bore handguns in this category is "hardcast." This is a term you have read about here on numerous occasions, as well as in the handgun media. I don't want to delve too deeply into semantics, but there are certain aspects of these bullets that anyone seriously considering their use should understand. There is much misinformation floating about, enough that the topic has attained to dogma status.

"Hardcast" came about to draw a distinction between high-performance cast bullets capable of handling even the largest of game, and soft, malleable lead bullets. While "hard" is a rather vague concept to define, there are some industry- and community-wide accepted levels of hardness to help the user determine whether an adequate bullet has been chosen for its intended purpose. The most commonly utilized measurement for a bullet's hardness is the Brinnell Hardness Number (BHN), made popular by Veral Smith of Lead Bullets technology (LBT). LBT sells BHN testers for bullet casters who want to test the hardness of their home creations.

A hardcast bullet with a Brinnell hardness of 20 or so and designed with a wide meplat and traveling at a modest velocity, will exit even the largest of game in most cases, even if the bullet encounters bone in its path. (Obviously, the alloy used will determine the characteristics of the bullet, such as malleability, hardness, brittleness, etc. For a complete guide to casting and the technology around the process and the designs of cast bullets, I recommend Veral Smith's book, *Jacketed Performance with Cast Bullets*. Veral goes to a depth and level beyond my capacity! You cannot go wrong following the advice.)

"Keith-Style" Bullets

In the realm of bullets for handguns, no term is misused and misapplied more often than "Keith-style." Of course, the reference is to the late El-mer Keith's great contribution to handgunning, with the design of a number of semi-wadcutter profiles that were known for their great accuracy potential (though you might not know that it was actually Phil Sharp, who experimented with this design in .38- and .357-caliber, in the 1930s). The Keith bullet also brought to light the wounding and penetration potential of a flat-nosed bullet profile, and, as a gun writer, Keith had an audi-ence with which to share his observations. (Odd-ly enough, dangerous game rifle hunters are now embracing the flat-nosed solid for its straight-line penetrative abilities and tissue damage, some-thing handgun hunters embraced decades ago. Better late than never, I guess.)

There are a couple Keith-profile bullet moulds available that are purportedly true to Elmer's original design parameters, but for every "real" Keith bullet, there are a hundred facsimiles of wildly differing qualities and variations on the theme. One of the most important attributes of Keith's bullets was their great accuracy. I realize that it is heretical of me to declare the Keith-style bullet as being way past its prime, but I feel there are a number of much better designs available to-day that overshadow Elmer's great contribution. But, how are they better?

Generally, today's designs are more *termi-nally* effective. Let me qualify that last statement with the fact that every revolver is a law unto itself; some bullet designs work better in some revolvers than others. If you find "your load," by all means, stick with it. But how are some newer bullet styles better with regards to terminal per-formance? Well, they possess larger meplat po-tential, but without the diameter-reducing step design of the semi-wadcutter, and the larger me-plat will produce a larger wound channel than a smaller meplat, an indisputable fact.

The Keith-style bullet remains popular with many shooters and hunters, as it still proves to be an accurate bullet style in many cases. And ac-curacy in and of itself goes a very long way to leaping over one of the biggest hurdles to killing game. If you are able to place the bullet where it belongs, and the bullet exhibits enough pene-tration potential, a dead animal will result. Still, we've come a long way since the great Elmer Keith was dabbling in bullet design, and some notable examples have taken center stage. SSK Industries, headed by J.D. Jones was one the first to offer truly heavy-for-caliber cast bullets, most notably for the .44 Magnum. And probably the greatest examples, from a design standpoint, are the bullets that come from Lead Bullets Technol-ogy, or LBT, the second-most misused nomencla-ture in the industry.

NOSE PROFILE

We talked about some of the popular and pre-vailing bullet designs in use and available com-mercially, but now we need to discuss their dis-tinct nose shapes. We revolver wonks tend to make a lot of references to the term "nose pro-file." What is nose profile? Simply put, it is the shape of the bullet's nose, or the killing end of the bullet, if you will. There are many different nose profiles that have been used over the years, including round-nose, flat-nose, hollowpoint, and pointed (or spitzer). Most commonly found com-mercial loadings for big-bore revolvers feature a jacketed expanding bullet of some type or a flat-nosed hardcast bullet design. If hunting is on your list of activities, better leave your round-nosed bullets at home. Round-nosed bullets notoriously tend not to track straight in testing media, making them less than ideal for hunting. The round-nose also limits the potential for creating a large wound channel. Round-nosed bullets should be avoided for all activities save plinking,

By far the most preferred and effective nose profile is the flat-nose. But isn't expansion a good thing? Yes, if you are starting off small. We are not. Big is a component built into our chosen calibers. We have bore diameters any expanding .30-06 bullet would be ecstatic to own. This is the single biggest advantage that we can boast—a sizeable diameter. Enter Lead Bullets Technology, or LBT.

Lead Bullets Technology (LBT)

Cast bullet guru Veral Smith opened Lead Bul-lets Technology back in 1984, but began experimenting with cast bullet design in 1980. This was when Veral acquired a mould lathe that allowed him to make variations in his bullet designs. Veral made identical moulds with one change in design at a time, enabling him to thoroughly vet each. His thorough design, trial and error, and exhaustive testing introduced a whole new vernacular to the handgun hunting world via a series of acronyms that would change the way we load our revolvers with cast bullets. As I mentioned, LBT is the second most misused term in commercial lead pistol bullet making. Unless the moulds come from Veral Smith and Lead Bullets Technology, or unless they are dimensionally true to Veral's designs, they cannot truly be called LBT.

The acronyms of which I speak are LFN (for Long Flat Nose), WFN (Wide Flat Nose), and WLN (Wide Long Nose). These are the three basic flat-nosed bullet designs that have superseded all that have come before, including the much vaunted Keith bullet, which was a semi-wadcutter design with a flat nose and a distinct shoulder. Veral Smith determined that certain meplat sizes were ultimately better than others, regarding penetration and terminal performance on game.

Veral was concerned with meplat area, velocity at impact, and the weight of the projectile. While Veral never set out to create a percentage factor, regarding meplat size, nevertheless, a formula emerged. The true specification of the Long Flat Nose (LFN) is a meplat of .125-inch under the bore diameter of the bullet, or roughly 74.5 percent. The Wide Flat Nose features a meplat that is .90-inch under the bore diameter, or 81 percent. A WLN is simply a WFN with a longer nose that retains the 81-percent meplat. With his designs, Veral sought to maximize powder room, bearing surface, bullet alignment at takeoff, and, particularly critical if used on live targets, the meplat size.

AUTHOR PHOTO

BELT MOUNTAIN'S PUNCH bullet on the left and CorBon's Penetrator on the right. These bullets were designed for uncompromised penetration and can be used on even the largest of land animals.

There is a common misperception that flat-nosed, non-expanding (actually, minimally expanding) hardcast bullets will produce a caliber-sized hole in game. This is simply not true by any stretch of the imagination. A large-meplat bullet, like an LFN or WFN, will produce a wound channel out of proportion to the bore size of the bullet. In Veral Smith's excellent primer on cast bullets, *Jacketed Performance with Cast Bullets*, he states:

"All tissue displacement is determined by the flat to nearly flat frontal area of the bullet. All wounding larger than bullet frontal area is created by displaced tissue spray. Violence of spray determines wound diameter, and spray violence is determined by volume of tissue displaced and speed at which it is displaced. The key to good kills with solids is enough displacement velocity to create rapid blood flow, and enough bullet weight to hold bullet velocity up to good wounding speed during the full depth of penetration."

Because of this "displaced tissue spray" created by the meplat of the bullet, the wounding area outside the bullet's frontal area actually misses the shoulder of a Keith or semi-wadcutter design. Veral found through much experimentation that the meplat does all of the work upon impact with live tissue and that the shoulder of the bullet never gets "wet" or makes contact with anything inside of the animal until the bullet's velocity nearly slows to a stop. Veral goes on to say that the "only utility of the SWC shoulder is to cut paper!" In other words, the shoulder limits the size of the meplat, which is largely responsible for the size of the wound channel

Belt Mountain, CorBon, and Barnes

Belt Mountain produces one of the finest flat-nosed bullet offerings, for absolutely uncompro-

AUTHOR PHOTO

THE 405-GRAIN load is on the far left, the challengers, from that cartridge's left to the right, included Jim Miner's 330-grain load, Cast Performance's 320-grain WLN, and Double Tap's 320-grain WFN.

mising performance on the largest and most heavily boned animals on earth. Dubbed the "Punch" bullet, it features brass construction with a lead core. The Punch is essentially a harder hardcast bullet, and it is the bullet choice for the handgun hunter going after elephant or other large, heavy-boned game that has the potential of crushing the hunter under foot. Mimicking a flat-nosed hardcast bullet, with respect to nose profile and terminal performance, the advantage the Punch bullet holds over hardcast lead bullets is material hardness that will maintain the nose integrity even when pushed to high velocities and/or when encountering hard obstacles like heavy bone. Whereas the hardcast bullet maintains integrity via velocity limitations, the Punch can be over-driven with no negative effects (save for the demise of the animal being hunted).

CorBon offers a similarly designed bullet for a number of handgun calibers that are also insensitive to higher velocities. Its line of bullets, similar to the Punch, are aptly named "Penetrators." Barnes Bullets recently entered this fray, as well, with a bullet relatively impervious to high impact speeds and hard materials. Barnes calls it the "Buster" bullet. Keep in mind that none of these bullets are merely "jacketed" bullets. They all feature a high content of brass with a lead core and are designed to maintain their nose shape no matter what they come in contact with. These bullets are worth any added expense you may incur in their use!

TOO MUCH OF A GOOD THING?

We spent a lot of time in the last chapter talking about larger-than-standard bullets, bullet design, and other factors that affect terminal ballistics on game. But is it possible to have too much of a good thing?

In many instances, we'd tend to answer that

question with a "Yes." There are good weight ranges for optimum penetration (assuming the nose profile is also optimized), but there is definitely a tipping point—both literally and figuratively. When the bullet is too heavy for the caliber, it can also be subsequently too long for the twist rate. Too, the case capacity of the cartridge is compromised, thereby limiting the velocity potential for stability and creating a whole chain of compromises. Arguments about optimal weights abound on Internet forums, so we decided to put some commonly held beliefs to the test. We performed a number of tests involving heavy-for-caliber bullets in two popular calibers, the .44 Magnum, and the .500 Smith & Wesson Magnum—both ends of the big-bore revolver spectrum.

The first testing we performed used the ubiquitous .44 Remington Magnum. The chosen extreme was a 405-grain hardcast lead bullet with a WFN-like nose profile designed for use in a .444 Marlin rifle (same bore diameter—think of it as a .44 Magnum on steroids) and Ruger Redhawk and Super Redhawk .44 Magnum revolvers. The decision was made to use load data that had been thoroughly tested and vetted previously, this data featuring a stiff load—as stiff as the limited case capacity allows, due to the massive bullet on top of it—of 2400 powder.

Keep in mind that this is a Ruger Redhawk or Super Redhawk proposition only. No other production .44 Magnum revolver features a cylinder long enough for this bullet, as it must be loaded to the second crimp groove in order to create enough case capacity for any meaningful velocity. A Smith & Wesson Model 29 will chamber this load, as will a Colt Anaconda, but the end of the bullet sits nearly flush with the end of the cylinder. There is absolutely no room for the slightest move-

THE 405-GRAIN bullet is seen here next to a loaded 320-grain .44 Magnum round. The extreme length of the 405-grain bullet necessitates seating to the second crimp groove to make enough room for the powder payload.

AUTHOR PHOTO

THE PENETRATION "BOX" consisted of 60 inches of bundled, water-soaked newspaper.

ment of the bullet out of the case (the dreaded pulled crimp), or it will tie up your revolver.

We were inclined to believe that this combination would experience issues with stability, both in flight and in the test medium. The commercially loaded ammunition came from Double Tap Ammunition, which provided the 320-grain WFN loads at an advertised 1,325 fps, and from Cast Performance, which provided 320-grain WLN bullets for us to load. We also tested 330-grain and 290-grain bullets designed by a good friend and partner in crime Jim Miner. Last, for grins and giggles, we tested an old standby, a 240-grain "Keith-style" (there goes that moniker again) load at a scorching advertised 1,500 fps from Double Tap Ammunition. We wanted to see how a truly old-school load would fare against more contemporary loads.

All the control loads have proven accurate and deadly on game. The decision was made to first shoot the 405-grain bullet into a wetpack within 10 feet. We would also shoot a number of commercially loaded 320-grain loads into the same wetpack, as well as a couple of handloads with homemade and designed cast bullets. If the 405-grain tracked straight, we would increase the distance of the impact in the wetpack, and if *that* proved successful in the same manner, we would test it for accuracy at distances of 50 to 100 yards. If all was still good, we would then take it on a wild hog hunt to see how it did on agitated porcine flesh.

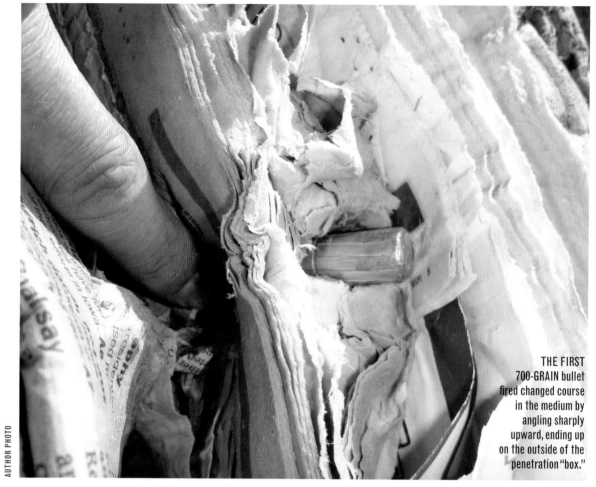

AUTHOR PHOTO

AUTHOR PHOTO

THE FIRST 700-GRAIN bullet fired changed course in the medium by angling sharply upward, ending up on the outside of the penetration "box."

PENETRATION TEST NO. 1—.44 MAGNUM/.475 LINEBAUGH

Bullet (grain)/Load	Velocity (fps)	Penetration (inches)	Notes
405/.44 Mag	960.6	22	exited box
405/.44 Mag	950.5	31	exited box
405/.44 Mag	944.7	28	began ascending
320 CP/.44 Mag	1,247	29	straight line
320 DT/.44 Mag	1,353	30	straight line
330 JM/.44 Mag	1,264	34	straight line
240 DT/.44 Mag	1,398	30	straight line
290 JM/.44 Mag	1,284.7	36	straight line
405/.44 Mag	937.7	34	straight line
405/.44 Mag	947	28	straight line
330 JM/.44 Mag	1,243	26	straight line
405/.44 Mag	966	28	straight line
430 JM/.475 L	1,355	54	exited-shot at angle
430 JM/.475 L	1,304	49	straight line

CP = Cast Performance; DT = Double Tap; JM = Jim Miner design

THE 405-GRAIN .44 MAGNUM bullets clearly exhibited instability in flight, as these two bullets passed through the target sideways.

The Test

Let's talk test media for a moment. We will certainly draw fire from those who believe we should be using ballistic gelatin on these tests, which we didn't, and they will question the conclusions we have drawn from our results. Despite the detractors, the choice we made to use wetpack over ballistic gelatin was one of practicality and economics. Not only is ballistics gelatin cost prohibitive, if you plan on performing a lot of testing, but unless you have the controlled environment of a laboratory at your disposal, it is not that easy to use correctly, particularly in its preparation. While wetpack does not completely mimic the flesh of animals, it does more than an adequate job of telling the tester what the bullet will do when it contacts flesh. It's a material that is actually tougher than animal flesh, and if your bullet performs well in wet newsprint, it will undoubtedly perform well on animals. It is certainly a good enough medium to monitor and track the stability of a bullet.

We soaked bundles of newspaper and phone books for 24 hours prior to the actual test. All the bullets would be fired into the same media to prevent any variations in the consistency of the media. We lined up 60 inches of wetpack, knowing that, if any of the tested bullets would traverse the wetpack's full length, we'd be surprised. All loads would be shot from the same firearm to prevent

THE 700-GRAIN BULLET (left) next to a loaded round with the same topper. Others tested from left to right were the 400-grain WFN from Double Tap, CorBon's 440-grainer, and Grizzly Cartridge's 500-grain load.

AUTHOR PHOTO

THE MAXIMUM overall length with the 700-grain .500 S&W bullet exceeds the author's comfort level, as even a slight crimp pull would tie the revolver up.

any variation. We also shot every load over a chronograph and recorded all data (see the chart).

First up was the 405-grainer, fired from a Ruger Super Redhawk with a 7½-inch barrel. As you can see from the chart, the first two 405-grain bullets travelled through a decent amount of wetpack, but both angled up and exited the box. This indicates poor stability. The third 405-grain stayed in the box, but also began traveling upward, stopping at 28 inches. The next five bullets of lesser weight than the 405-grain went deeper, including, rather surprisingly, the 240-grain "Keith-style" bullet. The next 405-grain did really well, staying in the box and traveling a full 34 inches in the wetpack.

The increase in penetration depth at this stage could very well have indicated that the paper was softening up and becoming pulpy; we have seen this happen before, on numerous occasions, while conducting penetration tests. Indeed, evidence of this was seen when another test bullet in this time

frame penetrated more than what has been accepted as normal in the test media.

We then subjected the 405-grain load to some accuracy testing, so we shot at two different distances to determine if the bullet would stabilize in flight. We had sizeable trouble putting it on paper. At 50 yards, we were able to shoot the closest thing resembling a group with three shots. Two of them had definitely key-holed. At this juncture we determined that 100-yard testing was out of the question. Some would argue that this load was meant for up-close and personal work, but I would argue that, if one has to wait until the animal is on top of them before firing because of a fear missing the target entirely, it's still a losing proposition. Sure, it penetrated well, but we found that, even then, the bullets were tumbling in the media and often times didn't out-penetrate "lesser" bullets (lesser, at least, in weight).

So, we concluded the big 405-grain was not worth the trouble of loading, not worth the additional lead necessary to make a bullet this big, and not worth the limited usefulness. I would much rather have a 300-grain bullet that shoots

THE LINEBAUGH SEMINARS

For more than a dozen years now, John Linebaugh has hosted a series of seminars in the spring, using various locations so that big-bore revolver nuts from every corner can gather to learn from the master gun builders, shoot revolvers, test penetration, and have some fun hanging out with other like-minded individuals for a couple days. The first seminar took place in 1999, in Dale, Texas, and was attended by about 50 of the faithful. John typically hosts five or six seminars a year, depending upon interest expressed. The largest turn out to date has been 169 attendees.

The seminars typically start with classroom presentations about general sixgun topics, including ballistics, accuracy, bullet performance, and effectiveness on big game. The format is free-form, and very informal. They usually start with a question posed, and the conversation goes from there. Flexibility is the name of the game, and John wants to keep it that way. The seminars are educational for all levels of participants, from beginners to old trail hands. Lots of shooting is involved, and participants are encouraged to bring their own guns and ammo and pit their pet loads against one another in a penetration test in wet newsprint and bone.

The penetration testing is the portion of the Linebaugh Seminars that has always interested me the most. Using wetpack, big-bore rifles are compared to big-bore handguns, and the results are often surprising. All results are recorded, and looking back over the statistics from the last few years, a definite and interesting pattern has emerged. For one, a .475 Linebaugh often makes a good showing, as does its big brother, the .500 Linebaugh.

This is clearly a hands-on experience, where participants get to shoot, learn, and shoot some more for three whole days. It is also a chance to get caught up with old friends and make some new ones. The seminar is a bargain at $300 per person, spouses and children under the age of 16 may accompany the attendee free of charge. For more information, call (307)645-3332 or log on to www.customsixguns.com.

accurately at 50 or 100 yards, that will penetrate to the same depth if not better, and that can be used in any and every production .44 Magnum revolver. Such a load could also be used for hunting and not simply relegated to the task of defensive shooting. Inconsistency also hurts this load combination. While it is pleasant to shoot, I would rather suffer recoil and accurately hit the animal bearing down on me. The recoil may be worth it.

We were divided on whether we should test this load further and decided not to, as its performance was so erratic. When it went straight, it penetrated well— not exceptionally well, but good enough for its intended purpose. Unfortunately, it only tracked straight approximately 50 percent of the time. Those are not odds I would bet on, particularly as its intent is stopping agitated bears or other toothy predators. If the 405-grain had shown penetration above and beyond all other competitors, we may have performed further testing, but the only advantage I can assign to this load is that the recoil is mild. However, since the weight of a Redhawk or Super Redhawk is substantial, even the hottest loads, in my opinion, are controllable, so it is a moot point.

One last note and observation about this test, before we put it to bed. The front of the wetpack, the portion we shot into first, was a soaked phone book, and the impact quality of each bullet was made clearly visible by the size of the hole created by the bullets striking the cover. While the 405-grain bullet simply made an unassuming hole, the 320-grain bullet from Double Tap, with its full WFN nose profile, actually created a crater upon impacting the phone book. This is obviously a function of both velocity and meplat size, but the initial "wound channel" was impressive, to say the very least. The faster bullets also proved to penetrate well, despite the higher impact velocities and the resistance it met on impact. While this test is far from conclusive and, frankly, just one test, it does demonstrate that, while there are more ways than one to skin a cat, some ways are very inefficient. This is one of them. Save your lead, load lighter, and learn to shoot straight.

Back in the January 1995 issue of *Guns & Ammo* magazine, writer Ross Seyfried tested the heavier-is-better theory using the .45 Colt round. He chose a 412-grain hardcast bullet in his hot-rodded, Hamilton Bowen-built five-shot Ruger Bisley, in hopes of improving upon the already impressive performance he'd experienced a decade before with 350-grain bullets on a Holy Grail dangerous game animal, the Cape buffalo. Ross wanted to prove to himself that the 412-grain bullet was the equal of the .475 Linebaugh on big game. After all, it was sporting the same sized meplat, a similar weight (412 grains versus 430 grains for the .475), and similar velocity levels (1,300 to 1,350 fps).

After dispatching a large Asian buffalo in Australia with his rifle (that's another story for another time), Seyfried used the opportunity to test the 412-grain bullet on the carcass (he didn't want to trust the bullet and load on a live hunt for dangerous game before it had been thoroughly vetted). The bullet failed to pass through both shoulders, while five years before, the .475 had whistled through both shoulders of a Cape buffalo. While shooting a dead animal usually presents the bullet with more resistance than a living, breathing animal, the test was still telling. Ross Seyfried concluded that the length of the bullet was poorly matched to the relatively slow twist rate of the revolver (1:20), thereby affecting the bullet's stability. The 412-grain bullets evidently stabilized adequately in flight, but not while penetrating through the test media, in this case bovine flesh.

With Seyfried's test in mind and the results of

GO DEEP!

Near the end of the test, we shot a 430-grain flat-nosed hardcast bullet of Jim Miner's design from his .475 Linebaugh BFR. The bullet left the barrel at a stout 1,355 fps. Because of the poor angle of the shot, this bullet exited the box. but it didn't and instead tracked straight—at the 54-inch mark! We still haven't found a .44 Magnum load that will compete with a good .475 in penetration testing!

our own first trial, our next "too heavy" test was conducted in the same manner as the first. We soaked newspaper for one day prior to the actual test, along with a number of phone books. Forty inches of soaked newsprint were set up on our private range, this time for testing the newest heavyweight champ, the .500 Smith & Wesson Magnum.

This cartridge has received a lot of hoopla in the gun press since its introduction in 2003. As a result, there is no shortage of commercial ammunition and loading supplies for the big round. Since this test was all about finding the tipping point with regards to bullet weight, we assembled a number of commercial hardcast loadings, including CorBon's 440-grain (the first max-effort and heavy bullet load that was released with the introduction of the Smith & Wesson X-frame), leaving the barrel at a scorching 1,625 fps advertised velocity. We also tested Grizzly Cartridge's 500-grain LFN at an advertised 1,550 fps, and Double Tap's 400-grain WFN load at a whopping 1,805 fps (this

PENETRATION TEST NO. 2 CHART—.500 SMITH & WESSON MAGNUM

Bullet(grains)	Velocity (fps)	Penetration (inches)	Notes
700	993.6	25	ascended almost exited
700	985	30	ascended and exited box
400 Double Tap	564	22	straight line
400 Double Tap	1,574	26	straight line
440 CorBon	1,513	27.5	straight line
500 Grizzly	1,179	40	straight line with exit
500 Grizzly	1,196	33	straight line

last velocity was attained with a gun using an 8⅜-inch barrel). The too-heavy load would consist of a 700-grain flat-nosed bullet over a stiff charge of 296 powder. This is a max-effort load for this bullet, according to load data we received from John Ross, and is a load that was quite compressed—and it's a good thing production .500 Smith & Wesson revolvers feature a long cylinder, as the 700-grain load has a *very* long overall length. The test gun was a Smith & Wesson X-frame with a 6½-inch barrel. All loads were shot over a chronograph and velocities were recorded.

See chart for results, but this test again confirmed our suspicions about diminishing returns and too-heavy bullets. We only shot a couple 700-grain bullets into the test medium and felt it was unnecessary to do more. Bullet No. 1 turned upward abruptly and was found outside and on top of the soaked newsprint, delivering only average penetration. The second bullet went deeper but, again, changed course, took a sharp turn up, and actually exited the penetration box.

The sweet spot, with regards to penetration from the .500 Smith & Wesson, is in the 440- to 500-grain range. Even the 400-grain WFN bullet did well. The first 500-grain LFN load from Grizzly Cartridge we shot punched through the *entire* box (40 inches). We'd intended to test more and lighter loads, but it was clear this wasn't necessary.

Comparing the two, it was clear that going heavier doesn't necessarily buy you any more penetration, and didn't enhance straight line penetration, which is of utmost importance. I see these really heavy bullets as novelties and nothing more. Testing for accuracy proved futile with these loads, when shooting off sandbags on the bench; aiming at a 50-yard target, the shots impacted in completely different places, clearly demonstrating stability issues with these extra-long bullets. This testing was not meant to be the last word on this topic and is, perhaps, insignificant from a statistical standpoint, but there are simply better options that are not nearly as extreme.

While, this is just one abbreviated test, it is revealing. The 700-grain bullet is *exceedingly* long, eating precious case capacity, and, in the case of the Smith & Wesson X-frame, the bullet's nose is

dangerously close to the end of the cylinder. I've raised this issue before, but, if you experience crimp pull, it won't take much to tie up your gun; assuming one would choose such loads/bullets for defense against dangerous animals, reliability is a real factor that should be taken into account. In all, the loads are compressed and, at least for me, a waste of lead, plus accuracy was also an issue. What good is a load combination that you cannot hit your target with? While not the final word, and statistically insignificant, the results simply reaffirmed our previous findings with regards to the lack of stability these long bullets exhibit.

Gunsmith and friend Lee Martin (profiled in another section of this book), developer of a line of unique wildcat revolver rounds, also tested the bigger-is-better theory in his own cartridge, the .450 Bonecrusher, which is a .500 Linebaugh case necked down to .45-caliber. Capable of rather impressive velocities that rival that of the .454 Casull but with lower pressures, Lee tested a number of different bullet weights in his pet cartridge. The heaviest tested was a 405-grain, flat-nosed cast bullet. Keep in mind that his test revolver features an 8½-inch barrel, and a fast 1:16 twist. Lee tested a number of different loads at varying velocities with the 405-grain bullet, and was unable to achieve acceptable accuracy. Furthermore, we had frequent key-holing, indicating poor stability.

In summary, too much of a good thing really does exist. "More's Law"—more is always better—is nearly always pressed into action, when limits are being tested. It's how we find the upper limits of any envelope. We had to see for ourselves what the upper limits of bullet weights are for these popular calibers, and we hope we have saved you the time, trouble, agony, and resources necessary to come to the same conclusions. In many cases, you really can do more with less. We think that, as general rule, if you want to move up significantly in weight in any given caliber, look at the next larger calibers and see where the heavyweight bullets start. In many cases, you will see greater terminal performance with an increase in diameter *and* weight, versus simply using heavier bullets and leaving the diameter the same.

BULLET TYPES, ENERGY, & OTHER MYTHS EXPOSED

We felt this topic deserved more attention than we have already invested. If you haven't already guessed, and especially after the testing described here, I am big proponent of hardcast flat-nosed bullets. For me and many others, they have worked exceptionally well. But, instead of just me, the author, giving you one biased side of the debate, I asked a fellow gun writer who has used jacketed expanding bullets extensively and successfully on large game animals to tell us why he feels jacketed expanding bullets are the right tool for every job in the hunting fields. Let me introduce you to Gary Smith, accomplished writer, handgun hunter, guide, and all around good guy.

THE CASE FOR JACKETED BULLETS
BY GARY SMITH

I began hunting with handguns more than 30 years ago and have long since lost count of how many big-game animals I've taken with pistols and revolvers. Most have been whitetail deer, but there have been a couple trips to Africa and other parts of the U.S. over the years. In the world of hunting and firearms, a few topics seem to evoke religious-like emotions, and the debate over cast versus jacketed bullets in big-bore handguns is one of those. I have witnessed otherwise rational men nearly come to blows arguing about the merits of cast versus jacketed bullets. It's just one of those debates that no one can quite settle once and for all. I have used hard-cast bullets on a number of occasions to take some very nice trophies, but, when it comes to big-bore, straight-walled cartridges, I prefer a jacketed expanding bullet for hunting all but the very largest game—and, even then, unless it is my misfortune to try and stop a charge with a handgun, I would choose a jacketed bullet first.

SIERRA 350-GRAIN jacketed hollowpoints in the .500 JRH round, as loaded by Grizzly Cartridge Company.

RIGHT: THIS IS A .41 MAGNUM WINCHESTER Platinum Tip bullet recovered from a good-sized hog. It shows excellent expansion and was lodged in the hog's gristle plate on the off-side. An unfired cartridge is shown for comparison.

My first handgun was a T/C Contender chambered in .44 Remington Magnum, and, after several months of practice, I felt I was ready to tackle deer hunting. My opportunity came one December morning, when a fat Virginia doe came within 50 yards. I can't recall whether the bullet was a Sierra or Hornady, but it was a handloaded 180-grain JHP. The shot was placed perfectly on her shoulder point, as she quartered toward me, and she made it only 30 yards before going down. I have since decided that a little heavier bullet in the .44 is more to my liking, but, if the 180s shoot well in your gun, they are certainly up to the task of taking deer-sized game.

PHOTO BY GARY SMITH

Some of those early, jacketed bullet designs were good, and some are still around. One in particular is the Remington 240-grain semi-jacketed hollowpoint. Back in the days, when there was such a thing as a cheap box of handgun ammo, the Remingtons were always available and, after changing to a 240-grain load in the .44, I shot quite a few of them down the pipe. I had largely forgotten about the Remingtons, until a couple years ago, when I found myself very pressed for time leading up to a hunt where I'd be using the Ruger Super Blackhawk Hunter in my .44 Magnum chambering. I started out that hunt intending to shoot a deer, but found myself in the position to shoot a cow elk—and, of course, the bullets I had with me were factory Remington 240-grain semi-jacketed hollowpoints. That bullet has a lot of soft lead at the tip, and I was a little cautious about shooting that large an animal with a soft lead hollowpoint bullet, but that was all I had with me and the gun was dead-on at 100 yards, so I had complete confidence in the gun and my ability, if I could get the right shot.

Sure enough, we spotted a herd of cows, and, after a short stalk, I was in position to take a shot from about 65 yards. I took a quartering-away shot, and the elk went about 50 yards and dropped. The Remington retained 75 percent of its original weight and mushroomed perfectly. The bullet didn't exit, but I did get 24 to 26 inches of penetration before the bullet lodged in the off-side shoulder. If you asked me, I probably wouldn't recommend a hollowpoint bullet for elk, because there are better choices in the .44, but it will work if you recognize

PHOTO BY GARY SMITH

THIS IS A 250-GRAIN Winchester .454 bullet recovered from a whitetail deer. Winchester has loaded some of its rounds with Hornady XTP bullets.

the limitations. In this case the quartering-away angle allowed me to avoid the heavy shoulder bones until significant damage had been done to the vital organs.

HARDCAST BULLETS—
ALWAYS THE BEST CHOICE?

One of the favorite rationalizations for using cast bullets is that a hunter doesn't need to worry about matching the bullet to the game, as a suitable hardcast bullet could be used for taking any game from moose to mice. This is certainly true enough, but I find that, as it is with most absolutes, there are usually a few problems.

While on my first trip to Africa, I used a .44 Magnum to take several animals, including zebra and wildebeest, with a 310-grain hardcast bullet. The wildebeest was broadside to me and I hit him on the shoulder at 50 yards—and that bullet whistled right through him.

This was my first experience with relatively large, thicker-skinned game and cast bullets, and the issue I had in those situations was a lack of blood trail. Neither the zebra nor wildebeest bled enough to follow the spoor, even though they were very well shot. The wildebeest traveled about 150 yards in a straight line, and, fortunately, the cover was open enough to make recovery possible by following the tracks. My observation was that the exit wound in the skin

was small, about .44-caliber, and simply didn't allow enough blood to flow out for easy tracking.

In the same vein, I nearly lost a good warthog with a high double-lung hit and would have, had it not been for a tracking dog finding the hog still very much alive about an hour later. I am certain an expanding bullet shot under the same circumstances would have done more damage to the lungs and the hog would have bled out within 100 yards. Regardless of what it has been shot with, though, finding even a fatally hit animal in all but the most open cover can be a big problem, unless there is a sufficient blood trail to follow. Throw in heavy brush and ground cover not conducive to seeing blood, and finding your game can become impossible until the buzzards start circling.

Mark Hampton, a good friend and fellow handgun hunter with vast experience, notes in his book that, "Big cast bullets in revolvers essentially leave a half-inch diameter hole, but, in most cases, they do not kill quickly … . Unless the shoulder or spine is broken or a brain shot is made, the chase will be on." I agree. If I ever hunt grizzly, rhino, or Cape buffalo with a revolver, I'll choose a gun in .475 or .500 and pick a heavy, bonded soft-point bullet for the first couple rounds, and then perhaps have a couple cast bullets in the remaining chambers in case I need the penetration they offer. Even on elephant, a hardcast bullet would not be my first choice for a frontal brain shot, though the Punch bullet and similar designs offered by a couple different companies are superior choices, in my opinion, because there is no risk of them coming apart.

Cast bullets have enjoyed a couple advantages over the years and the ability to mould your own bullet is perhaps the greatest reason that still exists for the active shooter. A custom moulded bullet can be very accurate, but even the best are no more so than a premium jacketed bullet. The downsides to moulding your own bullets are the time involved in our already busy lives and finding and preparing suitable lead. Tire shops no longer give you a bucketful of wheel weights just for the asking.

Cast bullets also used to be significantly

WINCHESTER HAS A mildly loaded .454 Casull round that is excellent for deer and other medium-sized game and minus the punishing recoil of full-house loads.

cheaper than jacketed bullets, even if you bought them already moulded, but that is no more, if you're buying top-quality bullets for hunting. If you're not a reloader, cast bullets offer even less in terms of savings, and, in many cases, the jacketed bullets will be cheaper, a lot cheaper. For example, a box of 20 loaded rounds in .475 Linebaugh with the Hornady 400-grain jacketed XTP is just under $30 at a popular online store, while a box of 20 Buffalo Bore 400-grain hardcast bullets is just over $60. If I had the time to put into finding lead and moulding my own bullets, or if I could achieve a significant savings over jacketed bullets, I would undoubtedly shoot cast bullets a lot more. Realistically though, how many times a year do you shoot something that requires the penetration offered by a 300- to 400-grain hardcast bullet?

In my opinion, having shot game up to the size of elk with revolvers using both jacketed and cast bullets, I will choose a jacketed bullet every time. To be the most effective at killing an animal, the bullet needs to expand and it needs to penetrate to the vital organs. If either of those two conditions

is not met, then you're making a trade-off. As with any bullet, regardless its design or material, there is a trade-off between penetration and expansion. The more it expands, the less it penetrates. Ideally, a bullet would fully penetrate on a broadside shot, but, if it hits large bones and stops in the off-side shoulder or just under the hide, I'll take that over a bullet that doesn't expand at all but penetrates fully. Jacketed bullet technology has come such a long way in the last 15 to 20 years, and it continues to evolve.

Many bullets offer excellent controlled expansion and enough penetration to bring down the largest game. Although it's now discontinued, the Nosler Partition HG has been a mainstay in my revolvers for quite some time. They were available in .357-, .44-, and .45-caliber in a couple different weights—and about the only thing in North America I wouldn't shoot with the 300-grain .45 bullet would be a grizzly in close cover. The Swift A-Frame is a very similar bullet to the Nosler design and, unless something better comes along, it will be my first choice when my stockpile of Noslers is exhausted in a couple of years.

Another company delivering advanced bullet technology and design is Winchester. Its latest achievement is a dual jacketed/dual bonded bullet called the Supreme Elite Dual Bond. The Dual

Bond is a very unique design, consisting of an inner jacket chemically bonded to an inner lead core, and an outer jacket mechanically bonded, or crimped, to the inner jacket. It's designed to open at a controlled rate into 12 segments, or petals, six on each jacket, with expansion of up to twice the original bullet diameter and retention of nearly 100 percent of its original weight, for a combination of knockdown power, solid penetration, and significant tissue damage.

Most handgun hunters will end up using the Winchester Dual Bond bullet on game under 250 pounds, but I wanted to try it on something a good deal larger—elk.

There is perhaps no place better to conduct bullet tests on live game than on a ranch in Texas. After a few hours of spot and stalk, and an attempted ambush that went sideways, I finally got a shot at a spike bull from about 60 yards with my open-sighted, 4¾-inch barreled .454. The elk stood at a slight quartering angle, and from the time I shot until the bull was down was just under 13 seconds. Impressive! The bullet penetrated the shoulder blade about four inches down from the top, took out two ribs, and lodged next to the stomach on the off-side of the body cavity. Penetration on the elk was approximately 28 inches and included some very significant damage to the soft tissue and bones.

Based on my observations with this elk, this bullet is a little light for large game because of its expansion characteristics, unless you limit your shots to broadside encounters and try to avoid heavy shoulder bones. I'm certain this bullet will fully penetrate deer and other medium game from all but very oblique angles, and will likely fully penetrate larger game on broadside shots with proper shot placement.

One final note on Winchester's bullet. To perform as designed, the Dual Bond should not expand below the cannelure or crimp groove. If it does, it can separate, which is why I wouldn't recommend it for large game, but think it's a great deer bullet in the .454 Casull.

Bonded bullets have become popular in recent years and show great promise for a handgunner who chooses a jacketed bullet. A "bonded" bul-

THIS COW ELK was taken by Gary Smith using a Freedom Arms .475 Linebaugh. He shot her with a hand-loaded 325-grain Speer bullet having a muzzle velocity of 1,500 fps. The shot was from 60 yards and into her shoulder, and she and went just 50 yards before piling up.

THIS WARTHOG was taken with a 310-grain hardcast bullet out of a Ruger Super Blackhawk Hunter in .44 Magnum. Nearly all the blood on this hog was caused by the fight that ensued with the tracking dog after the shot. Both lungs were hit, but the cast bullet just didn't do enough damage to kill quickly.

let has an inner core that is chemically bonded to the jacket, a design meant to control expansion and, theoretically, prevent the dreaded core/jacket separation. I have tried the bonded Speer Deep Curl in the .475 Linebaugh in the 325-grain bullet weight on several animals, including a huge cow elk that the bullet just crushed. The shot was a sharp quartering-to angle, and I was unable to recover the bullet when it became lost in the paunch, even though a couple of us looked for it for about 30 minutes. The elk's shoulder was broken, the lungs were ripped open from the bullet traversing them, and the liver was punctured and torn—the animal went all of 50 yards before piling up. I've also shot a few whitetail and several hogs with the Deep Curl, but have yet to recover a bullet to see how it expanded. Still, the exit

wounds have been what I would expect from an expanding bullet that starts out at nearly a half-inch in diameter. I can find no justification for moving up to the 400-grain bullet unless I'm after grizzly or other large and dangerous animals.

For medium-sized game up to about 250 pounds, I would choose a quality jacketed hollow-point bullet. If black bear or larger animals were on the agenda, then I would use a soft-point bullet in the middle to heavy end of the scale for the caliber, and it would be a bonded bullet, if available.

If you're already convinced that a cast bullet has some extraordinary ability to kill game, then nothing I can say will likely convince you otherwise, because, like I said, it's just one of those debates. However, if you're open-minded and honest about the size of the game you'll encounter, then a quality, jacketed bullet may be all you'll ever need. They will kill quicker if the cartridge and bullet construction is appropriate for the size of the animal, will generally cause more internal damage, and, most importantly, they will leave a

INCONSISTENCY KEEPS the author away from using jacketed expanding bullets on large game, because they may not expand and, when they don't, they perform a poor impression of a flat-nosed hardcast bullet.

THE AUTHOR argues that a jacketed expanding bullet may or may not do what it was designed to do—expand. This 240-grain Remington JHP expanded quite nicely.

good blood trail when a cast bullet often will not. If you do choose a cast bullet, you should make every attempt to shoot the shoulder of the animal, preferably both shoulders. The additional damage caused by bone fragmentation and the impediment of the mobility of the game will go a long way towards making a quick kill and recovering your animal quickly.

COUNTERPOINT: THE CASE FOR HARDCAST BULLETS

You will notice that I have not displayed any photographs of hardcast bullets I have recovered from game. That's because I have never recovered one! They nearly always exit, a factor in using hardcast bullets that I find useful and comforting.

There is no doubt that big-bore handgunners feel very passionate in their bullet choices, particularly with regards to hunting. One school believes that a violently expanding bullet at a high-striking velocity is the best method to quickly bring down game. The other school of thought—the one we will refer to, appropriately, as "old school"—believes that flat-nosed hardcast bullets are the choice for all seasons, all game, and all reasons. Both schools offer solid reasoning for their choices, but, in many cases, those from the old school camp didn't start out there, but rather migrated there through a series of failures.

Huh? I know that sounds a bit confusing, but many handgun hunters I know and have spoken with at length have admitted that, when they began pursuing game with a wheelgun, they chose hollowpoints or soft-points at maximum velocity. The problem with that line of thinking is that this load may kill one animal spectacularly one moment, and the next the hunter is tracking a wounded animal through the thickets. Why? There are a number of possible reasons. Your impact velocity may not have been high enough to induce expansion, in which case you end up with a solid-type bullet with a big open cavity at the nose that doesn't impart much damage. Let's face the facts, a hollowpoint that doesn't expand is going to perform a poor imitation of a flat-nosed hardcast.

A lot of thought has gone into the nose profiles of LBT's WFN- or LFN-type bullets, and they not only penetrate deeply, they also create a wound channel larger and out of proportion to their diameter. On the other hand, there is a common misconception that flat-nosed hardcast bullets produce a bullet diameter-sized wound channel. Obviously, this is simply not the case.

I was one of those big-bore handgun hunters who started off in the jacketed expanding bullet camp, and I met with my fair share of successes in the game fields. But, a spectacular failure on a small wild hog in Florida got me thinking—and experimenting. I didn't pack it in and just instantly swap out my ammo type. Instead, I used the same load the following day on a much larger animal (by 200 pounds!), and the bullet/load performed as advertised. Now, I was *really* confused. I hate inconsistency. Inconsistency makes conclusions hard to draw and decisions difficult to make. I don't want to wonder what will happen when my bullet strikes flesh, especially if the animal in your sights can fight back.

A lengthy conversation with good friend and handgun hunter John Parker convinced me to try something different. I started testing heavy-for-caliber hardcast bullets and found they were very consistent. The cast bullets didn't necessarily produce the initial devastation that hollowpoints are capable of producing, but, more often than not, they produced an exit hole, something the expanding bullet often did not do. And, not only did the flat-nosed hardcasts provide more than adequate penetration every time, they would do so from any angle presented. This advantage really helps, as you do not have to be nearly as picky choosing your shot. Over the years, I revisit jacketed expanding bullets to see if I have drawn the wrong conclusions, but that old word "inconsistency" keeps coming back to haunt me.

A fellow hunting buddy once made a trip to Texas, to a ranch to kill a bison for meat. The chosen animal wasn't very large (for a bison), at approximately 700 pounds. My friend's handgun of choice was a .500 Smith & Wesson Magnum, stoked with 500-grain soft-point jacketed bullets. A full 30 minutes after the first shot hit behind the foreleg, the animal continued grazing. Stunned, my friend finished the animal with a rifle.

On any other day, his load may have worked like a charm. Indeed, my friend tells me that other large animals have succumbed to this load/bullet combination. Why not this time?

More inconsistency, but, in this case, maybe not a case of bad ammo, instead, perhaps, a poor *choice* for that type/size of animal. There are a plethora of reasons for a bullet not to perform as designed, as hunting is performed under less than ideal conditions, shot angles differ widely, the animal may be alerted to our presence and adrenalized, or the bullet may have clipped a bone just enough and at the wrong angle to send it off its course by a millimeter. The list of possibilities goes on. There are so many factors that can negatively affect terminal performance. This is exactly why I choose the "safer" and more prudent route and go with the type of bullet/load that will likely work under *most* circumstances.

Professional Hunter Bud Rummel enjoys hunting with a handgun, when not guiding clients in Africa. He reported that, upon purchasing his .500 Smith & Wesson Magnum, in 2005, he wanted to try it out on a rather large bison at the Brady Ranch, in Florida. At the time, there weren't many available factory loads for the big .500, so Bud chose what he thought to be a good load, a 500-grain jacketed flat-point bullet. He got a 32-yard broadside shot on a mature bison bull, and, upon impact, the animal turned and began walking away, but then turned around and faced the perplexed hunter. It then lowered its head, began stomping the ground with a hoof, and raised its tail straight in the air. Having hunted discontented bovines in the past, Bud prepared himself for the charge that was imminent. Just then a cow bison walked in front of the bull, and the bull's attention was diverted momentarily. He sniffed the cow, began following her, and then fell over dead. Upon butchering, Bud discovered the bullet had hit no bone, yet failed to exit.

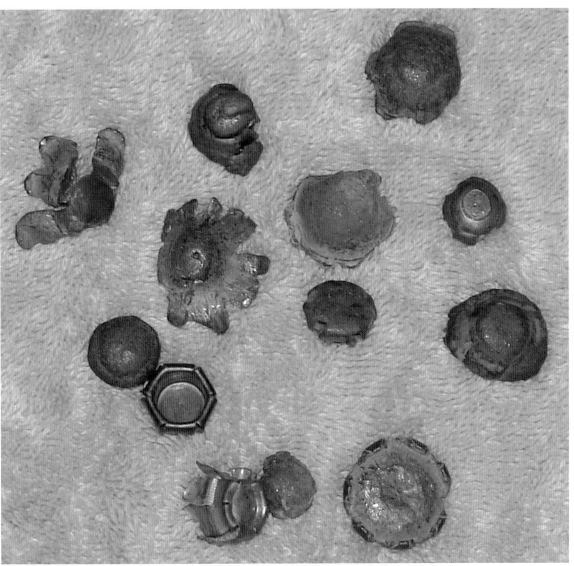

PHOTO BY JOHN PARKER

OVER-EXPANDED jacketed hollowpoints do not penetrate well.

Using this same load one year later, Bud again hunted the Brady Ranch, but this time Asian water buffalo was on the menu. He wound up shooting a 1,600-pound bull four times before it succumbed to its wounds. Fifty minutes passed from the first to the last shot and the expiration of the animal. No bullet exited, and none were recovered. A conversation with Smith & Wesson's (at the time) Tom Kelley pointed Bud towards Cor-Bon's 440-grain wide, flat-nosed hardcast loads, and he has used it successfully ever since on all types of dangerous game, including African lion.

Bud reports that this load performs consistently.

Tim Sundles, proprietor of Buffalo Bore Ammunition, communicated to us that, for certain applications, particularly thin-skinned game like deer, he prefers a bullet that mushrooms. He once had a customer call him and complain that he used Buffalo Bore's 420-grain LFN loads in his .475 Linebaugh for hunting deer. He placed the bullet through the shoulders of a trophy buck, and killed two does behind the buck! This was clearly a case for an expanding jacketed bullet. The gentleman paid a hefty fine for his poor bullet choice in that application. Tim told me, "When you expand a bullet, it is like a parachute, and you can say amen to penetration." For large animals, Sundles prefers a hardcast bullet with a large meplat, but warns against over-driving them.

I have heard the claim that hardcast bullets fail to produce much blood for trailing, but I would argue that an exit hole increases the likelihood of a good blood trail by providing another escape route for blood. If the bullet stays in the animal, it can only bleed from the entrance hole. But is it that simple?

Our good friend John Parker was hunting Asian buffalo with his cousin in Hondo, Texas, one year. They successfully killed a rather large Asian buffalo with a Freedom Arms Model 83 in .500 JRH, loaded with 425-grain, truncated cone, flat-nosed hardcast bullets at nearly 1,400 fps. They successfully put the animal down in less than one minute. Preparing to leave the ranch and head home, they decided to accompany a hunter who had just arrived in camp, as he went after a mature bull bison with his .500 Magnum Smith & Wesson. The well-meaning hunter's choice in ammunition was a commercially loaded 400-grain hollowpoint at an advertised 1,675 fps, a stout load by anyone's standards.

The hunter's first shot was true and nearly broadside at approximately 75 yards. The bull bison was obviously irritated, but relatively unfazed, when he ran off. While running away, the hunter got another shot off that struck the bull behind the rib cage. This did not slow the bison down. The hunting party pursued and, once they caught up with the wounded bovine, the hunter was able to get off one last shot, as the animal quartered towards him. After this shot, the bison finally dropped. Time elapsed was a full 20 minutes. Once the bison was skinned and opened up, it was revealed that none of the three bullets had managed to exit and that the first broadside shot, which entered the onside shoulder, had failed to reach the offside rib cage.

Many hardcast users have told me similar stories about starting in the shiny bullet camp and ending up in the lead bullet camp. The other way around doesn't seem to hold true, and I have found that proponents of jacketed expanding bullets tend to have very limited exposure to flat-nosed hardcast bullets and their use.

AUTHOR PHOTO

THE AUTHOR shot this cow moose with a .500 Linebaugh loaded with Grizzly Cartridge's 500-grain LFN loads at 1,100 fps. Damage from the big, hardcast bullets was impressive.

I would argue that, when your bullet is exiting the barrel at nearly a half-inch in diameter or more and the velocity is rather anemic (as compared to a rifle of nearly any caliber), your main concern should be to actually reach the vitals of the animal. In other words, penetration is the most important action the bullet must take. With such limited speed, the bullet can ill afford expansion and the subsequent increase in frontal area, which will radically slow the forward motion—if the bullet expands at all. If the bullet expands significantly and still has enough momentum to reach the vitals and destroy them, then you have a good situation on hand. If not, what you may have on your hands is a mess. Not good enough for me.

There is also the very real risk of over-expansion, which can really hurt penetration (see photo). This can happen when the bullet's construction is too soft or the bullet is driven faster than it was designed to run, or it can be a combination of the two, which can result in a fragmenting bullet. This is why it is of the utmost importance to consult the bullet manufacturer prior to choosing a bullet and find out what the working parameters of minimum and maximum velocities are.

It sounds as if I am no fan of jacketed expanding bullets. When they work as intended and as designed, the results can be spectacular, and I have witnessed this kind of performance. On the

AUTHOR PHOTO

IF THE AUTHOR HAD A DIME for every time he's heard the incorrect assertion that hardcast bullets simply zip through game and do little damage, he says he'd be a wealthy man. The author took this whitetail, in West Virginia, with a custom Ruger Super Redhawk in .475 Linebaugh, loaded with a 420-grain flat-nosed hardcast bullet.

PHOTO BY DR. LARRY ROGERS

DR. LARRY ROGERS of West Virginia, took this white rhino with his Linebaugh-built .475 Linebaugh Ruger. The 420-grain Cast Performance hardcast bullets performed flawlessly.

other hand, I have witnessed them not working as they should just as many times. I have trouble accepting this ratio of success to failure. But I am not picking on the manufacturers of these fine bullets. I am picking on the concept and theory behind them and their use, and I am picking on those who choose to use the wrong type of bullet on the game being hunted. I think we have come a very long way from a technological and material standpoint, and expanding jacketed bullets are better than ever and a far cry from what they were merely two decades ago. And I think that there are many very fine expanding bullets available to the handgun hunter today. I just think we are asking them to perform under conditions not necessarily the best for their capacities.

It is critical to match the bullet to the game/

application when hunting with jacketed expanding bullets—and I would argue this is *not* the case with flat-nosed hardcast bullets. Small calibers can definitely benefit from an increase in diameter—no doubt that this is a good thing from a terminal performance standpoint, but we big-bore revolver shooters don't suffer this inadequacy. That is the beauty of big-bore revolvers. They perform their tasks easily, that is they don't have to be driven hard—they don't require high pressure, high velocity, or big expansion.

Now, whitetail deer are a great candidate for the expanding bullet. These animals are narrowly constructed and really don't require maximum penetration. Even though they have an admirable and tremendous will to live, they aren't particularly hard to kill, though they will go a long way when wounded and not hit quite right. I use both types of bullets on them successfully, depending on the caliber of revolver I am using on the hunt. This is why Barnes Bullets, maker of some of the best, high-tech, monometal expanding bullets in the industry for both rifles and handguns, offers its Buster line of bullets intended for uncompromising penetration. If there was no need, they wouldn't manufacture them.

There are limitations to hardcast bullets, as with all bullets. As I stated earlier, the hardcast bullet will not withstand very high velocities. High velocity and contact with a hard object like bone can degrade the nose of the bullet, hindering its ability to penetrate deeply. If you feel you need to push your .454 Casull or other high-velocity cartridge to maximum speeds, there are better choices in bullet construction than hardcast lead bullets. In this case I defer to the Punch or

TWO FOR THE PRICE OF ONE

Using a .45-70 in Africa, for some unknown reason, raises the ire of many folks. Any shooting website with an African hunting forum seems to feature at least one contentious thread per year on this very topic, and often more. Nothing seems to bring blood more quickly to a boil than this particular topic. No one seems to openly object to the use of the old .45-70 Government against plains game, but, if used on dangerous game, it seems to automatically qualifies as a stunt.

Many have deemed the .45-70 underpowered for the task at hand, citing muzzle energy as being at a minimum. Not fair, I say. While if one subscribes to this calculated figure as a determinant of effectiveness, then, indeed, there are many better choices available for the task. Me? I don't buy it for a moment. If a .45-70 rifle is deemed inadequate, where does that leave our big-bore revolvers?

Enter Brian Pearce and his series on hunting in Zimbabwe with a Marlin Model 1895 .45-70 lever-action rifle in the pages of Rifle magazine. Brian's PH was more than a little skeptical of the little lever gun his client intended to use on Cape buffalo, but, when he witnessed its terminal performance on a number of big, tough plains game like the zebra, he agreed to allow Brian the use of the Marlin. Brian brought along both handloaded 405-grain soft-point ammo and CorBon's excellent 405-grain Penetrator jacketed flat-points. The CorBon ammo *clocked a chronograph verified 1,800 fps from the Marlin's 22-inch tube.*

Brian's PH and trackers put him onto an old bull, but the wise and cagey bovine led them on a cat-and-mouse chase through the brush, before joining a large heard of buffalo. When they finally isolated the old dugga boy, Brian got a 100-yard shot that was less than ideal, as only a portion of the bull was visible, but the shoulder was in his sight picture, so Brian squeezed. The Marlin barked, and the shot was true—and in typical Cape buffalo fashion, the bull took off at a run. Pearce's PH instructed him to keep firing until the animal connected with Mother Earth. The next two shots connected solidly, the third placed in the animal's hindquarters while it was going away. The PH, viewing the drama through his binoculars, gasped and announced that a cow was down, as well as the bull.

The necropsy revealed that all of Brian's shots had connected. The first shot, having travelled through the bull's shoulders, had exited and struck a cow that was seven yards behind the old bull, penetrating through her two shoulders and ending up under the skin of her offside shoulder! Two for the price of one! Would a .458 Lott shooting 500-grain solids at 2,300 fps have killed the bull any quicker than the .45-70? What about the cow behind him?

PHOTO BY JOHN PARKER

THIS HOLE IN THE RIBCAGE of a bull elk was produced by a 180-grain TSX from a .300 Win Mag. Impact velocity was estimated to be 2,600 fps at the range it was shot, which calculates out to approximately 2,700 ft-lbs of muzzle energy.

similarly constructed bullets that maintain the flat-nosed profile that penetrates so deeply and causes good wound trauma. But, to me at least, that is the beauty of the hardcast flat-nosed bullet. It doesn't *need* to be driven fast to be effective, meaning you can get away with lower velocities, pressures, and the consequent reduced recoil, making them a great choice for deer.

When the game becomes more densely constructed, bigger, and thicker-skinned than deer, the bullet requirements change. I have used both jacketed expanding bullets and hardcast flat-nosed bullets successfully on wild hogs, for instance. Hog toughness can go either way. Sometimes they drop instantly, others it takes some time and a whole lot of lead for the signal

to reach the brain and tell them they're deceased.

Indeed, I am amazed at the amount of lead some wild hogs can absorb prior to conceding defeat. I once shot a smallish 100-pound boar in North Carolina, with a Smith & Wesson .460 XVR stoked with CorBon 395-grain WFNs (see "Kevlar Hog" in the final chapter of this book). Two shots from the big .460 into the lung area, and the hog was leading me on a wild goose chase through the swamps. I emptied my Model 29 .44 Magnum into that tough little pig, before he finally gave up the ghost. When I finally stopped this boar, I was underwhelmed by his size, and overwhelmed by his toughness. I would argue that a pig of that size would have benefitted from a good, jacketed expanding bullet.

As you can see, wild hogs can be very tough, if not hit right, and I have had more than a couple express their unhappiness to me over the years. Wild hogs are built considerably more densely than deer. If you are facing a particularly large

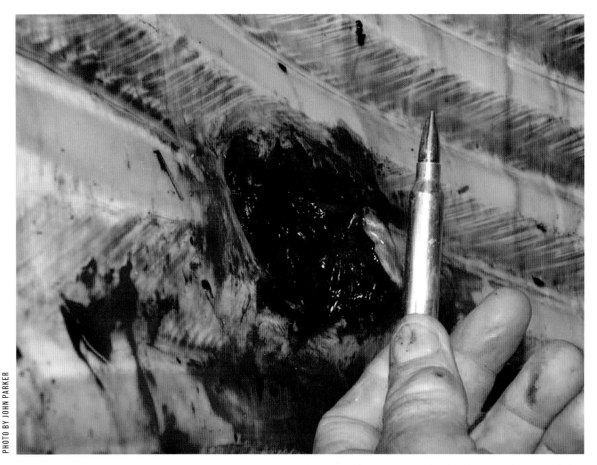

THIS HOLE, SAME BULL ELK, and also an exit hole in the ribcage, was produced by a 440-grain wide, flat-nosed hardcast bullet in .500 JRH, loaded by Buffalo Bore at an advertised 950 fps at the muzzle. The muzzle energy is calculated to be approximately 888 ft-lbs. Muzzle energy, as a determinant of lethality, is an exercise in futility.

boar, it may have a thick gristle plate that can challenge the construction of your chosen bullet. Their bones are also heavier than those of whitetail deer. Again, it's hit or miss regarding wild hogs.

ON VELOCITY

Fact: higher velocity produces a larger "splash" and initial wound channel size. Higher velocities also produce more resistance and a propensity to slow the bullet down at a more rapid rate than a bullet travelling at a more sedate velocity.

On the subject of velocity, there are also other factors to consider, such as bullet type. If a jacketed hollowpoint is being used, enough velocity is needed to expand the bullet, the intent of that bullet's design to begin with. On the other side, it is possible to push a flat-nosed hardcast bullet too hard and experience poor performance. When you hear stories of hardcast bullets breaking apart or not penetrating well, it may actually be a case of too much speed. Or it may also be a case of too brittle a bullet. If the nose shape is compromised by too high an impact velocity, the ability to penetrate will also be diminished.

There is a reason experts agree that moderate velocities seem to work better with hardcast bullets. Too much speed and you can exceed the material limitations of a lead bullet. Also, if your chosen bullet will travel lengthwise through a large wild hog and exit after leaving the muzzle at 1,200 fps, you gain no advantage driving that same bullet to 1,500 fps. What you *will* gain is recoil and discomfort, and you may actually compromise the bullet's penetrative ability.

We spoke with a number of knowledgeable

folks, most notably hunter Otto Candies, Jr., and John Linebaugh, who have noted a veritable "dead zone" from approximately 1,400 fps to roughly 2,100 fps. What is meant by this "dead zone" is that there is seemingly no real gain in performance from 1,400 fps through 2,100 fps, so any attempt to raise the velocity over this lower point will result in more recoil and noise and not necessarily an increase in performance, or only a minimal increase—and by performance, I mean depth of penetration. This is particularly evident when using cast bullets, which do not stand up well to high velocities. "Compound resistance" is the term for this phenomenon, whereby increasing speed does not equate to an increase in penetration—at least not linearly.

Our beloved revolvers will never attain rifle-like velocities, no matter how much pixie dust we load with, and, as mentioned earlier, loading them like they are a rifle will only lead to disappointment. That doesn't mean that they do not work at longer ranges, just that there are some limitations—and I would assume that, if you choose to hunt with a revolver, you aim to get closer than the hunter with a scoped rifle. "Closer" is the challenge I can surmise all revolver hunters choose and relish.

THE ENERGY MYTH

The fact that I am referring to energy as a myth flies in the face of conventional wisdom. After all, ammo boxes are stamped with energy figures, and ammunition retail websites offer ballistic comparisons between cartridges, with muzzle energy as the comparative figure. Gun magazine articles talk endlessly about the energy of hunting cartridges, and books about hunting are filled with references to energy as a determinant of effectiveness. Energy has been utilized to rate the lethality of cartridges/loads for some time now. But what is energy? Is it definable? Is it measurable?

Ask any proponent of energy to define how it enables a bullet to kill game, and he will respond in vague terms. Really press him, and he will accuse you of having a poor understanding of terminal ballistics. Yet, even many game laws call for muzzle energy minimums for specified game. Seems like everyone is in on the sham! The terms "energy," "energy dump," "kinetic energy," "muzzle energy," et al, are tossed around with utter, complete, and unfounded confidence by their proponents—until forced to explain.

A number of African big-game hunters I have been in contact with and who have killed numerous elephants in their days often cite that a minimum safe (effective) cartridge for hunting elephant must have a 400-grain bullet and 5,000 ft-lbs of muzzle energy. I have not killed an elephant with a revolver (nor with a rifle), so I defer to those with this experience. Now, in their significant experience hunting elephant, their summations have held true, as most of the cartridges utilized on elephant have met this minimum requirement. And, in the cases where they have not met this arbitrary minimum, it has been noted that the cartridges in question have not worked very well. So, having said that, what if I shoot an elephant with a frontal brain shot with a revolver in .475 Linebaugh loaded with a 420-grain bullet at 1,300 fps, and I have enough penetration to reach the brain and dispatch the elephant? Clearly, this load does not meet my colleagues' minimum requirement in one of the two criteria. Yet, surely my cartridge is adequate despite the "inadequate" muzzle energy. By the way, a 420-grain bullet at 1,300 fps "generates," or rather calculates, out to a whopping 1,576 ft-lbs. Supposedly it's not enough, even though it kills the animal door mouse dead.

Energy, as such, can *not* be measured. Muzzle energy figures are *calculated*. Fortunately, once the energies are calculated, you can file them away in the useless information bin. Yup, muzzle energy has no reflection on the lethality of one round over another. Any .22-250 rifle round loaded to spec will create a higher muzzle energy number than some loads for the .454 Casull. Which one would you rather have when facing down an angry grizzly bear? For me, it sure wouldn't be the .22-caliber round, despite its energy "advantage."

Just about every centerfire rifle cartridge can

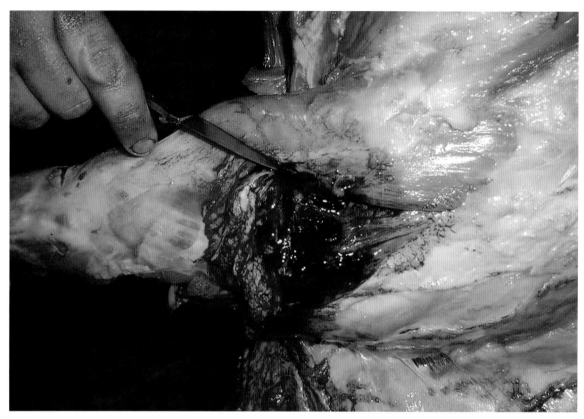

AUTHOR PHOTO

THE DAMAGE CAUSED by a flat-nosed hardcast bullet with a large meplat can be deceptive—externally. But they typically produce a large swath of destruction in their travel path. This 200-pound Florida hog was shot at 80 yards with a .475 Linebaugh slinging 420-grain WFN bullets.

boast better paper ballistics than a revolver. It doesn't require a doctorate in physics to see why, but big-bore revolvers don't rely upon velocity and rapidly expanding bullets to kill game. Big-bore revolver cartridges feature a large diameter and relatively heavy bullet, which are constants, while velocity is ever diminishing.

Bullet wound trauma expert, Duncan MacPherson, says, "… the assumption that bullet effectiveness (as measured by the damage that it causes) is proportional to energy is demonstrably not true in general, and all the evidence suggests that it is wrong for tissue damage. Kinetic energy absorption (i.e., the process of transformation of kinetic energy into heat energy), does not equate to damage in many physical processes … ." Furthermore, MacPherson says, "The reason that kinetic energy and damage are not always correlated is that dy-

namic damage is not due to energy absorption, but to stress (force per area)." In other words, energy proponents incorrectly attribute wound trauma to this mythical concept of energy. Kinetic energy does exist, but is mostly transformed to thermal energy, or heat, in layman's terms.

While perusing one of my favorite hunting/shooting Internet sites, I came across a discussion (actually, it wasn't quite civil enough to qualify for discussion status) about the ethics of using an "inadequate" (as deemed by some) cartridge on large game at long distance. In this instance, an antelope was wounded at 740 yards by a very experienced long-range hunter. His rifle of choice was one chambered in .243 Winchester and loaded with high ballistic coefficient 105-grain bullets. Seems the shooter flubbed the shot, wounding the animal, but corrected the dope of his scope and followed up with an impressive and fatal head shot.

Immediately, the self-righteous Internet ethics police attacked the brutally honest author of the post, not only about shooting game at that range, but for utilizing a cartridge that was deemed "minimal," "inadequate," "under-powered," etc. Despite all the evidence to the contrary, with regards to the terminal effectiveness of the .243 cartridge in question, the naysayers unloaded in anger about optimal game weight for the cartridge's muzzle energy and threatened to form an Internet lynch mob.

This type of argument seems to crop up on these websites every few months, which brings me to the point I am attempting to make: more often than not, these so-called inadequate and under-powered cartridges *can and do* reach and destroy the vitals of an animal, yet some still consider them inadequate. Simply amazing. In my experience, energy, paper ballistics, and conventional wisdom—and who dubbed it conventional or even wise, for that matter?—are more often than not critically flawed in determining the lethality of a cartridge on game. One needs not look further than the blackpowder cartridges of old, like the .45-70—which launched a 500-grain bullet at 1,200 fps at the muzzle)—and the terminal effects that load had at range on large game like bison. Bison populations out West were nearly wiped out for good with this "inadequate" cartridge.

Proponents of muzzle energy, I fear, interpret the results of their observations in a manner that is not objective. I recall watching a hair-raising charge by a Cape buffalo in one of Mark Sullivan's African hunting videos, where the aforementioned buffalo was zeroing in on Sullivan in high gear. A 900-grain solid from the hunter's .600 Nitro Express double rifle put into the chest of the advancing bovine failed to give the animal even minimal pause. Ultimately, Sullivan's second shot brained the beast, bringing the charge to an immediate halt.

"Energy dump" is a variation on the topic we have been discussing here. Proponents of energy dump claim that, if a bullet exits the animal, it has not deposited its full potential energy into said animal. If the bullet stops in the animal, though, did it deposit all of its energy in the animal, or did it simply not have enough momentum to exit? Can't answer that? Then you must consider that

the bullet may have over expanded, at the expense of penetration.

Our big-bore revolvers, in essence, mimic the ballistics some of the old blackpowder cartridges delivered, and I can assure you that they are considerably more than merely "adequate." Despite the rather anemic muzzle energy figures, big revolvers like the .45 Colt, .500 Linebaugh, etc., when loaded correctly, are damn effective on even the largest of game. If the cartridge in question has enough penetrative ability to consistently reach and destroy the brain of a mature bull elephant, then, to me, at least, the cartridge is more than adequate—particularly in light of the fact that the cartridges we are discussing feature large-diameter bullets that consequently produce a large wound channel. The deceased horse I keep beating here is that paper ballistics should be ignored when rating the lethality and effectiveness of any cartridge/load. Remember it's holes that kill, not energy.

CAST YOUR OWN

When it comes to lead bullets, handloaders like to buy bullets in bulk. But, a bullet is a precision tool, and you must use the correct tool for the job. Many have based their opinions of cast bullets on cheap, mass produced, one size-fits-all bullets having questionable quality and design and, when their results are less than spectacular, they shun cast bullets as being ineffective and slow-killing. One option to this dilemma is to cast your own.

Casting your own bullets does offer you several options to tailor your bullets to the game you are hunting. You can cast your bullets hard by adding linotype, or by water-quenching or heat-treating. You can cast them soft for expansion, or you can cast a soft nose on a hard bullet, giving you the best of both worlds. Casting can be very versatile if you are willing to put in the time and effort. And, as I stated before, I strongly recommend purchasing Veral Smith's tome on cast bullets, Jacketed Performance with Cast Bullets. You can save a lot of hard lessons by learning from Veral's own experiments and experiences.

CHAPTER SIX

SIGHTING SYSTEMS

You have made the decision to hunt with your new big-bore revolver, and now you are facing the decision of choosing a sighting system for this short-barreled firearm. Or maybe you will only be punching paper and not hunting. What is the best system available? That depends. There are a number of factors that determine what is best for you.

The handgun hunter and recreational shooter should ask themselves a number of questions, in order to make an educated determination and help narrow down the hundreds of choices out there. Are you hunting over bait from a stand? If so, how long of a shot do you expect and what is the maximum distance you could end up ultimately shooting? Will you be shooting off a rest (for maximum stability)? Are you hunting with dogs? How good is your vision? Another thing to consider is recoil and making sure the system you choose can withstand the considerable abuse generated by a high-powered handgun.

AN **ELUSIVE WILDLIFE** Technologies XLR 100 Kill Light mounted to the barrel of a Ruger Bisley Hunter.

PHOTO BY MARK WINNERSTIG

Your answers to these questions should all be factored into the sighting system you choose to use on your handgun, when hunting or shooting stationary targets. I have laid out three major sighting systems to consider and their optimal uses.

SIGHTING SYSTEM 1: SCOPES

There are a number of quality scopes produced specifically for handguns today, such as those offered by Burris and Leupold. What sets them apart from other firearms scopes is that they will have a long eye relief, enabling their effective use on a firearm that is held at arms' length.

Using a scope on a handgun requires some getting used to. All the shakes and wobbles we experience when shooting offhand are exaggerated when peering through a scope, particularly when using a variable scope set to a high magnification. With a handgun, you don't have the benefit of whole-body support for the firearm, thus ,the movement of the firearm is increased.

Because of the long eye relief inherent in handgun scopes, the light gathering capability of the exit pupil is compromised. Therefore, some

of the advantages gained by using a scope on a rifle don't quite translate over to a handgun scope. These are simply physical limitations that are not the fault of design or manufacture, but rather the location of the scope relative to the shooter's eye.

Scoped handguns are best used with a solid rest. For hunting applications, this makes them nearly optimal for use from a stand or blind over bait, where you'll have the rail of your stand or even shooting sticks to use. Scopes also offer, of course, the added benefit of magnification, allowing the hunter to better assess and judge the animal in their sights, and the ability to shoot at longer ranges more accurately. Likewise, the target shooter should be able to shoot more accurately with a scope on a handgun, as the sighting system is more precise from an aiming standpoint.

All that being said, personally, I don't care for scopes on big-bore revolvers, mostly because they are difficult to use in a hurry, i.e., it's difficult to quickly acquire a solid and thorough sight picture. Where you have the luxury of glassing an area and carefully picking your shot, scopes are fine. But, to me, this is a very limited option

PHOTO BY GARY SMITH

GARY SMITH TOOK this Texas wild hog with a Smith & Wesson Model 57 Classic in .41 Magnum, topped with a Leupold 2X scope.

that truly has specific times and places for use. If a scope is something you choose for your handgun, check with the manufacturer and make sure that the scope you're considering is made specifically for or is compatible with handgun use and can handle the recoil from big-bores in particular.

SIGHTING SYSTEM 2: RED DOT SIGHTS

This type of sighting system generally offers no magnification, but instead superimpose an illuminated red dot on the intended target. This is a personal favorite of mine for most hunting and shooting applications. The red dot can be adjust-

ed for brightness to compensate for changing light conditions in the field or out on the range, and it is probably the best solution for low-light hunting situations. Best of all, it is very easy to acquire in a hurry, a factor that's enhanced when you choose a model that features an adjustable dot size. This last option is also handy if you're shooting different sized game, where a large dot can cover up too much of the vital area and actually inhibit accuracy. I find the red-dot sights most advantageous in low-light conditions, where the black crosshairs of a regular scope may be hard to see.

There are essentially two types of red dot sights. The first is a tube type that resembles a scope and is adjusted and mounted in the same

ABUSING THE ULTRADOT 30

We spend a lot of time talking about and exploring the effectiveness of calibers, different bullet designs, velocity, accuracy, terminal performance, etc., but then we sometimes fail to acknowledge the fundamentals. All of the horsepower in the world won't do you a darn bit of good if you can't put your bullet on target. This is why your sighting systems is so important. I will take this opportunity to talk a little bit more about my favorite sighting system, the Ultradot 30 red dot.

I have been using an Ultradot 30 for more than four years now, with great success and satisfaction—and I haven't actually been very kind to my sight, having subjected it to thousands of full-tilt .475 Linebaugh loads through my custom Ruger Super Redhawk revolver. Keep in mind that the recoil generated by this firearm is brutal enough to have destroyed a set of aftermarket rings (though not the Ruger rings I used later), yet the Ultradot continued to function perfectly. If that weren't enough, I have dropped it out of a treestand, not once, but twice (hey, at least one time it wasn't my fault!), and it has never even hinted at losing zero. Adding insult to injury, it has been subjected to some serious load development trials—those who know me are aware that all my loads are full throttle and that I don't know the meaning of the word "down-load"—strapped to the top of my Magnum Research BFR revolver in .500 JRH. So, I haven't really shown my Ultradot any tenderness, yet it keeps coming back for more.

For those unfamiliar with Ultradot's products, the Ultradot 30 features an aluminum tube that's 30mm in diameter, hence the "30" in Ultradot 30. Ultradots, like most other red dot-type sights, do not possess any magnification.

The dot in the 30 is four-MOA in size, and the brightness can be adjusted in one-click increments (up to 11), via a dial adjuster on the left side of the tube. This enables the hunter (or target shooter) to adjust the dot's brightness to all light conditions they may encounter. Elevation and windage are adjusted, just as with an ordinary scope, by turning the dials on the two turrets. The entire assembly weighs just a touch over four ounces, and, believe it or not, the light weight allows it to better withstand heavy recoil. To top it all off, Ultradots come with a lifetime warranty, so that if anything ever goes wrong, your investment is covered.

Super Redhawks have scope mount scallops in the frame for use with their excellent scope rings. The rings that come with the revolver, though, are one-inch or 25mm, so you will need to upgrade to the 30mm rings offered by Ruger if you decide on the Ultradot 30. Or you can opt for the smaller 25mm unit, the Ultradot 25, and use the factory supplied rings. Personally, I prefer the larger field of view offered by the Ultradot 30.

Low-light conditions in the field are where the Ultradot 30 really shines. I have found that they extend your effective shooting time significantly over both standard tubular scopes and iron sights. I have comfortably taken a number of wild hogs, deer, and a moose in light that would have nixed the shot with another type of sighting system. All you do is put that bright little red dot on the shoulder and squeeze the trigger. Then go collect your bacon, venison, beef, goat, whatever.

Whenever I head out on a hunt, I bring a couple of extra batteries, in the event the one in the unit fails. For four years I have been carrying those same spares, but the original just doesn't seem to want to give up the ghost. I should probably replace the spares. Tough construction, reliable performance, lifetime warranty, shipped to your front door for right around $160.00. What's not to like about the Ultradot 30?

THE AUTHOR took this North Carolina black bear with a custom Super Redhawk in .500 Linebaugh, topped with an Ultradot 30.

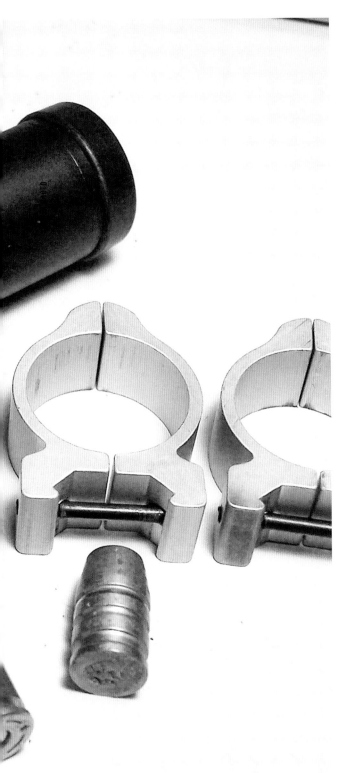

manner. The second are the holographic sights, which project a red dot on a small screen. The holographic-type sight is quite compact and may not add more than a few ounces to your shooting rig. Where this second type is weak is during inclement weather, as it may be difficult to keep the screen clean and procure an unobstructed view of your target. Red dot-type sights in general are light in weight and don't change the balance of your gun in any significant way. As with a standard scope, be sure to speak to the manufacturer prior to spending your money, to make certain the red dot you choose is up to the task of withstanding the recoil of your handgun.

In any case, a good warranty goes a long way towards customer confidence. The company known as Ultradot produces a whole line of economical and rugged red dot-type sights that come with a lifetime warranty. I am a big fan of this maker's products for a number of reasons, but mainly for their reliability.

I have had an Ultradot 30—it has a 30mm tube diameter, hence the designation—on a number of my heavy recoiling revolvers and can report that this sight has exceeded my expectations by a dozen miles. Thousands of full-tilt .475 Linebaugh and .500 JRH rounds have truly tested the integrity of that Ultradot. The poor unit now resides on my ultra-abusive,

PHOTO BY JOHN PARKER

ONE OF THE author's favorite red dot-type sights, the Ultradot 30.

ONE OF TWO COLLABORATORS on this book, John Parker took this large bison with a .500 Linebaugh and open iron sights.

lightweight Ruger Super Redhawk in .500 Line-baugh. I have not been kind to my Ultradot, but, like a loyal dog, it keeps coming back wagging its tail. See the sidebar at the end of this chapter for more insight on this optic.

The only drawback with any red dot-type sight is that battery failure can leave you high and dry when you can least afford it (think large, toothy animal with bad intent bearing down on you, or the trophy buck of a lifetime striking a

THE AUTHOR shot this 225-pound sow with a Ruger Bisley Hunter in .44 Magnum topped with an Ultradot 4 an hour before midnight one evening. Double Tap Ammo supplied the firepower in the form of 320-grain WFNs at 1,350 fps, while illumination was provided by Elusive Wildlife Technologies' XLR 250 Kill Light.

pose for you). Remember to always carry a spare battery and the tools (in this case a quarter!) necessary to change it in the field. From supported and unsupported shooting positions, the red dot shines.

SIGHTING SYSTEM 3: OPEN IRON SIGHTS

Here's one for the purists among us big-bore revolver fanatics. Virtually every hunting or target revolver comes with a set of adjustable iron sights up top (okay, there are a couple that come with fixed sights, like the Ruger Vaquero), and they work well, as long as you have adequate light. They are quick to acquire, but, maybe most importantly, since the user *isn't* peering through a tube, they then have a full view

AUTHOR PHOTO

AUTHOR PHOTO

ULTRADOT'S HOLOGRAPHIC red dot-type sight, the Pan-AV.

of their surroundings. Why is this important? Just ask those who hunt bear or wild hogs with dogs why it's crucial to see all that is going on around them in the ensuing chaos of a hunt with hounds. The handgun hunter must be able to respond quickly, assess the situation, pick their shot, and make absolutely certain that no dogs are in the way. Open sights, in this type of situation, have no equal.

One of the other greatest advantages open sights enjoy is their resistance to recoil—plus, they have no glass to break or batteries to die. Ultra reliability is another bonus. The only real limitation to using open iron sights is the shooter's vision and ability to line up the front and rear sights on the target. You may find that the older you get, the better you were.

In my humble opinion, the best adjustable rear sight available on the aftermarket is manufactured by Hamilton Bowen of Bowen Classic Arms. Those unfamiliar with Bowen's work skipped over the fourth chapter of this book! His

AUTHOR PHOTO

THE VERY BEST adjustable rear sight for a revolver is manufactured by Bowen Classic Arms. This is a must on any custom revolver, or any revolver for that matter where the shooter chooses to use open iron sights.

are, by far, the best adjustable rear sight available for a revolver. They are precise, easy to adjust, and well-made.

Whatever you choose, you need to practice enough to completely familiarize yourself with the sighting system. Some sights take some getting used to but, once you get there, their use should become second nature.

THE AUTHOR KILLED this sow at night with Hog Heaven Outfitters of North Carolina, using an Ultradot 30 mounted on his custom Super Redhawk in .475 Linebaugh. As long as there is a light source on the target, the red dot-type sight works very well.

HUNTING AT NIGHT

Hunting in the dark is illegal in many states. But, wild hog hunting is legal and available at night in some, as they are treated by most DNRs as varmints. (And, as such, they often have no set limits). I spend a lot of time hunting hogs in North Carolina, where it's legal to night hunt bacon.

My home away from home, at least as often as I can, is with an outfit called Hog Heaven Outfitters (www.hogheavenoutfitters.com) of Johnston County, North Carolina. More often than not, particularly in the hot summer months, I hunt at night with this outfitter. Now, if there is a light source where the hogs are feeding, any sighting system will work. But, if there is none, there's a great solution. You simply bring your own light to the party with one of Elusive Wildlife Technologies' Kill Lights.

What is a Kill Light? It is a small flashlight with a colored lens (the most popular shades are red and green), that attaches to either your gun barrel or to your optic (either a standard glass scope or tube-type red dot), via an easy mounting system. The light itself comes equipped with a number of different activation switches, including a traditional on/off button on the end, a pressure switch, and a remote switch (with cable). It also comes with two long-lasting rechargeable batteries and a charger. There are two flashlight sizes available, the XLR 100 and the XLR 250, the 250 being the stronger of the two. Once mounted, you are ready to bring your own light source to the fight.

I have used both the XLR 100 and the 250 on a number of nighttime hog hunts, and this well-thought-out system is an inexpensive alternative to the high cost of night vision optical equipment. These Kill Lights are appropriately named and work as advertised. In the field, before shooting, I turn my Ultradot on, flip the switch on the Kill Light, acquire my target, and let the lead fly. Works like a charm.

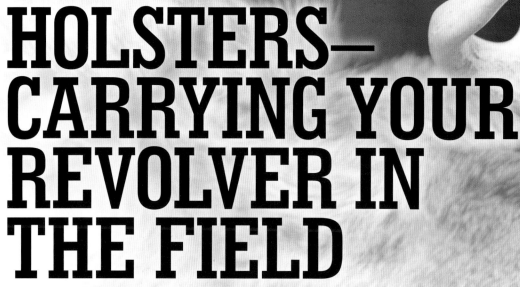

HOLSTERS— CARRYING YOUR REVOLVER IN THE FIELD

Whether you are hunting with a revolver as a primary tool or as a backup, you will need to have a holster to carry it in. The physical size of the revolver is what makes it so attractive for carry in the field, as long as you can comfortably strap it on. Once you do, you will free up your hands for other uses, like camp chores, clearing brush, or climbing up a ladder stand. A revolver in a holster is also particularly useful when skinning out an animal in bear country or when your rifle is propped up against a tree (and inevitably out of reach). It's an insurance policy leather-strapped to your body. We all know bear attacks are pretty rare, but, in many places, a rifle shot is a dinner bell for hungry brownies, so why not be a statistic in the win column?

I am going to limit this discussion to open carry in the field and not concealed carry. There are two basic types of holsters for outdoor carry that I would like to explore here, just know there are subcategories and variations on the theme. Revolver holsters are typically made of either leather or nylon, and the two types I'll be covering here are belt holsters and shoulder rigs.

Holster selection will be shaped by your needs. Obviously, the type and size of sidearm and whether it is equipped with a scope or red dot-type sight will determine where on your body you can feasibly carry it. Do you really want a 10-inch barreled revolver with a scope strapped to your waist? I didn't think so.

The type of hunting you are participating in (stand hunting, spot and stalk, with dogs, etc.), should also factor into your decision, as each will have differing equipment requirements. For instance, when you are chasing bears down with dogs, you want to travel light and your revolver needs to be quickly accessible. Ask yourself some questions, too. Are you carrying any gear around your waist? Are you using a day pack or a full-framed backpack? Are you wearing bulky winter clothes? Are you working in the woods in bear country and carrying along other tools?

Also of importance is preference. What type of holster works best for you? Which one is easiest and most comfortable to carry and offers the easiest access? This is very important, as you will want unimpeded access to your sidearm, particularly in an emergency situation. Hunting bears with dogs, especially, has taught me that the hunter of this game animal needs to be able to draw and fire their revolver at the drop of a hat, as the dynamic on the ground between bear, dog, and man changes constantly and rapidly. There is no time for fumbling to clear leather, as lives are at stake.

There are many different holster types that boil down to the user's needs and preferences, and a number of manufacturers produce very good quality holsters. To name just a few, you'll want to consider the products from Bianchi, Galco, Uncle Mike's, and Safariland, and smaller, high-end manufacturers like Mitch Rosen, 7X, Milt Sparks, El Paso Saddlery, and Simply Rugged are well worth taking a look at, too.

A WELL-MADE CHEST RIG should not impede access to your revolver, even when wearing a pack and a binocular harness. This chest holster system by 7X Leather is made for a 4-inch Smith & Wesson X-Frame

WES DAEMS

AUTHOR PHOTO

THIS RIG, BY PISTOL PACKAGING INC., out of Maple Plain, Minnesota, features a Bandito holster with a removable flap for carrying a scoped or unscoped revolver. The holster is of a two-ply construction of premium grade cowhide leather on the outside and a soft suede lining for comfort.

BELT HOLSTERS

Belt holsters attach to your chosen belt or come with a belt. You can carry your revolver holstered in such a manner on your strong side—that is, the side your dominant shooting hand is on—or in cross-draw fashion. It's your preference, really, and each has its pros and cons. There are many differing types of holsters in this category, and of all different manners of quality, but they all basically do the same thing.

An important feature, and perhaps the most important feature, is the retaining strap. The retaining mechanism needs to be strong enough to keep your revolver in your holster when performing physical feats like climbing, running, jumping (and even falling), but easy enough to negotiate with one hand quickly, when the need arises to bring your piece into action.

One of the less expensive brands that I have had much luck with are the holsters from Uncle Mike's. They are affordable and durable, and I particularly like the thumb-break of the retaining strap, as it is very intuitive to use. The downside to these and all nylon holsters is that the holsters will not form to the shape of your firearm, a feature that comes only with leather.

SHOULDER HOLSTERS

This is the preferred method of carrying when your revolver is larger and/or heavier than a back-up firearm (and, if your revolver rig threatens to pull your pants down in a belt holster, this is the direction you'll want to go). The gun suitable for a shoulder rig may also be wearing an optic like a scope or red dot-type sight, making the piece, again, too bulky for belt holster use. Of course, you may be wearing other gear around your waist that impedes the carry of a revolver on your belt. The shoulder rig makes perfect sense in these situations.

A shoulder holster is worn with the holster component opposite your strong side. This arrangement enables you to grasp your gun by reaching across your chest to your other side, and is a particularly good way to carry a larger and heavier handgun, as the weight gets distributed around your torso rather evenly.

Some shoulder holsters position the gun more towards your chest (or they can be adjusted to wear in this manner) and are slung over one shoulder with an attachment point to your belt (for stability) that descends from the bottom on the holster. Other designs attach to both sides of your belt to anchor the firearm to prevent it from swinging loosely, with straps that are positioned over both shoulders. These holsters are typically harder to get in and out of without twisting the straps. They almost require an additional pair of hands to set up.

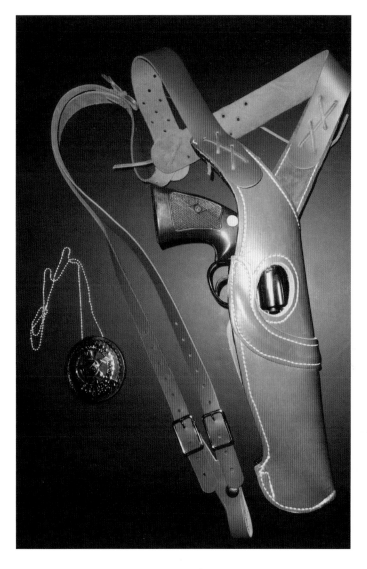

THIS ORIGINAL "DIRTY HARRY"-style shoulder holster was crafted by Jerry Ardolino of the Wild Guns Leather Company of Texas. This is one of the most comfortable shoulder rigs for toting a big-bore revolver, in this author's opinion.

A high-quality holster is a good investment that can provide many years of reliable service while hunting all manner of game, and such a piece of equipment also offers protection from the elements for your firearm. There are many options available, from regular production to custom rigs, so, before choosing a holster for field carrying your big-bore revolver, make a list of requirements to narrow down your choices.

SHOOTING OFF OF THE BENCH is the best way to develop a flinch.
The bench should only be used for sighting in.

SHOOTING THE BIG-BORE REVOLVER

Big-bore revolvers are great to look at and even more fun to handle, but we have them to shoot them, right? At least that's why my safe is dominated by big-bore revolvers!

I will put this up front. Your big-bore revolver will require a dedicated commitment by you, the shooter, to master. You can shoot them until you are comfortable, but getting to that level requires regular practice. Put it down for six months, and it may feel like you are starting over again.

I typically get to a level of competence and then, before the hunting season opens, I will take out a favored gun and shoot just a couple shots to make sure that I and the firearm are still "on" for the hunt. This last-minute tune-up, because I shoot regularly, doesn't require an extended shooting session.

UNLESS SIGHTING IN or checking zero, steer clear of the bench! Heavy recoiling revolvers, like the Ruger Super Redhawk in .454 Casull, abuse the shooter when used off of the bench.

Big-bore revolvers are not for the neophyte. Now, I am not trying to discourage the person who has the will to acquire a big-bore, just that it may take some dedicated work to get to the point that you can comfortably shoot your chosen sidearm. That said, it is best to work your way up the food chain and not immediately jump into a .500 Smith & Wesson Magnum as your first big-bore revolver. These handguns can be intimidating to the uninitiated, to say the least, especially as they're often still intimidating for the ones who do know what to expect! Further, starting with one of the biggest for your first big-bore revolver can be such an unpleasant experience that it may permanently sour an individual on big-bore revolvers. How? Heavy recoil can induce the development of a flinch. Flinches are quite common among shooters unfamiliar with heavy recoiling firearms, and developing one happens more often than you may realize. Keep in mind that something like a .475 Linebaugh generates rather brutal recoil impulses, when loaded to its potential—that's a 400- or 420-grain bullet running in excess of 1,300 fps. This level of recoil is in a whole different class than even the heaviest load in .44 Magnum is capable of generating.

IT'S ALL IN THE GRIP

One thing to consider, regarding heavy recoil, is the set of grips on your revolver. In order to make your big-bore revolver as manageable as possible, it is important to have a good set of grips that fit your hand well. This will make all the difference in the world, as far as shootability is concerned.

If you're lucky enough to find a set of aftermarket grips that fit you as if they were made for your hands, don't hesitate to buy them, for they'll likely cost less than a custom set of grips. If you cannot find aftermarket units that fit your needs, though, I am of the opinion that custom grips are a worthwhile investment. Good grips can mean the difference between being able to enjoy your big-bore revolver, or dreading to touch it off. The choice is yours.

YOU MUST MAINTAIN your focus and grip when shooting big-bore revolvers. Get distracted or relax your hands, and it's entirely possible to have that monster come back and clock you.

PHOTO BY JOHN PARKER

THE BENCH

Familiarization with your new big-bore should not take place on the bench. In fact, the bench is a surefire way of ensuring the new big-bore shooter will develop a flinch and learn to simply dread pulling the trigger. When fired from the bench, every bit of the big-bore's recoil is directed into the shooter's hands, arms, and psyche, as the gun's movements are restricted by its position on the bench and shooting bags. Limiting a guns natural movement during recoil transfers more of the abuse to the shooter. So, don't do it. Instead, go off-hand, as it were. Your first familiarization shots should be performed offhand, where the revolver has the freedom of movement. The bench has its place in testing, sighting in, and load development, but shooting off the bench for shooting skills and familiarity practice should be kept to a minimum.

LIMITS

Also of importance is simply limiting the number of rounds you shoot per session with a big-bore. Overdoing it will undoubtedly lead to the development of a flinch. As Ross Seyfried said in his article entitled "Negotiating With The Superpowers" in the September 2008 issue of *American Rifleman*, "When you use full-power ammunition, only fire a few shots each session. When I am practicing with my .475, I limit myself to less than 10 cartridges per day. The effect of recoil is truly cumulative, and each shot adds weight to the next. If you shoot too many, your self-control will rebel."

HANG ON TIGHT

Everyone develops their own techniques with their big-bore revolver. One method does not fit all, but this is a good place for me to offer some techniques that have worked the best for me over the years. Feel free to try and modify them accordingly. Regardless of which method you decide on, I do recommend using a lot of muscle tension, at least initially, until you figure out how much the revolver will move when you touch off a round. This way you are not caught off guard and surprised by getting your forehead creased—don't laugh, it happens all the time. Yours truly had a two-inch gash opened up in his scalp, when I let up just a little bit of muscle tension firing my custom revolver in .50 Alaskan. A revolver such as this *demands* the shooter's absolute attention and concentration. And talk about a flinch-inducer. Getting hit in the head can easily help create a flinch in the shooter as they anticipate getting hit again, not a good way to start a relationship with your new big-bore revolver!

TRIGGER CONTROL

This topic has been beaten to death in the popular gun media, so you probably don't need to hear about it again here, but trigger control is very important with every gun you shoot. When you put your trigger finger into the trigger guard and actually on the trigger, make sure it's the *pad* of your finger centered on the trigger and the *only* part of your finger touching the trigger. If you allow the side of your finger to touch the trigger, it can inadvertently push the gun sideways when you squeeze the trigger towards you. Once you have accomplished mastering the feel of this, you can begin the steady and slow pull back on the trigger.

The trigger break should surprise you, and you should not anticipate the recoil; anticipation will move your point of aim away from your intended point of impact. Many times, new shooters will flinch in this manner, so I will load their revolver with an undisclosed and mixed up number of live rounds and empty cases. This serves two purposes. First, I can observe the shooter to see if they're anticipating the shot. Second, this helps train the shooter to relax and squeeze, as they don't know what's coming next.

SHOOTING DOUBLE-ACTION

Some of you may share the affinity I have for double-action big-bore revolvers. That said, those same people may also share my dislike for actually shooting them double-action. So what's the point of having a double-action revolver you don't shoot double-action? Good question. If you would find yourself in the un-fortunate position of winding up under an animal bent on your destruction, a double-action revolver could prove invaluable—particularly if your thumb has been chewed off (okay, I added that for dramatic effect). Let me again qualify my statements and offhand comments by saying that I have never found myself in such an unfortunate position, but surely you can see where a double-action in just such a situation (i.e., a bear attack) would offer a distinct advantage over a single-action revolver. Simply press the barrel up against fur and squeeze—repeatedly—until said fur-bearer stops wailing the life out of you.

Now shooting a big-bore double-action revolver isn't impossible, and whether you ever intend to shoot your gun in double-action mode, knowing how to is useful, when fast follow-up shooting is necessary. To practice this skill successfully, one must not simply pull through the arch of the trigger—well, you can, and you may be successful, but this method doesn't work for me. No, for me, it's better to squeeze back on the trigger, cycling the cylinder nearly to the end of its motion and cocking the hammer back, a skill that's called "staging the trigger." When doing this, there is a slight pause, right at the end of the hammer cock, before finishing the pull of the trigger. This will allow for much more accurate shooting. Pulling all the way through in one motion can upset the revolver's position and pull you off target, especially as the double-action pull of big-bore revolvers is, more often than not, fairly heavy.

WEAVER STANCE

This is a pretty basic stance most handgunners are familiar with, but I've found there are better ways to shoot your big-bore revolver off-hand than in this position, at least for me. Those unfamiliar with the Weaver stance need to know that it entails pushing the revolver forward with your strong, or shooting, hand, while simultaneously pulling in the opposite direction with your support (weak) hand. Equal tension is given to the push and the pull, the counteraction providing a stable hold. This necessitates standing almost squarely in front of your target, but this

THE WEAVER STANCE has long been popular with handgun shooters, but the author feels there are better ways to shoot revolvers with heavy recoil. Here he uses a modified Weaver stance.

simply doesn't work for me. I am of the opinion that standing flat towards your target doesn't give the shooter the stability necessary to accurately shoot or provide a good foundation to withstand the recoil of big-bore revolvers; you do *not* want to be able to rock back on your heels. The Weaver stance also involves locking your elbows, yet another aspect I object to when shooting big-bores. When it comes right down to it, I really don't have believe that the Weaver stance offers the shooter the best way to stay balanced during heavy recoil. So, let's examine my offhand shooting technique. As I stated earlier, what works for me may not work for you, but, hopefully, this will give you a foundation to build upon or, at least, something to try.

I stand nearly sideways, with my left foot forward. This is a fighting stance, and my knees will be slightly bent. I grip the revolver in my right hand, with my left hand under the buttstock to pro-

THE AUTHOR likes to place the thumb of his supporting hand over the right hand, which strengthens the grip on the revolver and is less likely to break his grip/hold on recoil.

THIS PHOTO SHOWS the other side of the modified Weaver stance.

A TREE CAN provide an excellent anchor for the shooter. Simply sit on the ground with your back against the tree, lift your knees, place your feet flat on the ground (providing additional stability), and place your elbows on the insides of your knees. This is the author's favorite shooting position, if no other rest is available.

vide support. My left arm's elbow moves in and against my rib cage for support, creating a solid rest.

This is a much more stable position than is the true Weaver stance, where the revolver is almost free-floating in your hands. Note that I also do not lock my elbows, giving them the ability to move with the recoil. Yet I do not hold them loosely, rather I control the gun without fighting it. Try it, modify it, find out what works for you, but the only way you're going to do that is by burning powder.

REST

When hunting with a big-bore revolver, I strongly recommend using a rest when available, be it the shooting rail of a treestand, a log, your back pack, or the hood of your truck. The importance of a stable rest cannot be over emphasized and, when hunting, it can make the difference between a hit and a miss or, worse, a wounded animal.

THE AUTHOR TUCKS his left (lead) elbow in tight against the ribs to offer a stable platform.

Another view of the sitting position, this one clearly showing the placement of the elbows for maximum support.

AUTHOR PHOTO

AUTHOR PHOTO

SITTING ON FLAT or almost flat ground without a rest can still make for a stable shooting position. With your legs crossed, you simply place your elbows in the crooks of your knees.

When using a rest, I've found it best to rest your hands on the object, instead of resting the butt of the revolver; resting the butt may have an effect on the bullet's point of impact, causing you to shoot over or under your intended target. The frame of the revolver can also be rested on a solid object for stability. It is vitally important to practice all these positions and make sure you are proficient in their use before attempting them on game. We owe game animals our utmost respect, therefore we must be prepared. Again, one never knows what they will encounter in the field on the hunt, so it is best to be prepared and intimately familiar with your equipment and shooting positions/techniques.

SIT

Sitting positions are also very stable, particularly if you have something like a tree, a tree stump, a rusty Ford pickup, or a fallen tree to lean against. You can use the insides of your knees to support your elbows, creating quite the stable platform. You should also plant your feet flat on the ground, providing even more stability.

When sitting on flat ground, where you have no back support, cross your legs, with your lead leg (in my case, my left) facing slightly towards your intended target or direction of fire. Next, your elbows will rest on the insides of your knees, supporting your revolver.

KNEEL

Another relatively stable shooting position is the kneeling position. Your legs should be placed at a 90-degree angle from each other, and your hindquarters should rest on your back foot/heel. Your support elbow (left arm if you are right-handed) should rest in front of your knee and not on top of your knee. While not as stable a position as the sitting position, where both your arms are rested, this is a position you can quickly get into when need be, particularly when pursuing game.

THE KNEELING POSITION can be quickly acquired, making it useful when pursuing game. Make sure you rest your buttocks on the heel of your foot, so that you are firmly planted. Your lead elbow should rest ahead of your knee, not on top.

PRONE

I don't recommend shooting in the prone (lying down on your stomach) position, as it is usually one that's too awkward to gain control over a heavy kicking revolver. If you have a rest, on the other hand, this position is extremely stable. I've used it in a pinch, but I personally don't recommend it unless you have something to rest the revolver on at full extension (again, to avoid creasing your forehead). Sometimes terrain will dictate the use of the prone position, and it may be the only way to get a shot off on the trophy of a lifetime. Practice this shooting position in advance.

STICKS

Shooting sticks are another option for the handgun hunter. Used extensively in Africa, shooting sticks have yet to gain the same popularity in North America. But they make a lot of sense, providing an expedient and very stable rest no matter where you are. They are used in Africa so much, because they flat-out work, and when a visiting hunter is putting down five to six figures for the hunt of a lifetime, any and every advantage is welcome to make the outcome a success. I used shooting sticks for the first time on a moose hunt in Maine, and they worked well. I will use them again on future hunts. Be sure that you practice with them prior to using them on a hunt, and remember to rest your wrist where the rifle stock would normally rest when firing, or the frame of the revolver, to mimic the sandbags when resting on the bench.

OFFHAND

When practicing for the hunt, I tend to do so mainly offhand. Why? Because offhand is the most difficult position to master. I spend most of my time on the 100-yard line and shoot pig silhouettes. The pig silhouette measures roughly 16 inches wide by 12 inches tall—it's a pretty small target at 100 yards. Sounds odd, but when you can consistently hit targets that size at 100 yards, you are prepared for the worst-case scenario in the field.

Preparing for the worst-case scenario is a recurring theme in my hunt practice regimen. Some folks have different loads for different game, while I prefer to have one load that can do it all and perform well under the worst possible conditions. And that is how I view practicing for a handgun hunt. Prepare for the worst, and the "normal" shots come easily.

SAFETY

Let's talk safety a moment, particularly when out on the hunt. Let's assume that you know a deer is approaching your position, so you prepare to take a shot. You have carefully and quietly pulled the hammer back, but you are keeping your finger away from the trigger. Now, let's say the deer changes course, forcing you to change your position to a spot a little closer, even though the shot is imminent. Do you decock your revolver and risk the deer hearing you cock it again? That won't be necessary, if you simply place the thumb of your supporting hand between the hammer and the frame of the revolver, creating a positive stop (see the photo on the next page). This way, you can safely move into a new position and be ready to let lead fly.

When shooting your big-bore revolver, you should seek to lessen the damage it is capable of inflicting on you. Especially if your revolver is equipped with a muzzle brake, it will be markedly louder than if it were not so equipped. That means you should never shoot without hearing protection. Hearing loss is irreversible, so protect what you have. Wearing audio-enhancing ear protection, like Walker Game Ears, are quite useful when hunting. These nifty devices allow you to hear approaching game from farther away than with without them and still protect your ears during gunfire.

It is a good idea to also wear a shooting glove(s) to protect your hands and wrists. Recoil is not your friend. In fact, heavy recoil can inflict irreversible nerve damage to your hands. You should do all you can to prevent potential damage. I use a pair of dedicated shooting gloves from Pro-Aim (www.pro-aim.com) that feature a gel pad in the palm, a Velcro wrist strap, an exposed trigger finger and thumb, and a hard plastic splint along the side of the glove for additional wrist support. While the gloves may not completely stave off the damaging effects of recoil, they do offer a modicum of protection.

RECOIL

There is no way around it. These things kick. Unless you are limiting your loads to the very bottom of the loading manual and the lightest bullets, your big-bore revolver will let you know, in no uncertain terms, that you have touched off something special. Let's face the facts. Had you wanted a .38 Special, you would have purchased a .38 Special.

As I've stated elsewhere, the entry level big-bore, the .44 Remington Magnum, is truly a threshold cartridge. Some find it comfortable and manageable, but others find it to be their limit in tolerance for recoil. In a correctly weighted revolver, the .44 can actually be a pleasant round. (I didn't mention the .41 Magnum here, as it is not nearly as popular, manufactured as often, or widely distributed as is its bigger brother, the .44 Magnum, but it's a consideration if you want to find one on the used market.) On the upper end of the scale are the various .500s. Generally, they are in their own class of punishment, but some more than others. Whichever round you choose, it pays to work your way up to maximum level loads, assuming you handload. And, again, shooting gloves are a good idea to minimize the damage recoil can inflict, making the experience more pleasurable. It pays to take good care of your hands.

I have included a recoil table here, to give you an idea of what you will be facing with the generally popular loads in their respective calibers. One thing I must add is that, in the case of the .454 Casull, some loads may appear mild on paper, but the table does not take recoil impulse into consideration. As I've said in previous chapters, the .454, loaded to spec, is an unpleasant round, with pressure being the culprit.

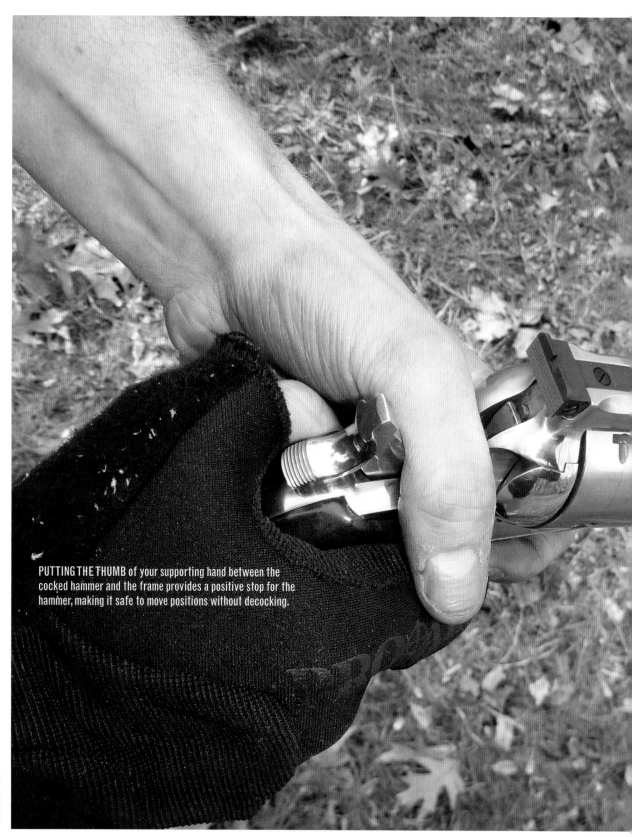

PUTTING THE THUMB of your supporting hand between the cocked hammer and the frame provides a positive stop for the hammer, making it safe to move positions without decocking.

Unless you are a hardened shooter, a glutton for punishment, numb from the waist up, or simply an adventurer, I would steer clear of the Casull as a starter caliber.

ELMER KEITH AND THE LONG SHOT

The legend of Elmer Keith's 600-yard shot on a wounded mule deer has been the topic of much controversy and debate among big-bore revolver shooters and rifle shooters alike, for decades. The story goes like this.

Elmer Keith was deer hunting with his partner Paul Kriley, when they located a good buck some distance away. Keith instructed Kriley to move over to the next ridge, which would put him within 500 yards of the deer. Kriley made the hike and shot the buck with his .300 Magnum. The deer dropped, slid down the mountain, but then regained its feet and began climbing a hill and moving away from the two hunters, one of its front legs obviously damaged from the shot. Kriley kept shooting, and missing, when Keith joined in the salvo with his Smith & Wesson revolver in .44 Magnum, shooting Remington factory 240-grain semi-wadcutters. Keith was shooting prone, using the front sight blade held over the rear. His first shot clearly missed, but he saw the impact (low) of the second shot. He adjusted by holding even more front sight up over the rear, and this time it appeared the bullet connected. The shot changed the buck's course, turning him back towards the hunters.

Now 100 yards closer, Kriley shot again and again missed with his rifle (a recurring theme in this tale). The buck wisely changed direction again, once more heading away from Keith and Kriley. Keith let another 240-grainer fly at a later paced-off 600 yards, when the deer disappeared from their sight. The hunters trailed him, and the deer once again got up and fled. The two hunters eventually recovered the animal and, upon skinning it out, discovered that two of Keith's shots had connected with the mulie, one striking it in the jaw, the other through the rib cage and out the offside, successfully ending the chase.

A GOOD SET OF shooting gloves, like these from Pro-Aim, offer protection for your hands and wrists from the heavy recoil of your big bore revolver.

AUTHOR PHOTO

RECOIL TABLE

Caliber	Bullet (grains)/Velocity	Revolver Weight (lbs)	Recoil
.41 Mag	250/1,400 fps	3	19 ft-*lb*s
.44 Mag	240/1,400 fps	3	19 ft-lbs
.44 Mag	320/1,350 fps	3	28.56 ft-lbs
.45 Colt	265/865 fps	3	7.89 ft-lbs
.45 Colt	335/1,300 fps	3	29.84 ft-lbs
.454 Casull	265/2,000 fps	3.5	41.23 ft-lbs
.454 Casull	300/1,750 fps	3.5	37.67 ft-lbs
.454 Casull	335/1,550 fps	3.5	35.26
.460 S&W	265/2,200 fps	4.5	41.56 ft-lbs
.475 L	425/1,400 fps	3.5	44.75 ft-lbs
.500 JRH	440/1,350 fps	3.5	45.90 ft-lbs
.500 L	400/1,500 fps	3.5	50.12 ft-lbs
.500 L	450/1,400 fps	3.5	52.57 ft-lbs
.500 L	525/1,200 fps	3.5	50.39 ft-lbs
.500 S&W	370/1,900 fps	4.5	55.91 ft-lbs
.500 S&W	440/1,650 fps	4.5	54.29 ft-lbs
.500 S&W	500/1,500 fps	4.5	54.78 ft-lbs
.50 AK	525/1,600 fps	4	94.47 ft-lbs

So, did it indeed go down the way Elmer Keith told the tale? Is it possible to effectively shoot a ballistically challenged (compared to a rifle) revolver 600 yards and not only hit what you are aiming at, but also end the life of your quarry?

Gun writer Brian Pearce set out to recreate the Keith long shot back in the pages of the October 2009 issue of Handloader magazine. They say the devil is in the details, and Pearce spared no effort in making sure the recreation would be not only legitimate, but period correct down to the finest of details. Brian started by buying a pair of pre-Model 29 Smith & Wesson .44 Magnum revolvers with 6½-inch barrels. He then acquired a case of Remington 240-grain semi-jacketed hollow-point ammunition, circa 1957. He also duplicated Keith's handloads for this test.

An interesting side note is that Brian chronographed that vintage .44 Magnum ammo, and it averaged 1,451 fps out of the two revolvers—tales of early .44 Magnum ammo being hot were evidently not exaggerated!

Having shot many big-bore revolvers and hunted with them for years, I know what they are capable of. I never doubted Elmer Keith's claims, nor did Brian Pearce. Brian simply wanted to show the naysayers that it was definitely a possibility, even if one has trouble wrapping their head around the claim at least conceptually.

Evidently, Elmer Keith had sighted his handguns in at 50 yards, which is where Pearce zeroed his two Smith & Wesson .44s. Both produced an average of three-inch groups, but one produced a 2½-inch group. Brian practiced on steel plates at 600 yards with both revolvers, before the test got officially under way.

A life-sized deer target, replete with antlers, was designed and manufactured by Pearce's 11-year-old daughter, and was painted black on cardboard. Brian researched the correct measurements of a mature mule deer buck, and had the dummy deer constructed to those dimensions. An eight-inch orange dot target was pasted over the lung area of the deer target, and the whole thing was mounted on two eight-by-eight-foot sheets of plywood and set up at the 600-foot mark, as confirmed by a Nikon laser rangefinder.

Brian opted for shooting off of a sandbagged bench instead of from the prone position, as Elmer Keith purportedly did. (Keith reported that he'd chosen the prone position to get out of the muzzle blast area of his hunting partner Kriley's .300 Magnum rifle.) Brian's first test shots struck several feet low. In order for him to maintain as precise a sight picture as possible, Brian adjusted his rear sight up as far it would go. This prevented him from raising the front sight higher, but allowed for a better sight picture. Recall that Elmer reported that he'd held up the entire front sight and part of the base, when he actually connected with the mule deer.

Brian elected to fire 20 rounds, rather than the four that Keith reportedly fired. This would allow Brian to collect more information, as to the feasibility of this event. For some unknown reason, Brain experienced the occasional flier, when a bullet would betray him and impact a few feet higher or a few feet lower. This may be attributable to the age of the ammunition; having passed the half-century mark, the bullet lube has undoubtedly deteriorated to a degree. After each five-shot group, Brian went downrange to check his target. All 20 rounds had hit the eight-by-eight-foot pieces of plywood, and seven had struck the deer.

So, did Elmer Keith actually finish that deer off at that range with his revolver? He was an intuitive shooter, with more skills than imaginable. Brian Pearce not only showed it could be done, but he did it with inferior ammunition. When he concluded his test, Brian broke out one of his old favorite pre-Model 29 .44s with his own handloads, shooting a true Keith-design cast bullet. Let's just say that his 600-yard groups tightened up considerably. Brian showed that not only were Keith's shots possible, but also probable.

THE PIONEERS

No book on big-bore revolvers would be complete without mentioning the late, great Elmer Keith. Elmer was a true pioneer, one who was not only instrumental in the development of the ubiquitous .44 Remington Magnum, but also one who made hunting with a handgun an acceptable practice; as an esteemed member of the gun journalist fraternity, Keith had a built-in pulpit from which to preach.

CHAPTER NINE

A grand thinker from humble roots and the author of nine books, Elmer showed the world what was possible with a modern handgun, but, there are many other pioneers who've contributed significantly to the hobby and helped bring us to this lofty level. Men like JD Jones of SSK Industries, as well as Lee Juras, to name just two you may have heard of. Three in particular and in addition to Keith, though, deserve particular attention, especially due to their contemporary contributions.

After Keith, first up is Dick Casull, who was hot-rodding the .45 Colt and building five-shot revolver conversions as far back as the 1950s—way ahead of all others. And it was Casull's association with Wayne Baker that brought such great revolvers as the Freedom Arms Model 83 to fruition, as well as the .454 Casull round.

The next man I wish to talk about is Larry Kelly. Larry was the founder of Mag-Na-Port International and an important pioneer in the sport of handgun hunting.

Last but certainly not least is Ross Seyfried, the well-known gun writer. How does Ross merit a place in this segment? For one, he went boldly where others feared to tread in the pages of the popular gun media, when he took his .45 Colt revolver to Africa and killed the mighty Cape buffalo without backup, and he introduced the shooting public to John Linebaugh and his creations. Intestinal fortitude, foresight, a knack for storytelling, and an attention to detail few possess, let Ross Seyfried vocally promoted handgun hunting where Elmer Keith had left off, bringing it to the mainstream.

THE GODFATHER—ELMER KEITH

Born in Hardin, Missouri, and raised in Montana, Idaho, and Oregon, Elmer Meffield Keith came into this world on the eighth of March, 1899. Keith was a rancher, a real live cowboy, firearms enthusiast, and innovator, as well as the author of such notable titles as *Sixgun Cartridges and Loads, Big Game Rifles and Cartridges, Sixguns,* and *Hell, I Was There!* to name but a few. Known for his 10-gallon hats and the perpetual cigar clenched in his teeth, Keith grew up at the turn of the century, giving him the unique perspective of a bygone era ebbing into a brave new world. He was a hard man in a hard world.

Keith's writing career began in 1926, with the publication of his first piece in the NRA's *American Rifleman* magazine, and then he went on to make a name for himself on the pages of the aforementioned *American Rifleman, Guns & Ammo, Outdoor Life, Western Sportsman,*

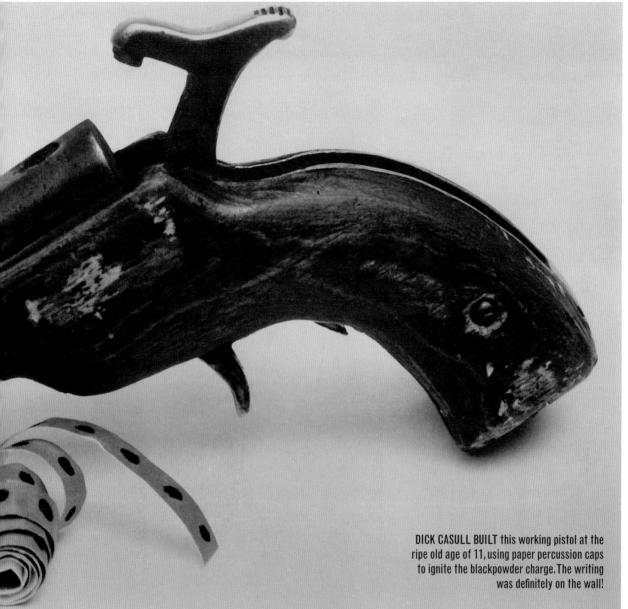

DICK CASULL BUILT this working pistol at the ripe old age of 11, using paper percussion caps to ignite the blackpowder charge. The writing was definitely on the wall!

and *Guns* magazines. In all, his experiences spilled out in the pages of the gun publishing trade in a writing career that spanned 50 years, and he developed a loyal following through his reputation for his straight talk without sugar coating. He wrote hundreds of articles on a wide range of topics, including waterfowl and big-game hunting, load development, self-defense, shotguns, rifles, handguns, and muzzleloaders, until 1981, when he suffered a debilitating stroke.

In handgun circles, Keith is best known for the role he played in bringing the .44 Remington Magnum to fruition, and he also had a hand in the development of the .357 and .41 Magnums. Keith discovered early on how useful and convenient a revolver could be out in the field, and gained some notoriety when he wrote of finishing off a wounded mule deer with 600-yard shooting, with a Smith & Wesson .44 Magnum revolver (see the sidebar in the previous chapter).

Dick Casull gave us the .454 Casull and the Freedom Arms Model 83, both milestone contributions to the hobby. A self-taught master machinist and inventor, Casull advanced the hobby of big-bore revolvers in leaps and bounds.

PHOTO BY DICK CASULL

Elmer died on February 14, 1983, in Boise, Idaho, leaving an indelible mark on the shooting world. One thing we know for certain is that, when Elmer Keith left this world, they broke the mold.

THE TRAILBLAZER—DICK CASULL

Born and raised in Salt Lake City, Utah, Dick Casull began his journey with modest means, but he would leave an indelible mark on the hobby of big-bore revolver shooting. After World War II, the Casull family, like many after the war, went through some economic hardships. As a teenager, Dick hunted to help put meat on the table. In those days, Dick reported, a man could purchase a Colt's Single Action Army for $20—considerably less than the expense of a rifle. He didn't have the money for the rifle, so he "settled" on a Colt's revolver chambered in .32-20. Dick cited that the .32-20 was lacking in power for larger game animals like deer, and, by the age of 17, he'd moved up to a larger, more effective caliber on game. That cartridge turned out to be the one that would not only change his life, but the industry as a whole. It was the .45 Colt.

By 1953, Dick had the desire to make the .45 Colt an even more flexible round. When asked why he'd chosen the .45 Colt over Elmer Keith's favorite .44 Special, he informed me that the Winchester .45 Colt brass of the day had solid heads versus the .44 Special's folded head cases. The solid design better enabled the case to withstand the higher pressures Dick was experimenting with.

While discussing this very topic with a friend, Dick came to the realization that, if he built a five-shot .45 Colt cylinder for the SAA revolver, there would be a lot more meat around each chamber and. He also saw that he could actually increase the outer diameter a bit to add even more strength. With the seed planted and a piece of 4110 bar stock in hand, Dick fashioned his first five-shot Colt's cylinder.

A self-taught master machinist, he built his

THE TOP REVOLVER in this photo is the 454 Proto that Dick built in 1957 out of 4140 bar stock. The entire revolver was hand-built from scratch. The bottom revolver is a Colt's SAA with a five-shot cylinder in .45 Colt that Dick built, in 1953. It was the first gun for which he built a five-shot cylinder.

five-shot cylinders on a lathe (his tooling was also of his own design and construction), wanting to get more out of the revolver by loading it hotter, but knowing that the box stock Colt's SAA just wasn't up to the task. Dick actually blew up a couple revolvers while experimenting to find out where the limits were and, in doing so, discovered exactly how the gun would fail. It must have been some relief, when Dick found out that the blast would go straight up, rather than blowing out the cylinder downward or to the sides, thereby typically leaving the shooter unscathed—scared witless, but not scarred. (During his testing, Dick took an old tire, cut a slot into it, and attached the revolver's grip to the tire with hose clamps. A string was used to trip the trigger and fire the gun, letting the designer stay safely out of the way.)

In 1957, the Proto 454 was born. Dick built the entire revolver from scratch, the frame cut from 4140 steel, the cylinder from 4150 steel. He then heat-treated the entire assembly. A stint working with the late, great P.O. Ackley had further honed Dick's gunsmithing skills by this time, and he credits Ackley with teaching him much of what he knows today. When Dick was building his better .45, he had Ackley machine a 1:24 twist barrel blank, as the 1:16 twist barrels he was testing didn't shoot very well. In this new configuration, Dick reports that the revolver would easily stand up to the pressures of today's ammunition.

Dick began experimenting with triplex loads in his beloved .45 Colt, these loads consisting of a light charge of Unique on the bottom of the case, followed by a heavy charge of 2400 topped with a couple grains of Bullseye. Once the load was compressed, it was able to launch a 230-grain jacketed bullet to nearly 2,000 fps!

In the 1960s, Dick was working for Rocky Mountain Arms, manufacturing mini-revolvers of his own design, as well as cap-and-ball rifles. One day, an entrepreneur by the name of Wayne Baker came in to Rocky Mountain Arms to purchase something and got to talking to Dick. By the end of their conversation, Wayne tried talking Dick into moving to Wyoming to help him build Freedom Arms.

Rocky Mountain Arms had originally wanted to build Dick's single-action revolver in his proprietary cartridge, the .454 Casull, but the company ended up folding. When Dick showed his designs to Wayne, Wayne decided he wanted to build it. In 1975, Dick and his wife made the move to Wyoming, and helped Wayne Baker set up his new shop. Freedom Arms started with the manufacture of Dick's mini-revolver design, which they refined a bit. Then, in 1983, Dick and Wayne Baker gave the Freedom Arms Model 83 to the world, offering it up in Dick's .454 Casull chambering.

With the introduction of the Model 83 came the addition of ammunition to be used in this new revolver, as there were no other manufacturers of the round (at least not at that time). Dick designed the case to include a small rifle primer, which allowed him to beef up and strengthen the head of the case because of the small primer pocket, as well as also extend the overall length of the case, in order to prevent the uninitiated from becoming fragmentation casualties through accidental chambering of the new wonder cartridge in their old and weaker .45 Colt revolvers. Dick even designed the bullets that Freedom Arms was to load into this ammunition.

In 1992, Dick Casull and Freedom Arms parted ways, but Dick had more plans up his sleeve, and after securing some investors, began producing the folding-trigger gun of his design and the .38 Casull. These remained in production for about five years, when, after such a rich and full career building his dreams and ideas, Dick retired with his wife, Jeri, in Wyoming.

THE AMBASSADOR OF HANDGUN HUNTING—LARRY KELLY

The story behind Mag-Na-Port International is really the story of the late Larry Kelly. Born on the east side of Detroit, in 1935, of middle-class family of Irish and Italian decent, Larry enjoyed hunting, fishing, and trapping at every opportunity, as a young boy. Larry dropped out of school in the eighth grade, and, by the time he'd turned 21, he had a wife and three little mouths to feed, yet no job. Hard times necessitated hunting and fishing for the sustenance of his family, and he gained acute skill, born of necessity, in both areas.

Having earned quite the local reputation as a hunter, he was frequently approached by businessmen for the use of his guiding skills and dogs. The stars aligned one day, when the vice president of a company based on the East Coast moved to the Detroit area and desired to go hunting. The executive hired Larry and, after a successful day in the field, the pair sat down and talked.

The gentlemen wondered why Larry was unemployed, and Larry explained that he had no education or training, limiting his possibilities. Nonetheless, the man was impressed with Larry and offered him a job. Larry accepted and, before long, he'd acquired some machining skills and found yet another job, eventually working both jobs full-time, while paying down medical expenses for his wife and daughter. More time passed, and Larry moved on to work for a company that specialized in EDM (electrical discharge machining) technology in the creation of fuel guidance control valves for the Apollo space program. Exposure to this technology gave Larry an idea on how to tame the punishing recoil and muzzle rise of his handgun. A number of years later, he and two partners established Apollo EDM, which quickly became one of the leading EDM companies in the Midwest.

Larry experimented with all types of port shapes on firearms barrels and discovered what worked best on rifles, handguns, and shotguns. The EDM process made clean and precise cuts that did not interfere with the lands and grooves of a barrel. The porting process and shapes worked well enough that, in 1971, Larry applied for a patent. He applied the porting to his very first handgun,

PHOTO COURTESY MAG-NA-PORT

THE LATE, GREAT LARRY KELLY, handgun hunter extraordinaire and co-founder of Mag-Na-Port Arms, posing with a large brown bear he'd taken with a revolver.

a Ruger Blackhawk in .44 Magnum, and quickly became the industry leader in recoil-reducing porting.

Mag-Na-Port Arms was born of Larry Kelly and Apollo EDM partners Bill Kain and Tom Beacroft. Larry contacted gun writers in an effort to market his Mag-Na-Port system and, after appearing on the January 1972 cover of *Guns & Ammo* magazine, the phones began ringing off the hook. Mag-Na-

Port Arms had arrived, and Larry soon sold off his part of Apollo EDM to pursue Mag-Na-Port on a faultier basis.

Though early on Mag-Na-Port was a one-man show, Larry loved hunting with a handgun. He used photos of animals he had taken while handgun hunting in his advertisements, and, before long, business was booming. With licensing agreements in Australia, Canada, and Europe, Mag-Na-Port became international.

By the early '80s, his son, Ken, wife, Barb, and daughter, Doreen, started working alongside Larry, and Mag-Na-Port officially became a family operation. The success of the company opened the door for Larry to hunt more and to hunt in more exotic locales, to include Alaska, Africa, and all over the Lower 48.

It was in the year 1978 that Larry Kelly made his first trek to the Dark Continent, where he hunted the Zambezi Valley of what was then Rhodesia. He was able to take a number of large game animals, including elephant, lion, Cape buffalo, and a slew of plains game. In 1980, Larry was invited by the Zimbabwe Game Department to hunt, whereupon he expressed the desire to take an elephant with a .44 Magnum revolver. J.D. Jones had prepared ammunition especially for this quest of Larry's, that ammo consisting of SSK-KTW Super Penetrators for the .44 Magnum, and some 300-grain Hornady solids for the .375 JDJ T/C pistol Larry was also planning on pressing into service. Larry faced a doubting game warden, when it came to the wisdom of using a .44 Magnum on the world's largest land animal, but was able to quell the warden's doubts with a demonstration of the round's capabilities on steel plates. It was on this safari that Larry successfully killed two bull elephants with a handgun, one with the .44 and the other with the aforementioned .375 JDJ.

A couple safaris later, in August of 1982, Larry completed his collection of the African Big Five by handgun, while on safari in South Africa. It is critical to note that, during this time, Larry Kelly began serious discussions with a number of ammunition manufacturers about the lack of sufficient and dedicated hunting ammunition for handguns. Many couldn't see the need for such specialized loads, but one man did. Peter Pi, of CorBon ammunition, began working up loads for Kelly, and, shortly thereafter, CorBon introduced the CorBon Penetrator, along with flat-nosed hardcast loads for handgun hunters desiring maximum penetration. Larry had always said that, when a bullet expanded, it was like slamming on the brakes—he wanted, *demanded*, maximum penetration.

Larry completed a dozen safaris in Africa, his last in 2001. He hunted all over Europe, Asia, and South America with a handgun, and shared his adventures through myriad magazine articles. He joined Safari Club International (SCI) in 1977 and became one of the very first Life Members, when the organization made the option available. Larry served on the board of directors of the SCI Detroit chapter for a decade, and also as vice president for a number of years. Larry, along with wife, Barbara, ran the Outstanding American Handgunners Awards Foundation for more than five years. In 1983, Larry Kelly founded the Handgun Hunters Hall of Fame & Museum, and, in 1986, he received the Outstanding American Handgunner Award. The North American Hunting Club (NAHC) recognized Kelly as an NAHC Living Legend, for his contributions to the sport of hunting. In 1989, Larry Kelly was inducted into the Safari Club International Hall of Fame.

Semi-retired from the day-to-day grind, in 1991, Larry suffered his first heart attack, which necessitated bypass surgery. His children, Ken and Doreen, had been running the company for a number of years by then, allowing Larry to take it easy and recoup.

While Larry Kelly initially made his mark with barrel porting, Larry's expertise in the hunting fields with a handgun prompted him to produce custom handguns that were reliable, effective, rugged, and specifically for the handgun hunter. Larry left this world for a better place in December of 2010. He is surely missed, but his legacy lives on.

MODERN-DAY WARRIOR—ROSS SEYFRIED

If anyone has led an unusual and interesting life, one that includes ranching, writing, guiding in the States and Africa, and trail blazing, it would be Ross Seyfried. We have cited a number of his seminal works throughout this book, and for a good reason. If Ross wrote about it, then it was thoroughly vetted and tested—you could take his conclusions to the bank. Without his contributions to this hobby, the likes of John Linebaugh may never have been known.

Growing up on a ranch in eastern Colorado, Ross got his first revolver, a Smith & Wesson Model 19 in .357 Magnum, when only a freshman in high school. He tried every load available commercially, including those with the highest velocity and lightest bullets, and reports they didn't live up to his expectations, so ineffective were they. An avid reader of Elmer Keith's works, the young Seyfried sat down with a pen and paper and wrote Elmer about his testing results. Elmer promptly replied back that the .357 was useless and that he should acquire a .44 Magnum—and *that* is exactly what he did.

Ross eventually carried a 4-inch barreled Model 29 in Africa, loaded with the requisite 250-grain Keith loads, but found it left him wanting more, after using it on many wounded game animals. Then, John Linebaugh entered his life, and the game changed for Ross.

Linebaugh convinced Seyfried that he had the perfect revolver for hunting big game and that it was a sizable step up, over, and beyond the revered .44 Magnum. An incredulous and doubtful Seyfried invited Linebaugh to his ranch to give a demonstration—with the promise it would be done at a safe distance. Not only was Seyfried impressed with this display of power, he was determined to find out for himself how this rejuvenated .45 Colt would perform in Africa, a place he considered a wonderful "laboratory" for testing this creation. The results spoke for themselves, culminating with Ross killing a Cape buffalo with a .45 Colt—and without a big double rifle backing him up.

Holding the position of gun writer with one of the biggest, most respected, and influential gun publications of the day, *Guns & Ammo* magazine, doesn't hurt when you seek a platform to float new ideas to a weary and skeptical audience. But, Ross walked the walk, and that put him in a position to speak to a wide audience. In a writing career spanning more than 30 years, Ross has contributed hundreds of articles to *Guns & Ammo, American Hunter, American Handgunner, Double Gun Journal, American Rifleman, Field and Stream*, and *Outdoor Life* magazines, and, most recently, to the online magazine of *Guns America*. In addition to thrilling us with his tales of the hunt, he introduced us mere mortals to such exotic and previously unknown calibers like the .475 and .500 Linebaughs and the mythically powerful Maximums. He showed us that, not only could the biggest and most ferocious animals be conquered with revolvers, but that the effectiveness of these rounds and revolvers was no fluke, as demonstrated by his repeatable results.

Ross Seyfried's contributions to big-bore revolver development, shooting, and hunting cannot be understated. He was a seriously competitive shooter, having won the 1981 World Practical Pistol Championships. Until recently, he served as a guide and outfitter in Oregon, and he has also been a licensed professional hunter (PH) in Tanzania and Zambia, providing him a position of authority from which to speak.

Ross reports that he has come full circle. After many rodeos with some truly big and nasty calibers, he is back to the .45 Colt, claiming to have crossed that line of old age and practicality. We spoke at length, and in a candid and unguarded moment, he mentioned that his greatest regret in life was not being able to hand Elmer Keith a five-shot .45 Colt. "Not only would he have loved it," Seyfried said to me, "he was a man who would have

CHAPTER TEN

HUNTING WITH THE BIG-BORE REVOLVER

GARY SMITH took this zebra stallion in South Africa with a Ruger Super Blackhawk Hunter in .44 Magnum, stoked with 310-grain Garret Hammerheads, in 2002.

Let's face the facts. There are more pleasant revolvers available for the casual shooter, plinker, and paper puncher. Where big-bore revolvers truly shine are in the game fields. They serve well not only as primary hunting tools, but as back-up tools to protect the hunter (or hiker, or rock-climber, or whatever) against predatory animals that would like to make a meal of them. For me, this is at the heart of owning big-bore revolvers. This is where the rubber meets the road and the lead meets the vitals.

Anyone semi-competent with a scoped rifle can successfully kill a game animal from 100 to 300 yards—it's just not that complicated. And I'm not taking away from the skills required to shoot a rifle, but, again, it's not that complicated. Field craft is the name of the game, when handgun hunting. It requires more patience and dedication to the craft of hunting to stalk within close range of an animal. That challenge is what has drawn me to hunting with a handgun—the bowhunters among you will completely understand the thrill of getting close—as one must to be cognizant at all times of the wind and cover, in order to get close. And when it comes to those animals above us on the food chain, a revolver puts the "dangerous" in dangerous game hunting.

My collaborators and I have assembled a number of hunting stories, with accompanying photos and hunter profiles, introducing the reader to the players. Some of them you will readily recognize, others may have remained anonymous and safe, but for the misfortune of knowing me! We have focused on big game, here, to illustrate the fact that big-bore revolvers, loaded properly, are capable of taking even the largest and most dangerous game on earth. (You will see some impressive trophies in this segment of the book.) Big game or small game, taxidermy specimen or meat animal only, every animal you take with a revolver is a trophy, and each will be a real source of satisfaction and pride.

The second part of this chapter will focus on the revolver as a back-up instrument. To kick this segment off, I will recount a situation involving book collaborator and close friend John Parker and the grizzly bear he had to dispatch, when the animal decided to challenge him for the moose he had killed. Then, we'll also look at some other high-profile cases, where dangerous animals were stopped with big-bore revolvers. You will readily see that these guns are up to the task and worth the inconvenience to carry.

PART I: ON THE HUNT

I have been a hunter for years. For me, no form of hunting excites me nearly as much as handgun hunting big game. Bowhunting is simply too quiet for me. I like shattering the stillness and peace of the forest with the blast from a big revolver. I make no apologies for it (I know I should get my head examined!) Handgun hunting can offer some of the thrills of bow hunting, with respect to getting close to your quarry, but with the added bonus of multiple shots. Handgun hunting tests a hunter's skills and ability to negotiate terrain, to utilize cover and concealment, to stalk close to the quarry, and to use the wind correctly.

When you examine the paper ballistics of any high-powered revolver cartridge, you can begin to doubt their effectiveness of game, let alone large and dangerous game. But paper ballistics are a very poor way to measure the lethality of a round. We discussed this issue in detail in Chapter 4, yet I feel the compulsion to reiterate. I have yet to meet a game animal that can read, and barring an encounter with an animal educated in terminal ballistics, they all succumb to their wounds, as long as their vitals have been destroyed. Reach the vitals, destroy them, and a dead animal will be the result. Keep in mind that smaller rifle calibers rely on expanding bullets to make the bullet larger in diameter and result in more tissue disruption and a consequently larger wound channel. Big-bore handguns come "pre-expanded," as Ross Seyfried articulated so many years before the idea became mainstream. When starting with more than a .40-caliber, there really is no need for expansion, as the diameter of the bullet will, by default, make a large wound. Now, combine that diameter with a heavy-for-caliber weight to aid in penetration, and a good nose profile featuring a wide meplat, and the resulting wound channel mimics that of a hunting

CALDWELL SMITH taking aim with a Freedom Arms Model 83 in .454 Casull.

PHOTO BY GARY SMITH

MAGAZINE MOGUL Robert Petersen killed the first polar bear ever with a .44 Magnum, a nickel plated Smith & Wesson Model 29. The large bear required five shots to bring down.

THE SMILING RICHIE BOCHENEK took this 42-inch Cape buffalo with his JRH-built .500 Maximum Ruger. The revolver features an 8 3/8-inch barrel with muzzle brake, topped with a Burris 2.5-7 scope and stoked with 525-grain Cast Performance hardcast bullets over a heavy charge of WW680. The bovine took three shots to earn mortality—all bullets exited.

rifle shooting expanding bullets at high velocity. In fact, a wide-meplat flat-nosed bullet will create a wound that is larger in diameter than the bullet caliber. Don't believe it? With every animal I kill, I make the effort to examine the damage produced by the bullet/s. It is eye opening to see what a revolver bullet at moderate velocity is capable of doing. Remember, there is still no replacement for placement. You still have to hit the vitals no matter what you are shooting, be it a .38 Special or a 105mm Howitzer (okay, well, maybe not the Howitzer!)

You will notice the photo to the left of a very large stuffed polar bear that was taken by the late Robert Petersen,

magazine mogul (Petersen's magazine titles included *Guns & Ammo, Petersen's Hunting,* and *Hot Rod,* to name a few), adventurer, and worldwide big-game hunter. The bear he took has the distinction of being the very first polar bear to be taken with a .44 Magnum revolver. It required five shots in the chest and shoulder area, but the Norma 240-grain Triclad steel-jacketed bullets did their job. The Petersen polar bear mount is in the lobby of the NRA headquarters building, along with the nickel-plated shooting iron that immortalized it keeping vigilant watch and reminding visitors that big-bore revolvers are viable game-getters.

THE NORMA TRICLAD was a steel-jacketed soft-point, weighing 240 grains and having a truncated cone nose profile. This bullet was never intended to expand, but rather to penetrate deeply.

ROB MILLETTE—THE MISSISSIPPI HITMAN

Civil Engineer, land surveyor, and all-around good guy, Rob Millette began shooting revolvers at the ripe old age of six. He began hunting small game with a revolver in the late '70s, but got serious with the pursuit of big game with a big-bore revolver in the late 1980s. He also grew up on a cattle ranch in south Mississippi, where he learned how valuable a tool a revolver can be when dealing with cantankerous bovines and having had to stop a few at point-blank range who had the intent of stopping him into the ground.

Rob's first big-bore was a Ruger Super Blackhawk in .44 Magnum. Even today he has a serious soft spot for fine single-action revolvers, and an even softer spot for fine single-action revolvers by John Linebaugh. He has hunted all over North America and also South Africa, where he hunted a number of plains game with a revolver, including gemsbok, kudu, eland, Limpopo bushbuck, and zebra. North American game he's taken includes mule deer, whitetail, feral cattle, wild boar, elk, and all manner of small game. Rob's favorite all-around calibers are the .45 Colt and .475 Linebaugh. He told me, "There is no animal either of these calibers won't handle with aplomb."

THIS WATERBUCK was taken by Rob Millette, in South Africa, with his Freedom Arms Model 83 in .454 Casull. Rob's revolver throws Freedom Arms' excellent 260-grain jacketed flat-point bullets to nearly 2,000 fps!

What does the future hold for the Mississippi Hitman? He's already corrupted his five boys and daughter in the fine art of handgun hunting, and his hunting plans include Argentina, Alaska, and a return to the Dark Continent. Mississippi Hitman is a well-earned nickname.

ALLAN GRIFFITH—MOOSE MEETS .45 COLT

Retired U.S. Army officer, father of four, and Southern California born and bred, Alan Griffith calls Mapleton, Utah, home these days. A pas-

ROB MILLETTE downed this gemsbok with his mighty Freedom Arms .454.

PHOTO BY ALAN GRIFFITH

ALAN TOOK this 62-inch moose with his trusty .45 Colt Ruger Blackhawk.

sionate hunter, Alan hunts all types of game in many disciplines, including bow and rifle hunting for big game.

Back in 2009, Alan headed to Alaska, along with his best friend Dan McPeak of Folsom, California, to join up with outfitter and guide Brian Simpson of Wittrock Outfitters. Alan had his CZ bolt-action rifle in 9.3x62 as his primary hunting weapon, and a stainless steel Ruger Blackhawk in .45 Colt with a 4⅝-inch barrel as backup. He carried his Ruger in a customized Mernickle Field II holster, worn on his hip in cross-draw fashion. Alan decided that, if conditions were optimal, he would forego the use of the CZ and use his big-bore revolver. Not intending to hunt moose, as he really wanted a grizzly bear, Alan started getting really interested in the other species after seeing two 60-plus-inch bulls up close. Alan decided then that, if a good bull was spotted and the guide could get him into good handgun range, he would take the shot.

The hunter and guide finally spotted a worthy bull that was traveling with an entourage of three cows (some guys have all the luck!), and the group eventually bedded down in a willow draw. As the hunters approached the bedding area, Brian whispered last-minute instructions, going over the dos and don'ts and ifs. After creeping close for a while, the pair stopped for a full 20 minutes, looking, listening, and waiting for something, anything, to happen. It didn't.

Over the next 10 minutes, Brian cow called three times. Nothing. Nada. Nil. Brian handed back to Alan the rifle of his he'd been carrying in case of bears, moved 10 yards away, and picked up a long willow branch with which he began raking the adjacent brush. That did the trick. Alan saw the bull rise to stand just up slope from them with one of the cows. He could also see that the bull's view of the hunters was obstructed, but that the cow had a straight-line view of the two men.

Brian, not having seen the moose rise, turned and started heading back to where Alan stood. Alan quickly gestured with his hand for Brian to stop and pointed two fingers in the direction of the happy couple on the hill. Brian, the seasoned guide, immediately understood. Brian slowly raised his binos, assessed the bull, and mouthed the words "He's *huge*!" That was enough for Alan!

In what seemed like an eternity, the cow that had been staring at Alan turned her head and lowered it, giving Alan the opportunity to duck down and out of sight, and move up the slope 50 yards. The hunter paused at the edge of the willows, trying to figure out a way to get closer, when Brian sounded off with the most perfect bull grunt and raked the willows once more. That was all it took! The bull became agitated and started heading down slope. What Alan didn't know was that Brian was in a near panic as he stood there, no rifle, and only a willow branch for a weapon. He didn't know that Alan was getting ready to show that bull just how effective a .45 Colt can be.

The bull traveled to within a mere 40 yards away and directly across a draw from Alan, but a willow branch stood between the two. The moose kept moving, and Alan lost sight of the bull in the draw before he reappeared, coming around the up-slope side of the bush. At that moment, Alan set down his rifle and found a good shooting lane into where he believed the moose was heading. He then drew his Ruger, got into a standing, modified Weaver stance, thumbed back the hammer, and waited for the vital zones to materialize. As soon as Alan saw shoulder, he put one tight behind it.

The bull grunted loudly and humped up. Without hesitation, Alan put two more 335-grain WFNs (over a stiff load of Lil' Gun) into the vitals. All of a sudden, the bull whirled around and faced Alan. Alan was convinced the bull was coming to exact revenge, but it continued to turn around, eventually stopping and facing away from him. Now it was Alan's turn to panic, as he feared his moose would get away, and he let fly the last three rounds he had, and though he only hit the bull moose once, the bull moved another 10 yards, stopped, and toppled over, never moving another muscle. It was over. Never a dull moment when handgun hunting!

DUSTIN LINEBAUGH AND THE LONG SHOT

In 2006, Dustin made the long trek from Cody, Wyoming, to Alaska, for the hunt of a lifetime. He

A PROUD DUSTIN LINEBAUGH (left), with guide, Tom Buller, and friend Jerry Hammic, and the grizzly bear Dustin shot at 176 yards with his .475 Linebaugh Vaquero. Dustin's load consists of a 425-grain LFN hardcast bullet over a charge of H110. The moderate load pushes the bullet out of the barrel at 1,200 fps.

was there to hunt North America's most dangerous predator, the grizzly bear, with a handgun.

Sitting with his guide on an open hillside, glassing the tundra and alder patches below, Dustin soon caught sight of a big grizz ambling out of an alder thicket some 600 to 700 yards below the pair. After a little more glassing and a quick deliberation, it was decided that this bear was indeed a great trophy and worth pursuing.

The hunting party quickly set out to close the distance between shooter and bear and stalked to within a rangefinder-confirmed 176 yards. The bear knew that something was going on, but Dustin felt the confidence born from lots of handgun hunting experience and, when the bear stopped and sat on his haunches facing Dustin, the hunter let a 425-grain LFN fly.

The shot centered in the bear's chest, breaking his spine and exiting. The bear went down and immediately began rolling around, trying to get up. Dustin wasted little time sending two more bullets into the bear broadside, quickly ending the ordeal. Who said big-bore revolvers are range limited?

GARY SMITH—FOUNDER OF *HANDGUN HUNTER MAGAZINE*

Gary Smith is the founder of *Handgun Hunter Magazine* (www.handgunhunt.com) and has been

VIRGINIA NATIVE GARY SMITH dropped this trophy buck in Loudoun County, Virginia, with his Ruger Super Blackhawk Hunter in .45 Colt chambering handloaded Speer jacketed hollowpoints.

hunting extensively with handguns for more than 30 years. He created the online publication in the year 2000, to promote the sport of hunting with handguns, to serve as a repository of information for the benefit of handgun hunters worldwide, and to demonstrate the safe and responsible use of handguns for sporting purposes. Gary's favorite big-bore revolver calibers include the .44 Magnum, .454 Casull, and the .475 Linebaugh. His favorite revolvers are single-actions and include the Freedom Arms Model 83, Ruger Blackhawk, and Super Blackhawk.

Smith considers hunting with a 4- to 5-inch barreled revolver to be just about the ultimate in challenge in handgun hunting. He told me, "I have nothing but respect for the guys who can make accurate shots beyond 300 yards with a single-shot handgun, but it's not my preferred way of hunting. I like to get relatively close before taking a shot, if possible. I've taken deer out to about 300 yards and I probably will again, but I get more satisfaction from an animal taken at 50 yards with a revolver."

Smith competed in NRA handgun silhouette matches for many years and also worked for several years as a range safety officer. Gary is a native of Virginia, but now lives in Texas, and in addition to a full-time job in the high-tech industry, he also works as a guide for the Texana Ranch, in Hunt, Texas.

LARRY WELCH—
BEAR HUNTER EXTRAORDINAIRE

Larry Welch is a wildlands firefighter by trade and a houndsman by birth. Hailing from eastern North Carolina, the home of the biggest black bears on record in the Lower 48 (and some of the best barbeque in the southeast!), few people I know of have Larry's depth of experience hunting black bears with dogs.

Hunting with dogs lends itself well to handguns, as an easily packed, lightweight firearm is

LARRY WELCH, pictured above working on his skills at the range, took this doe with his custom Ruger Super Redhawk in .475 Linebaugh at just over 100 yards.

an asset in this fast-action sport. Not only does it free up your hands to handle the dogs, if necessary, but a smaller firearm makes threading your way through the briars that much easier.

Larry's big-bore of choice is a Ruger Blackhawk in .45 Colt, fitted with a Bisley grip frame, while his bear-busting load is a 325-grain flatnosed hardcast bullet pushed to just under 1,200 fps. While Larry has also used the .44 Magnum with success, he reports that the .45 Colt just does the deed a little better. But stay tuned, as Larry recently got his hands on a custom Ruger Super Redhawk in .475 Linebaugh, and he plans on thinning out the North Carolina black bear, wild hog, and whitetail populations in the coming years with this new gun.

DARREL HARPER—IN HIS OWN WORDS

I have been dreaming of taking a brown bear with a handgun for a number of years now. After one disappointing attempt a couple of years

100 yards
500 S&W
38 Gr 296
375 Gr XP3
Rem Pr
*- Brass

DARREL THOROUGHLY prepared for his brown bear hunt. He made sure that his revolver, load, and shooting ability wouldn't be limiting factors. The .500 S&W revolver is capable of good accuracy out of the box—this three-shot, 100-yard group measures less than two inches and was fired from the prone position.

prior, I was fortunate enough to return to Alaska, for a second chance at harvesting a big brownie with a handgun, in 2011. I booked the hunt with Grizzly Skins of Alaska, owned and operated by well-known outdoor writer Phil Shoemaker. His hunting area is located on the Alaskan Peninsula, which has a history of producing large bears.

I was reminded that just getting to Alaska can be an adventure in itself. I, along with my carry-on backpack and the duffel bag I had checked, arrived in King Salmon, Alaska, only an hour or so behind schedule. Unfortunately, the Pelican case containing my optics, shooting sticks, guns, and ammunition did not. I decided to go ahead and fly into base camp for the night and wait it out.

The next morning, I phoned the airport in King Salmon and was informed that my gun case had arrived. That afternoon, I was flown back to King Salmon to pick up my gun case and, after returning to base camp, I went out to the range to check the zero on both of the handguns that I had brought along for the hunt. I wanted to take a bear with my .500 S&W revolver but, since this was the hunt of a lifetime for me, I'd also brought along my custom XP-100 chambered in .376 Steyr. Even though the revolver was capable of longer shots, I placed a 100-yard limit on shots with it, and I was comfortable with the .376 Steyr at distances twice that far. After some slight scope adjustments on both firearms, my guns were ready for hunting.

I was flown to a spike camp about six miles away from base camp and about three miles from the nearest salmon stream. Opening morning found our trio of hunter, guide, and packer perched on a spotting hill, glassing for bears. Things started off slowly. We first spotted some bears fishing in the river and, after a while, we began seeing others roaming the hillsides closer to our position. One bear was only about 800 yards away, and it lay down right out on the open tundra and took a two-hour nap! We also saw several herds of caribou off in the distance.

Around 12:30 p.m., we spotted a big bear that we decided was definitely one worth going after. With my guide leading the way, we confined ourselves to the alders as much as possible, moving *only when the bear was looking away. When we got to within 350 yards of the bear, we ran out of cover and began belly crawling, trying to remain out of sight of the bear as he continued to amble our way. When the bear was about 200 yards away, the guide asked the packer to remain behind, in order to minimize movement. I moved up front, and we continued to crawl towards the bear.*

Finally, we came to the edge of a small stream that the bear also seemed to be headed to. I had brought along a rolled up sleeping bag pad to use as a field rest from the prone position, and I now placed it on the ground in front of me. The bear was only 135 yards away by this time and still heading in our direction. I could see that, if he continued on his present course, he would drop out of sight momentarily while he passed through a tiny patch of alders. However, that would allow

IN ORDER TO HELP contain scent that would alert bears to the presence of humans in the area, the animals are first spotted from a distant hill with optics. After a quality bear is located, a stalk is planned to intercept the bear and get within shooting range.

enough time for me to pop my earplugs in and set up for the shot with the .500 S&W. Once he cleared the alders, he would be standing in an opening that I had ranged at 100 yards—inside my comfort zone for the revolver with a steady rest. It was a perfect setup!

As predicted, we lost sight of the bear. Five minutes passed, then 10, then 20, then 30—no bear! We finally realized that he had decided to take a nap once he'd entered the alders. My guide motioned for the packer to join us, and he soon belly crawled up beside me. You can imagine how nerve-wracking it was to have the bear of a lifetime sleeping in an alder patch, out of sight, only 125 yards away! I prayed that the wind direction would remain constant and that he would continue on his prior course after he woke from his nap.

Finally, two and a half hours later, the bear stood up in the alders and continued in our direction. He stopped once he entered the clearing, but it would have been a steep quartering to shot, so I held my fire, waiting for a broadside shot opportunity. He moved on, and as he

PHOTO BY DARRELL HARPER

PHOTO BY DARRELL HARPER

DARREL HARPER'S glorious bear taken with his .500 Smith & Wesson revolver!

reached the top of the creek bank across from us, I hoped that he would continue down to the water's edge, which would have given me a 75-yard shot. Unfortunately, just as my guide had anticipated, he chose the path of least resistance and turned to go downstream in order to find a less-steep bank to descend to the water. Just before leaving the clearing, though, he stopped in a quartering away position again just 100 yards away. I looked over at my guide, who was prepared to back me up with a .375 Ruger rifle, and I was given the go-ahead to shoot.

I placed the crosshairs of the 2X Leupold scope just behind the bear's right shoulder and squeezed off the shot. The bear growled and whirled around, biting the area where he'd been hit, and I was able to fire two more shots, before the bear retreated into a small patch of alder about 15 yards away. After a few seconds, the al-

ders quit shaking. My guide and I both covered the area with our guns, and then, after a few more minutes, the handshakes and congratulations on the successful hunt began.

My guide and I crossed the creek, circled high above the alder patch where the bear was lying, and descended on the area cautiously, spotting a patch of brown fur in the grass beneath the alders. But the bear showed no signs of breathing, as my guide stuck the barrel of the .375 Ruger in the bear's eye, while I covered with my freshly reloaded revolver. After many years of waiting, I had finally fulfilled my quest for a handgunned brown bear!

JIM MINER—THE DEER SLAYER

Born in Cleveland, Ohio, Jim Miner was exposed to hunting at an early age, via frequent rabbit hunts with his neighbors. Jim always liked revolvers, but was in heaven, in 1956, when the .44 Remington Magnum made its debut. Jim mail-ordered a Ruger Flat Top and shot it for a year,

JIM MINER striking a familiar pose.

JIM MINER and the author (left) out shooting big-bore revolvers.

before he decided he just had to have the new N-frame Smith & Wesson chambered in the powerhouse cartridge. Jim shot nothing but factory ammo until he collected enough brass to start reloading, as the handloader couldn't yet buy brass for the newest magnum.

In 1982, Jim bought a new stainless steel Ruger Super Blackhawk from his local gun shop, with the express purpose of competing in IHMSA (International Handgun Metallic Silhouette Association) matches. This was the first year the Ruger had been offered with a 10½-inch barrel. IHMSA was where Jim learned the fine points of handloading (and trigger control!) and he went on to win the Ohio State IHMSA title, in 1983, with a score of 79 out of 80.

Jim moved his family to West Virginia, in 1986, when his company relocated him and this marked the first year he would hunt deer with a handgun. He mainly used his proven Super Blackhawk, but also took bunches of deer with an Old Army cap-and-ball revolver. Occasionally he dabbled in archery and muzzleloading, but the handgun hunting bug bit him hard. He later bought a Ruger Vaquero in .45 Colt, a BFR in .45-70, a .475 Linebaugh, and another in .500 JRH. Jim loves casting bullets of his own design, machining the moulds in his own basement, and he spends as much time on the trigger as possible.

AUTHOR PHOTO

ONE OF DOZENS of whitetail deer that have fallen to the lethal combination of Jim Miner and his revolver.

Retired from the airline industry, this big-bore revolver hunter does his best to help control the deer populations of his corner of West Virginia.

MIKE RINTOUL— OWNER, RINTOUL ENTERPRISES

Former Marine, Vietnam veteran, and mechanical engineer, Mike Rintoul, of Alton, Illinois, is the owner of Rintoul Enterprises, the parent company of such notables as Cast Performance Bullets and the Grizzly Cartridge Company, producers of some of the finest ammunition to grace our shores. Mike produces high-quality hardcast bullets in all the popular calibers and weights, and he has catered to the discriminating handgun hunter for years, offering ammunition for virtually any and every big-bore revolver cartridge one can imagine.

As the photo indicates, Mike likes hunting big game with a revolver—*really* big game.

DOCTOR LARRY ROGERS (AND FRIEND)

Hailing from Cabin Creek, West Virginia, Doctor Larry Rogers' life story is one of success. Larry grew up during tougher times than many can imagine, in a coal mining camp, until he was a teenager. He and his family got their first indoor bathroom, when Larry was 12. His humble roots have kept him grounded, just as they have also motivated him to succeed on his own.

Larry Rogers has been a doctor of family practice for 37 years now, but makes sure that work doesn't impede his hunting. He recently passed two milestones in his active hunting career, to wit 11,000 groundhogs and 2,000 deer with a handgun. You see, Dr. Rogers takes part in cull/crop deprivation hunting every year, and he keeps meticulous records. A more experienced big- or small-game hunter is hard to imagine.

Larry's dad is to blame for his handgun habit, having given Larry his first handgun, an H&R revolver in .22 LR, at the impressionable age of eight. Larry carried it in a low-slung cowboy hol-

PHOTO BY MIKE RINTOUL

MIKE RINTOUL brought down this giraffe with three shots from his .500 Linebaugh. His PH was so impressed with the short gun's terminal performance, he felt that Mike wasn't the least bit under-gunned.

ster, and there wasn't a local squirrel or ground hog that was safe. By 1977, Larry had killed his last buck with a rifle (at 420 yards, on top of that). From then on, it was all handguns all the time, to include specialty pistols and revolvers. In college, he bought his first revolver, a Ruger Blackhawk in .357 Magnum, a gun he kept in tow through medical school.

They say an individual is defined by the events in their life, but even more evident than defining oneself is finding out who your friends are. On January 2, 2002, Larry's house burned to the ground, and with it, 65 guns. Fortunately, no one was hurt, but Larry was heartbroken, having lost the tools of his other trade.

This is where your friends either become mere acquaintances or they show you they really have your back. You see, Larry Rogers is close friends with J.D. Jones. Or at least he thought he was— J.D. actually proved to be a *lot* better than a close friend. He promptly sent an employee to West Virginia, to collect the fire damaged guns. Jones' plan was to restore every firearm that was restorable and, in the end, actually managed to rescue and renew four of them. He then told Larry that whatever handgun he wanted built, J.D. would make it for him as quickly as possible. Anyone would be hard pressed to have a better friend, as J.D. helped Larry maintain his sanity through those trying times.

To date, Larry has made six trips to Africa, and has taken all manner of big game with a handgun, including elephant, hippo, and rhinoceros. Larry's immediate plans call for a trip back to Africa in 2013 for elephant with his John Linebaugh-built .475 Linebaugh Ruger. We have no doubt the good doctor will succeed.

MAX PRASAC—THE KEVLAR HOG

A number of years ago, while testing Smith & Wesson's .460 XVR for an article I was writing, I

PHOTO BY DR. LARRY ROGERS

DOCTOR ROGERS travelled to Alaska, to dispatch this very large brown bear with his Taurus Raging Bull in .500 Smith & Wesson Magnum stoked with Barnes 375-grain XPBs.

dragged the XVR down to my favorite North Carolina hunting spot with Hog Heaven Outfitters. I took a box of 395-grain WFN hardcast loads by CorBon with me and used half a box sighting in the .460. Recoil with these loads, rated at 1,525 fps, is considerable and not for the faint at heart.

That afternoon, I sat on a stand about 40 yards from a feeder, hoping to drill a hog with the big Smith & Wesson. As luck would have it, I was up in the stand for no more than an hour, when four boars showed up for a snack. I chose one, put the sights behind his shoulder, and squeezed. The Smith roared and the hog stutter-stepped off to the side, so I put the sights on his other shoulder and let another fly. This time he made his way into the brush on the edge of the clearing. I gave him about 10 minutes before I headed down for what I hoped would be a short tracking job, my old Smith & Wesson Model 29 .44 Magnum now in my hand and outfitter Milt Turnage showing up to give me a hand.

We found some blood at the edge of the clearing and descended into the darkness of the brush. We tracked all the way to the edge of the swamp to partake in what became a harrowing chase through deep black water, thick brush, painful briars, and clouds of mosquitoes. I shot a total of six times with my trusty .44 Magnum and was charged once by the angry porcine, before he finally conceded death from a shot behind the ear—good thing, as I was out of ammo. I emerged soaking wet, mosquito bit, empty-gunned, and with a destroyed camera and cell phone and a hog that resembled a block of Swiss cheese, but I couldn't have been happier. The first shot from the .460 had been true and a double-lunger, but we think this hog may have succumbed to lead poisoning. Just goes to show how tough some animals can be.

EDWARD K. FOLMAR—BADGER REVENGE

Born and raised in Chicago, Illinois, Edward K. Folmar made his living and met his wife in California, before retiring to Idaho Falls, Idaho. Now, Ed and his lovely wife, Deena, hunt full-time—exactly the way retirement is supposed to be!

THE "KEVLAR HOG" weighed a whopping 101 pounds dripping wet, that weight undoubtedly a good portion attributable to lead bullet content. He absorbed more lead than the author would like to admit.

AUTHOR PHOTO

PHOTO BY ED FOLMAR

ED USED HIS Taurus Raging Bull in .454 Casull loaded with 300-grain Hornady XTPs and topped with a Leupold 4X scope to take this bison.

PHOTO BY ED FOLMAR

THIS BEAUTIFUL WATERBUCK fell to Ed Folsom's Smith & Wesson Performance Center .460 Magnum stoked with Hornady 200-grain loads. The revolver is topped with a Bushnell 2-6X scope.

While doing a tour in the Air Force, in 1959, Ed was a member of the pistol team. He acquired his very first big-bore revolvers, a pair of Ruger Flat Top .44 Magnums, while working for Uncle Sam, and mainly punched paper and busted rocks in those days. He moved to California, in 1964, bought a Ruger Hawkeye and a Super Blackhawk .44 Magnum, and got started hunting ground squirrels, jack rabbits, and the occasional varmints. As time went by, Ed started going after bigger animals with a handgun, including elk, bison, brown bear, and African plains game. To date, Ed and his equally accomplished handgun hunting wife have been on four safaris to Africa, culminating in a trophy bull elephant that Ed shot with a T/C Encore chambered in .450 Marlin. Ed finished the animal with a shot from his Freedom Arms .454 loaded with 320-grain Punch bullets.

As successful as he's been as a handgun hunter, it was a missed badger, of all things, that haunted him for some 30 years. An opportunity ultimately presented itself for Ed to redeem himself when, out on an elk hunt, he spotted a badger off in the distance. He had a Ruger Hawkeye with him, and Ed got his badger at a confirmed 152 yards. Ed holds that badger up as one of his most prized trophies to this day.

What's next for the retired full-time hunters? Deena's going to keep racking up one-shot kills with her T/C Contender in .35 Remington, and

PHOTO BY ED FOLMAR

ED AND HIS WIFE, Deena, spend their spare time in the hunting fields, as is evident by this Montana bison that fell to Ed's Freedom Arms Model 83 in .454 Casull. Ed used CorBon 320-grain Penetrators on the big bovine.

Ed just had a custom Ruger Vaquero in .475 Linebaugh built by Dixie Firearms that he intends to use on another bull elephant. We have no doubts he will be bring his trophy home.

LYNN THOMPSON—
THE RUGGED INDIVIDUALIST

Cold Steel proprietor Lynn Thompson is hell on wheels, and one needs only to watch his video on hunting water buffalo and wild hogs in Australia, *Handgun Hunting Down Under,* to know that the man is an exceptional shot with a handgun. Multiple fleeing targets at varying ranges are scenarios in which Lynn thrives. Even more remarkable, upon viewing this video, is the fact that the revolvers Lynn uses are *borrowed*! Australia does not allow the visiting hunter to bring their own handgun in-country, so you can forget about familiarity.

As I write this, Lynn has just returned once

PHOTO BY LYNN THOMPSON

THIS RHINOCEROS FELL to Lynn Thompson's .454 Freedom Arms Model 83.

again from hunting Down Under, but this time he was using one of Cold Steel's *spears* to dispatch water buffalo—you read that right! A natural talent is obviously all present and accounted for, but Lynn attributes a strict practice regimen to his wildly successful handgun hunting career.

We spoke at length with Lynn, and he gave us some of his insights into handgunning the largest and most dangerous game in the world, which,

PHOTO BY LYNN THOMPSON

COLD STEEL KNIFE company owner Lynn Thompson shot this Cape buffalo with a Freedom Arms Model 83 in .454 Casull.

for him include the Big Seven via a revolver in .454 Casull.

Lynn started the company we know as Cold Steel, in 1980, a number of incidents providing him with the impetus to start his own knife-making business. Lynn stated in no uncertain terms that, "There are two things that motivate me— make me afraid, or make me angry. Then watch out, as I am coming with a vengeance."

Back in the day, Lynn had a number of businesses, including a K-9 security enterprise. One day, an 80-pound Doberman pinscher decided he didn't like Lynn and bit the hand that fed him. Lynn was in a very precarious situation. He defended himself as well as he could (the martial arts are a pretty significant skill set of his), but he realized that a knife would have been of great benefit, short of carrying a handgun in his kennels. He emerged from the dog fight only slightly worse for the wear, but the incident left an indelible mark on his mind. That was where motivating factor No. 1, fear, came in.

While Lynn was training in knife fighting, a well-known brand-name knife he was using broke. Thinking it a fluke, he grabbed an identical spare, but proceeded to break the tip off of that one, as well. Anger, factor No. 2, then presented itself to Lynn. Now the formula was complete to start his own knife-making company, and Cold Steel was born.

Lynn began killing critters with a handgun when he was 13 years old, following the purchase of a $32 single-action .22 LR revolver. He soon realized that he had a knack for this handgun hunting thing, killing rabbits and woodchucks by the truckload. By 16, he'd bought himself a K-22 Masterpiece and continued ridding California of its rabbit population.

Because he was a student and perpetually short on money, Lynn bought a Lee reloading set and dies to feed his growing revolver collection, which now included a Smith & Wesson Model 19. By the mid-'80s, the handgun hunting fire was further fueled through Ross Seyfried's handgun hunting adventures in the pages of *Guns & Ammo* magazine, particularly the story of Sey-

THIS CROCODILE MET his demise at the business end of Lynn's mighty .454 Ruger Super Redhawk. Likewise, this fine African elephant, the world's largest land mammal, was also no match for the man and his gun.

fried's Cape buffalo hunt with a .45 Colt (weren't we all?).

Fast forward to 1989, when Lynn bought out his partners and gave himself the vacation he had vowed to take since graduating from college, in 1977. Lynn journeyed to South Africa with a .454 Casull, a couple boxes of ammo, and one whole month's time, during which 32 animals fell. Now Lynn was *really* hooked.

Lynn Thompson has the distinction of purportedly being the only one to have taken Africa's Big Seven, consisting of African elephant, Cape buffalo, lion, leopard, rhinoceros, hippo, and crocodile, with an open-sighted revolver. He has hunted Africa 14 times and frequents Australia to hunt feral donkeys, kangaroo, wild cattle, feral hogs, and water buffalo.

Lynn subscribes to a disciplined practice regimen every Sunday after church, whereby he burns lots of powder. He starts off with a .22 LR revolver and gradually works his way up to his beloved .454 Casull. He is a firm believer of "aim small, miss small" and practices at different ranges off-hand, shooting small targets like shotgun hulls.

Lynn prefers handgun hunting to all other forms, and he feels that, if one is hunting dangerous game, then it should be hunted at dangerous (read, "close") distances. That said, Lynn doesn't feel that a handgun offers any handicap over a rifle and actually feels better served by the short-barreled weapon. He told me, "A revolver is much easier and faster to bring into play in an emergency situation than any rifle."

MIKE WINNERSTIG—IN HIS OWN WORDS

"Handgun hunting" and "Sweden" are concepts that, unfortunately, do not square very well. Although there is a very strong tradition of hunting in Sweden—the annual harvest of more than 80,000 moose being its most visible aspect—this is circumscribed by many very restrictive laws. Thus, handgun, bow, and muzzle-

COLD STEEL'S LYNN THOMPSON and a hippo he took with his .454 Freedom Arms revolver. The lion was done in by a Super Redhawk chambered in the same round.

loader hunting are illegal activities (with a few exceptions, such as killing trapped animals with a .22-caliber revolver).

However, there is also a well-established competitive shooting tradition and, by European standards, a fairly high percentage of the population owns one or several firearms. One of the traditional, national competition tournaments is called "magnum field shooting." This entails shooting at long-distance (up to 180 meters, or slightly less than 200 yards) paper targets with big-bore revolvers, normally .357 Magnum through .454 Casull calibers.

I am currently a researcher at the Swedish Defense Research Agency, and I started out my pistol shooting career when serving as a reserve Captain in the Swedish Army. I am also the vice chairman of the Swedish Pistol Shooting Association, an organization with around 25,000 members (the equivalent of 900,000 members in a U.S. setting). After a lot of magnum field shooting, I began reading U.S. gun magazines on hunting with handguns and realized that, given the precision of his guns, hunting with them would not at all be impossible.

In the spring of 2008, I started planning for a full customization of one of my older and lesser-used guns, a .44 Magnum S&W Model 29-2 produced in 1976. The idea was to get it optimal for both the scoped class in Swedish magnum field shooting competition and for handgun hunting in the US. Receiving the gun back from a local Swedish gunsmith, I saw that

PHOTO BY MIKE WINNERSTIG

MIKE TOOK this four-horn ram, at the Wilderness Hunting Ranch in Pennsylvania, with a 300-grain XTP from his custom Smith & Wesson .44 Magnum. The distance measured 77 yards.

PHOTO BY MIKE WINNERSTIG

MIKE INCLUDES the family on his hunts whenever possible. Here his daughters Miranda and Amanda share in Mike's success in bagging this whitetail doe in northern North Carolina. The shot was 91 yards.

a full transformation had taken place. Now, the gun had not only a scope, but also laser, light, bipod, carry sling and even bayonet options!

I tested my handloaded ammunition extensively and settled on two hunting loads, a 300-grain Hornady XTP on top of stiff charge of Vihtavuori N110 for use on game up to red stag, and a 310-grain Oregon Trail LaserCast LFP over a load of N110 for wild boar and heavier game. (The latter load is pretty hot, at more than 1,300 fps.)

I primarily works with analyses of the U.S. foreign and defense policies, so he travels frequently to the States. During a number of these business trips, I've been able to take a few days off for handgun hunting trips in Pennsylvania, Texas, and North Carolina. The results: one wild boar, a four-horn ram and several whitetail deer, with all but the boar one-shot kills. Ranges have been everything from 15 yards to more than 90 yards.

Back home, I moonlight as a freelance gun writer, and stories of my U.S. handgun hunting adventures appear in Swedish gun magazines. So far, they have mostly been received with great interest by the readers, but there is still a long way to go before handgun hunting is recognized as a legitimate sport in my native country. But, as they say, a drop hollows out the stone.

MIKE GIBONEY—BISON MADE EASY

Born and raised in Springfield, Missouri, Mike Giboney grew up hunting small game and fishing

in the Ozarks. In the early '90s, Mike made the move to Texas, to work in the high-tech industry. Like so many of us, he was inspired by Ross Seyfried's article detailing the killing of a Cape buffalo with his .45 Colt, and Mike promptly fell in love with big-bores.

Still a big fan of the .45 Colt, since 2006, Mike has been hunting with his BFR in .500 JRH and was able to help Jack Huntington evaluate that cartridge in the field, by taking the first head of game ever with the Buffalo Bore 440-grain cast load. Fittingly, that game animal was a bison. As the picture clearly demonstrates, even loaded way down (440-grain bullets at a "walking" pace of 950 fps), the .500 JRH makes for great buffalo medicine.

OTTO CANDIES, JR.— "TACK"-DRIVING BULLETS

Otto Candies, Jr., has hunted around the world with rifles and handguns, but prefers the challenge of the revolver as a primary hunting tool. One of the first hunters to explore the capabilities of the .475 Linebaugh, Otto has cleanly harvested a number of African bull elephants, the largest and one of the most dangerous of all land animals. Otto's propensity for handgunning elephants lead to a creative bullet solution for maximum penetration on extremely large game. Prior to the advent of bullets like the Belt Mountain Punch, Otto used hardcast bullets with upholstery tacks driven into the nose, giving the bullet a steel tip

PHOTO BY MIKE GIBONEY

MIKE GIBONEY took this bison with a mildly loaded .500 JRH BFR, the load pushing a 440-grain hardcast bullet at a subdued 950 fps. Even an animal as large as a an American bison is no match for a correctly loaded big-bore revolver in experienced hands.

that was better able to withstand impacts with heavy bone. Ever innovative and adventurous, Otto Candies, Jr., never fails to impress!

BROCCOLI BANDITS— A HUNT WITH THE AUTHOR

In August 2011, I received an opportunity to hunt cow moose in northern Maine. A number of crop deprivation tags were offered to local outfitters in, to assist broccoli farmers there with protecting their crops from the damage produced by North America's largest ungulate, the moose.

My outfitter was Don Burnett, co-owner of #9 Lake Outfitters of Bridgewater, Maine, and I would be using a custom revolver built for me by Jack Huntington. The foundation for this custom was a Super Redhawk in .454 Casull that I had purchased a decade earlier. It was a good and accurate revolver with its 7½-inch barrel and had accounted for the demise of a number of wild hogs. But, I decided the gun would be sacrificed to the big-bore god, in this case, the .500 Linebaugh.

My intent was to turn this revolver into a back-up piece that could double as a primary hunting piece if need be, so I specified a five-inch barrel,

with a nod towards packability and light weight. The end result was a revolver that weighed a couple ounces less than my six-inch Model 29 Smith & Wesson—and, subsequently, kicks like an angry mule on performance enhancing drugs. Very hard to shoot, even with the "mild" loads I had settled on (Grizzly Cartridge's 500-grain LFN hardcast bullets at a leisurely 1,100 fps), the revolver was put on the back burner of priorities due to a busy editorial schedule. But, one month prior to my moose hunt, I decided the short Super Redhawk would be my chosen piece for moose in Maine. A much used and abused Ultradot 30 was mounted via Ruger's excellent 30mm rings, and two sessions with the .500 indicated exceptional accuracy despite my sore hand. I was ready.

We were given permission to hunt on a couple local farms, and after thoroughly scouting the roads and tree lines surrounding the broccoli fields, we were encouraged by the fresh and abundant moose sign. The morning of opening day was uneventful but, on our way out, we noted a number of well-traveled game trails leading into the fields. That afternoon, my guide, Mike Hogan and I set up downwind of two game "super highways" on one corner of the field, a position that gave us a commanding view of the road that wound its way around the perimeter of the entire field. We quietly settled in after positioning my shooting sticks in a spot that gave me clear fields of fire in all directions of the tree line, and the mosquito feeding ensued.

The greatest thing about moose is that their size betrays them—they are incapable of moving through thick brush without making a racket. Roughly 20 minutes before the last legal shooting light, we heard movement in the brush to the rear of our position. Expecting a moose to emerge to the right, Mike and I were surprised when a large cow cautiously exited the forest to our left. I quickly settled in behind my custom Ruger Super Redhawk, pulled the hammer back, and settled the red dot on what I estimated to be her shoulder. I had practiced out to 100 yards and was confident at that range. Once my breathing was under control, I held my breath and slowly squeezed. The Ruger barked, and I heard the telltale *thwack*, as lead struck moose flesh. Not waiting to see if my shot was true, I lined the red dot onto the dark blob that was now farther away, and let the next round fly—and the next, and the next. My final shot found moose flesh and sent the cow crashing head first into terra firma. I reloaded, grabbed my flashlight, and ran down the road towards my moose.

All of my five shots had connected, though it turns out none were needed beyond the first, which got both her lungs. That said, I am of the mind-set that a hunter should keep shooting until the animal is no longer standing, especially when that animal weighs four times more than any deer.

After field dressing her, we loaded the cow moose onto a trailer and set off to get her tagged and weighed for. She tortured the scales to the tune of 629 pounds dressed, meaning she weighed more than 700 pounds on the hoof. Do you realize just how many steaks the bride of Bullwinkle yielded? I need a bigger freezer!

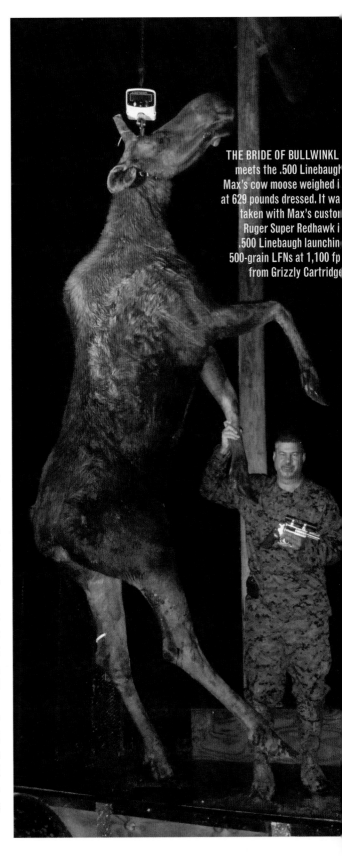

THE BRIDE OF BULLWINKL meets the .500 Linebaugl Max's cow moose weighed i at 629 pounds dressed. It wa taken with Max's custoi Ruger Super Redhawk i .500 Linebaugh launchin 500-grain LFNs at 1,100 fp from Grizzly Cartridg

READY FOR MAINE Moose! The Huntington-built .500 Linebaugh Super Redhawk was sighted in an inch high at 50 yards with Grizzly Cartridge's potent 500-grain LFN loads.

JAMES SWIDRYCK—JAMES FROM JERSEY

James from Jersey actually hales from New-port News, Virginia, before his father, a ship designer, moved his family to Manhattan, New York. He has remained in the area since, calling New Jersey home, despite his southern roots.

Unlike most, James actually started hunting with handguns initially, and it wasn't till much later that he even considered using rifles. James bought his first firearm in 1973, a Colt's Government Model 1911, and was hooked from the start. Eight years later, in the early '80s, James participated in his first handgun hunt after being invited by his foreman to pursue deer in Pennsylvania. James didn't own a rifle, but he discovered it was legal to hunt with a revolver. From that point on, James took 13 deer in succession prior to his first with a rifle.

Then there was a seismic event that rocked James to his very core. James was on a hunt at the YO Ranch, in Texas, and he was quite by chance paired up with Bill Grover—*the* Bill Grover, of Texas Longhorn Arms fame. James, young and impressionable and not then the confident hunter he is today, was more than a little nervous to be in the company of such greatness. He was particularly intimidated, when he witnessed Bill hop out of the hunting vehicle, take a knee, steady the revolver, squeeze, and drop a deer in its tracks. The shot was 165 yards (measured), done with open iron sights! This event steeled James' resolve to be all that he could be with a sixgun in his hand.

James has had the good fortune of hunting Africa twice with his favorite Freedom Arms Model 83 in .454 Casull with a 7½-inch barrel. James commented that "There is nothing on this planet you cannot take with the .454." He couldn't be more correct.

PART II: SAVING YOUR BACON

In North America, dangerous game animals aren't that common. Still, nearly any and every wild animal can potentially pose a danger, especially when wounded or feeling threatened. But beyond those generalities, the biggest threats to the well being of humans in North America are bears.

I have a very good friend, hunting partner, and

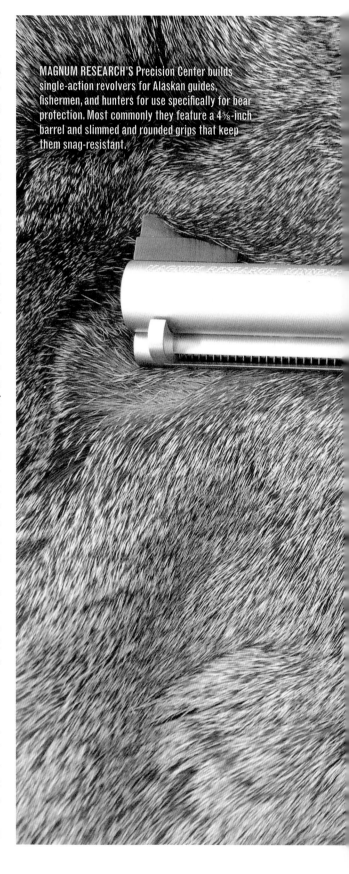

MAGNUM RESEARCH'S Precision Center builds single-action revolvers for Alaskan guides, fishermen, and hunters for use specifically for bear protection. Most commonly they feature a 4⅝-inch barrel and slimmed and rounded grips that keep them snag-resistant.

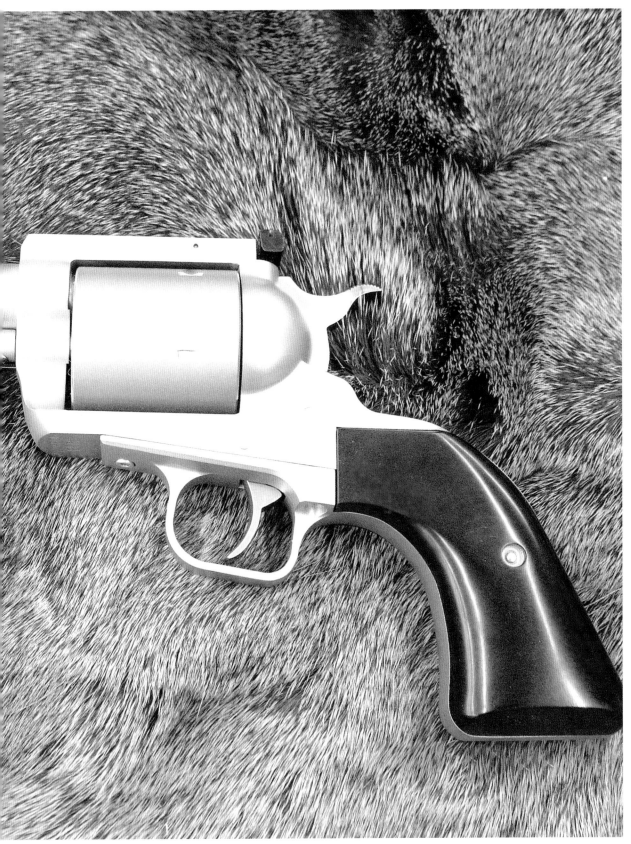

JOHN PARKER knows the value of a revolver for backup work. The bear to his left intended to do him harm, but was stopped with a 390-grain hardcast bullet from his Hamilton Bowen-built .475 Linebaugh revolver. As a side note, this was the first .475 revolver Bowen ever built.

book collaborator who had a close brush with an arctic grizzly, and his revolver saved his bacon. This was back in 1988, when John Parker and his friend Jimmy were in Alaska, hunting moose with rifles. John carried a Hamilton Bowen custom Ruger Bisley in the then-new .475 Linebaugh. John shot a bull moose one afternoon and, losing daylight, bagged what meat they could and packed it back to camp. Later, approaching the downed carcass to gather the remainder, the hunters found it had been partially buried by a bear.

John propped his rifle up against a tree (out of reach, I might add), and got to work chopping out the moose's antlers, while his buddy wisely stood watch. Without warning, an adult male grizzly cleared the brush, making a beeline towards John and Jimmy. When it reached the 40-yard mark, Jimmy realized the bear had no intention of stopping. He made an executive decision, shouldered his .338, and put a 250-grain Nosler Partition in the brownie's on-side shoulder. The bear went down, but then immediately jumped up like it was spring-loaded. It was also very unhappy. John, not waiting for an invitation, cleared leather and let a 390-grain hardcast bullet fly, catching the back of the bear's rib cage. The bruin went straight down and exhaled its last breath.

We all know that the chances of actually being attacked by a bear are slim, but that small percentage still carries with it substantial negative

LYNN THOMPSON, proprietor of Cold Steel, was spear hunting in Australia but stopped this charging water buffalo with a Ruger Super Redhawk in .454 Casull, while spear hunting. Lynn never steps out into the field without a revolver.

PHOTO BY LYNN THOMPSON

PROFESSIONAL HUNTER BUD RUMMEL with a 371-pound lioness he took in Zimbabe. Rummel used a .500 Smith & Wesson from the S&W Performance Center, and stalked to within 22 yards of the dangerous feline to put a 440-grain hardcast flat-nosed bullet in her.

PHOTO BY BUD RUMMEL

HUNTER'S PROFILE - BUD RUMMEL, PROFESSIONAL HUNTER

While in college, Bud Rummel had a good friend invite him to go hunting in Montana. Taking on the hunt with an outfitter, Bud became a little disappointed, when his hunt was over after three shots. He'd carried an old Mossberg in .243 and brought with him only 16 rounds of ammo, but he had his pronghorn antelope down in less than an hour on the first day, and on the opening day of mule deer season, he made a repeat performance. The second day he got another buck (back then you were allowed two bucks). Three shots, and three animals down. The outfitter was so impressed with the young Rummel, that when Bud asked if he could stay on and help the rest of the season, the outfitter answered with a resounding "Yes!" That was the start of Bud Rummel's guiding career.

In 1994, Bud went to Zimbabwe to learn the safari huntingbusiness as a booking agent. What was supposed to be six-week visit stretched into a nearly six-month stay, and Bud was drifting away from the booking agent end of the industry and into guiding. In 1996, he began participating in Zimbabwe's apprenticeship guide program. He met his wife-to-be there, marrying in 1997, and it was around that time that Bud began hunting for meat with a revolver. In 1998, Bud received his PH's license and that same year bought an 8,600 acre ranch. They stayed for a couple years, but with the political climate there extremely stressed, in 2000, the Rummels made the trek back to the U.S. It wasn't until 2004 that Bud started going back to Zimbabwe seasonally to work as a PH.

Bud is one of those lucky individuals who has managed to turn his passion into his profession. He frequently hunts with a handgun these days, and when Smith & Wesson unveiled its .500, back in 2003, Bud knew he had to have one. As the photos indicate, Bud has taken a number of large and dangerous animals with handguns and reports that the .500 Magnum, loaded correctly, is more than capable of taking any and all game on every continent. We tend to agree.

consequences. It is, in fact, substantial enough to justify strapping an additional 3½ pounds to your belt. Consider a big-bore revolver to be a leather-wrapped insurance policy, if you will.

For absolute reliability, I would like to limit this discussion about backup guns for hunting to revolvers. Nothing against semi-autos, but they simply do not rank in the same league when it comes to reliability, and are not typically available in calibers that I would consider "fight stoppers."

So what is a "fight stopper?" Typically, it's the biggest caliber you can accurately shoot without a flinch or fear of recoil. For every person, the choice is different. Experts agree that, when in a tussle with an angry bear, you will most likely have time only for one well-aimed shot (thus, magazine capacity is a moot point). I like to think of the .44 Magnum as the minimum reliable caliber, and it's also a good choice if you don't reload, as there is an abundance of factory ammunition for this popular caliber. The old warhorse .45 Colt is perhaps the most overlooked backup round, probably due to the rather weak factory load offerings (which are, in turn, due to the many older .45 Colts in circulation). Loaded to its potential in a modern firearm, there is little the .45 Colt cannot tackle. Moving up to the .454 Casull, .480 Ruger, .475 Linebaugh, and the .50-caliber cartridges requires a serious commitment by the shooter to master them. These large calibers are not for the neophyte; they require lots of practice to become competent with, as the recoil can be debilitating. Larger diameter bullets create larger wound channels, but still need to be placed accurately to be effective.

I spoke about bear defense with the good folks at Magnum Research, makers of the BFR (Biggest Finest Revolver) line of single-action revolvers. Director of Manufacturing Jim Tertin told me that Magnum Research builds a number every year from their custom shop, the Precision Center, for use in the Alaskan outdoors by fishermen, guides, and hunters, specifically for use in bear defense. Typically, customers specify a 4⅝-inch barrel and slimmed and rounded grips that make the guns snag resistant. The most popular cartridge by far is, unsurprisingly, the .475 Linebaugh, followed closely by the potent .500 JRH. The ubiquitous .44 Magnum and .454 Casull come next. (I didn't mention Smith & Wesson's powerful .460 and .500 Magnums, as they require a much larger framed revolver and would serve better as a primary hunting tool than as a back-up piece.)

Dog hunters know how much easier it is to carry a revolver than a rifle, especially when trailing dogs through the North Carolina briar, hot on the heels of a cantankerous black bear. It frees your hands, for one, enabling the hunter to keep up while moving through thick brush. Another good reason for a revolver when hunting or camping is that you can keep your revolver in your sleeping bag and actually use it. Try doing the same with a rifle. Just doesn't work.

There are no guarantees in life, but it pays to equip yourself for the worst-case scenario. I know carrying a revolver in the field will add to the weight of your load, but I like to think my life is worth the added discomfort.

LYNN THOMPSON— BRING ALONG A KNIFE *AND* A GUN

Cold Steel's Lynn Thompson knows something about using revolvers as backup weapons, as he's been faced with the prospect of being flattened by an agitated bovine on several occasions.

Recently, Lynn took another trip to Australia, intent on taking a water buffalo with a seven-foot spear. When a lone buffalo was spotted, Lynn began putting on a stalk. He worked has way down a dry stream bed to within five yards of his intended target, where he then encountered a large termite mound that provided the concealment needed to get spear-chucking close. The hunter crouched low, intending to pop up on the side of the mound and deliver the spear to the buffalo. The animal was quartering away from Lynn, (who later surmised later he should have waited longer, but hindsight is always much more clearly defined than the present), who popped up and threw the spear, but the buffalo, sensing motion before the throw, blocked the hunter's spear and charged directly at the threat with its own two spears. Lynn stepped to the side, while simultaneously tugging the 7½-inch-barreled Ruger from its holster. He

THE AUTHOR HAD THIS REDHAWK built by Jack Huntington for back-up duty. It started life as a .45 Colt, but was fitted with the .454 Casull cylinder out of a Ruger Super Redhawk. The author loads this revolver with heavy hardcast bullets from Double Tap Ammunition.

AUTHOR PHOTO

RENE ANDERSON stopped this 100-pound wolf with her Smith & Wesson Mountain Gun in .44 Magnum, while she was bowhunting for elk.

AUTHOR PHOTO

THE ORIGINAL INTENT of the Huntington-built Ruger .500 Linebaugh Super Redhawk was backup duty, but when the author discovered just how accurate it was, he pressed it into duty as a primary hunting tool by adding an Ultradot 30 red dot-type site.

fired as soon as he cleared leather, catching the worked-up bovine in the head. That shot was lethal, but Lynn continued delivering lead to his attacker, striking the animal repeatedly in the head and spine until the six-shot cylinder was empty. The best part of that almost too-exciting hunt? Lynn managed to catch the whole event on film, as can be seen in the sequential photographs on the previous pages.

CRY WOLF!

The reintroduction of wolves into the U.S. territories where they once roamed and hunted has met with mixed results. In May of 2009, the U.S. Fish and Wildlife Service delisted wolves from the protections of the Endangered Species Act in Montana, Idaho, and Wyoming, and, after a se-

ries of court battles, Montana and Idaho opened wolf seasons. (Other states in the Lower 48 appear to be following suit, including, as this book goes to press, Wisconsin.)

More and more communities are now seeing an outcry from disenfranchised locals who have a front row seat to the destructive behavior these animals are capable of. One such person is Rene Anderson, of Headquarters, Idaho. An avid hunter of more than 30 years, a grandmother, and a former hunting guide, Rene had a hair-raising encounter with a wolf, while hunting elk in the woods of Idaho.

Rene's preferred mode of hunting is archery, but she never does so without her Smith & Wesson Mountain Gun in .44 Magnum strapped to her belt, a habit she picked up guiding for a dozen years. The habit proved prophetic.

Rene's husband had dropped her off on a ridge and moved off to hunt another area by himself. Alone, Rene used an elk call to attract any nearby elk. What she wasn't counting on, or expecting,

COULD THE Smith & Wesson Lew Horton Model 29 with its 3-inch barrel and rounded grip frame be the predecessor of Ruger's Alaskan and Smith & Wesson's .460 and .500 PDs?

RUGER'S Alaskan revolvers came in three different chambering, .44 Magnum, .454 Casull, and .480 Ruger. The .480 was eventually dropped from the line.

was a wolf responding. Rene recollects hearing the wolf crashing through the brush, before seeing it in a low crouch moving up a hillside finger towards her. The sight of the prowling wolf iced her blood, especially when she noted she'd been upwind of the animal the entire time—the canine must have been aware of what Rene was, yet was still determined to attack.

Fixated on the advancing wolf, Rene lost momentary sight of the animal as it entered a thicket. She glanced around and estimated where it would clear the brush, immediately set her bow down, drew her revolver, and aimed it towards the opening. The wolf reappeared just where she had anticipated and made eye contact with Rene, sending a chill up her spine. But that chill was all she had time for. The wolf was approximately 150 feet away from making contact with Rene and closing the distance fast, so fast it was a mere 10 feet away when Rene fired. The round struck the canine on the left side of its head, causing it to fall between two logs, yet it was still alive, and Rene emptied her revolver, stilling it for good. The wolf tipped the scales at 100 pounds.

Rene conveyed to me that, in her opinion, "Everyone who spends time in the outdoors should carry a handgun. They are quicker to bring into play than a rifle." She also reports that there has been a surge in revolver sales locally, as folks have been reminded that the Disney portrayal of wild animals couldn't be further from reality, especially where predators are concerned. "We are programmed from an early age, by the shows and movies we watch on television, to view animals like wolves and bear as benign creatures. The reality is that these animals pose a real potential threat and should be approached and treated with caution" opined Rene. We couldn't agree more, Rene.

BREAKING AND ENTERING

The late Larry Kelly, profiled in the "Pioneers" chapter of this book, had a hair-raising encounter with a grizzly bear, while hunting caribou in Alaska. Waiting out a severe storm on the beach of Bristol Bay in a crude, 100-year-old shack made of driftwood and plastic sheeting, Larry and his guide Bob Gerlack were hoping for the wind to die down enough for the pilot to pick them up and move them to another area.

The wait was a long one. On day four, Larry had to answer the call of nature and headed outside, strapping on his Smith & Wesson Model 29 beforehand. He immediately noticed a large bear moving towards the beach and in the direction of the cabin. When it hit the beach, it began running towards the stunned hunter. His guide Bob came outside with a camera after hearing Larry's announcement, but immediately returned for his rifle, a .375 H&H bolt-action. Larry had already drawn his .44 Magnum, and when the bear angled up the hill towards the front door, some 30 yards away and closing fast, Bob fired a warning shot over the head of the advancing brownie, while screaming at Larry not to shoot the bear. (The guide was in the process of acquiring his master guide's license and could ill afford any controversy with the Fish & Game Department. They couldn't shoot the bear unless they were sure the bear meant them harm.)

After the first shot, the bear stopped abruptly and sat down. Then he looked at the perplexed Larry and his master guide-to-be and promptly made a beeline right at them. The guide fired into the ground in an attempt to turn the bear's charge, as both men retreated to the back of the small cabin, Larry knocking over the stove and Bob crashing into a table as they backed up. Still, the bear came through the door, and when he hit the two-foot mark, Larry fired two quick shots into his chest. The bear turned to the side, and Larry put two more broadside shots into it. (Little

did Larry know that, during the dustup, Bob was frantically trying to clear his jammed rifle.) The bear turned and started heading out the door, Larry put his last two rounds in the retreating bear's backside and, his jammed rifle finally cleared, Bob began slinging lead, his .375 booming. Ten feet outside the cabin, the bear finally collapsed.

Larry's Model 29 was loaded with 240-grain jacketed hollowpoints that were clearly not designed for use against such a large and tough animal, these bullets having penetrated only a few inches and experiencing core separation. When all was said and done, the two weary hunters had connected on the bear with a total of 14 shots combined. This incident was a turning point for Larry and his bullet selections for big game—particularly big game that bites.

MAN'S BEST FRIEND?

They say the dog is man's best friend. In the case of veteran salmon fishing guide and proprietor of EZ Limit Guide Service of Soldotna, Alaska, Greg Brush, his Ruger Super Redhawk Alaskan in .454 Casull turned out to be his best friend and companion, particularly after his dogs fled the scene, when the party was just getting started.

Greg was out taking his three dogs for a walk near his home in Soldotna when, alerted by just a snapping twig, he turned around to find 900 pounds of fur-covered teeth heading his way in a hurry. Brush barely had the time to draw the SRH he carries on his hip when he leaves the house. With the bear at less than 15 yards, Brush fired from the hip, but missed his adversary. He continued firing, and running backwards, and his fifth shot connected as he stumbled and began to fall—he had to actually side step the large bear as it came crashing down. The .454 had performed its task perfectly. Man's new best friend? You bet.

The likelihood of actually having a predatory or defensive bear encounter are slim to none, but it is better to have a weapon and a plan in the event of the rare and unfortunate attack. Brush's bear was estimated to be between 15 and 20 years old and underweight by some 400 or 500 pounds. It had grass packed in its molars and little fat on its body. At that time of year, the bear should have

ALASKAN FISHING GUIDE and proprietor of EZ Limit Guide Service of Soldotna, Alaska, Greg Brush is pictured here with the bear he shot out of self-defense, in 2009. It's a blessing that Brush was carrying his .454 Ruger that day. The 900-pound grizzly was underweight by some 400 to 500 pounds and, apparently starving to death, thought Brush would make a much-needed meal.

been packing on the pounds for the nearing winter. Instead, it was starving and saw Greg as its opportunity for an easy meal.

Greg Brush is the perfect example to follow for individuals who spend their days in bear country. You must know the dangers, the risks, and the pitfalls and have a practiced plan in place—and you must *always* carry your chosen form of protection. If you pick and choose the days you carry, you may end up on the wrong end of a bear and have no way of leveling the playing field.

Bear attack behavior specialist James Gary Shelton, in his book *Bear Attacks II – Myth & Reality*, states, "If you can legally carry a handgun and your work necessitates it, then a .44 Magnum is minimum. A .357 Magnum will not do the job on a frontal charging grizzly." Shelton believes that bigger is better, when relying on a handgun for bear defense. I cannot imagine that a properly loaded .357 *isn't* capable of stopping a fight with a large bear, but the small diameter leaves little margin for error, and without absolutely perfect shot placement, it just may be inadequate. Personally, I believe that if you can shoot a larger caliber well, then a large caliber is your best bet. Obviously something is always better than nothing, but you might as well stack the deck in your favor.

You have read about a number of situations where large-caliber revolvers, loaded correctly, offer more than enough terminal performance to be effective against the largest of dangerous game. The fact that large-caliber handguns are typically harder to master than rifles perhaps has attached a bit of a stigma to the use of them for defense against large, dangerous game. On the same token, the same logic can be applied to the .470 or the .500 Nitro Express rifle rounds, meaning that they are very capable of delivering the goods, but only in the right hands. Not everyone is capable of proficiently wielding (or paying for!) a large British double rifle chambered in a cartridge the size of a fine cigar.

Also often overlooked is the concept of having a plan in place for those rare possibilities. If you decide that bear spray is what you will carry while out in bear country, you should practice and play out every possible scenario in your head prior to heading outdoors. This will lessen the possibility of surprise and increase your chances for survival. If you make the decision to carry a large bore revolver, you owe it to yourself to be completely familiar with your firearm, and you must practice, practice, practice. When you are through practicing, practice some more.